Discovering Bhutan

DISCOVERING BHUTAN

Land of Gross National Happiness

Janet Ward Schofield

Sentient Publications

First Sentient Publications edition 2025
Copyright © 2025 by Janet Ward Schofield

All rights reserved. This book, or parts thereof, may not be reproduced in any form without permission, except in the case of brief quotations embodied in critical articles and reviews.

A paperback original
Book design by Laura Johanna Waltje

Library of Congress Control Number: 2024946383
Publisher's Cataloging-in-Publication Data

Names: Schofield, Janet Ward, author.
Title: Discovering Bhutan : land of gross national happiness / Janet Ward Schofield.
Description: Includes bibliographical references and index. | Boulder, CO: Sentient Publications, 2024.
Identifiers: LCCN: 2024946383 | ISBN: 9781591813385 (paperback) | 9781591813392 (ebook)
Subjects: LCSH Bhutan. | Bhutan--Description and travel. | BISAC TRAVEL / Asia / India and South Asia | TRAVEL / Special Interest / Religious | HISTORY / India & South Asia
Classification: LCC DS491.4 .S36 2024 | DDC 954.98--dc23

SENTIENT PUBLICATIONS
A Limited Liability Company
PO Box 1851
Boulder, CO 80306
www.sentientpublications.com

Contents

Preface ———————————————————————— 1
I Went to Educate and Treasure What I Learned ——————— 7
Geography is Destiny ———————————————————— 22
Meet the Monks ——————————————————————— 40
Unseen Forces at Work: Local Deities, Ghosts, and Astrology ——— 62
The Dragon King and I ———————————————————— 79
Being Bhutanese ——————————————————————— 96
Growing Up, Growing Old —————————————————— 119
The Long and Winding Road ————————————————— 142
Land of Yaks and Yetis ———————————————————— 163
Is Happiness a Place? ————————————————————— 183
Afterword —————————————————————————— 204
Glossary ——————————————————————————— 208
Book Club Questions ————————————————————— 210
Photo Credits ———————————————————————— 212
Acknowledgements —————————————————————— 213
Endnotes —————————————————————————— 215

*For the people of Bhutan,
who welcomed us with such warmth and grace
and for my husband, Doug,
whose adventurous spirit led us to more than a decade
in that remarkable land.*

Preface

Few people from the modernized global world have ever been fortunate enough to visit the remote, endlessly fascinating, and spectacularly beautiful kingdom of Bhutan, often called the Last Shangri-La. This tiny Himalayan kingdom's unique and intriguing culture is so different from that experienced by most Westerners that it can both expand and challenge their understanding of the world in which they live.

The Bhutanese frequently remark that their country is not a great many years away from its medieval roots. Indeed, Bhutan's king abolished serfdom only in 1958. Without visiting Bhutan, it is hard to imagine a retired king, married to four sisters, bicycling around the capital city, or children who avoid swimming in pristine lakes due to fear of mermaids. Come with me on a vicarious journey to this enchanting land and you will see for yourself a world where such things are possible—and even make sense. You will also see how this impoverished country's unique culture has led to its remarkable environmental policies as well as to the origination of an internationally influential holistic approach to development called Gross National Happiness (GNH).

I am lucky enough to be one of the miniscule number of Westerners ever allowed to live and work in this reclusive hermit kingdom for over a decade. *Discovering Bhutan* is a portrait of a rapidly changing culture that is very different from the ones most Westerners know. The country's unique culture is illustrated here by colorful tales of my many extraordinary experiences there, some amusing, others touching or even astonishing. This book also provides travelers to Bhutan with insights and information that should greatly enrich their experiences there. But it is not a guidebook.

Although *Discovering Bhutan* is fact-based, it is filled with personal stories bringing the country's people and places to life. Anecdotes about my experiences, such as being charged by a stampeding herd of yaks and sleeping in structures ranging from a royal residence to the floors of a rural school, a monastery, and even a small, dilapidated storage shed, provide readers with vivid descriptions of life in far flung and intriguing parts of this stunning country. Tales of interactions with dozens of individuals, ranging from illiterate yak herders to a teenage monk reputed to be the reincarnation of a deceased holy man, to the country's Fifth King, add richness, depth, and human interest to the material on Bhutan's environment, religion, folkways, educational system, monarchy, and social structure.

If you want to learn about what took me and my husband to Bhutan and the nature of our work and life there, you are invited to read the rest of this preface. If you prefer to start your vicarious journey immediately, skip straight to Chapter 1 from here. No matter which option you choose, I hope you find the country and its culture as captivating and thought-provoking as I do.

The story of our move to Bhutan starts with a personal disaster. I had worked happily as a professor of psychology at the University of Pittsburgh in the U.S. for more than thirty years while my husband, Doug, and I raised three wonderful daughters. But fate intervened and Doug developed cancer. Being terribly ill, he had to sell the financial services business he had founded decades earlier. After recuperation from extended and debilitating treatment, he saw little likelihood of finding a fulfilling new job. With no job prospects and our youngest daughter having just left home for college, the two most important centers of his life, work and family, were gone or drastically changed. Things seemed grim.

International travel had been a longtime avocation for both of us. So, we decided that living and working overseas might be a way forward. Asia was our target for many reasons, including our previous very enjoyable travel and work experiences there. An intensive job search yielded several offers. Bhutan clearly provided the greatest challenge in terms of adjusting to doing without many things we had taken for granted, including dependable electricity and internet access, drinkable tap water, advanced medical services, toilet paper in public restrooms, and even pastries worth the calories they contain. But the location and the work seemed ideal in other important ways. For example, language barriers were not an issue because English is the primary language used in Bhutan's education system as well as in many other contexts there. So, we decided to join the small team establishing Royal Thimphu College, the first private college in Bhutan.

The college was founded to provide Bhutanese students with an education emphasizing analytical thinking, skill development, and international exposure rather than memorization, which was still commonly emphasized there. A Bhutanese man, Tenzing Yonten, and his remarkable wife, H.R.H. Ashi (Princess) Kesang Wangmo Wangchuck, the sister of Bhutan's Fourth King, were cofounders of the college. Tenzing served very actively and productively as the college's founding director. Consistent with her many other activities intended to improve the lives of Bhutan's people, Ashi Kesang provided the land for its twenty-five-acre campus—which had earlier served as a royal hunting ground—and took a personal interest in beautifying the landscape there. Bhutanese with suitable experience to establish and run a college consistent with the founders' goals were quite scarce. When Doug and I arrived in the spring of 2009, virtually all faculty and most other personnel were still to be hired.

Very shortly after we landed in Bhutan at what the Australian magazine *Travel and Leisure* has called "the scariest runway in the world," it became clear that the college would be a high energy environment. After more than twenty-eight hours of grueling travel, I dropped off luggage at the apartment where Doug and I initially lived and then went directly to Royal Thimphu College's temporary workspace, because construction of the college's buildings had only recently begun.

The founding director politely inquired whether I felt up to diving right in. Anxious to make a good impression, I assured him I was. An extremely fit thirty-six-year-old, he bounded straight up four full flights of stairs to the college offices at what seemed to me like warp speed. Determined not to let Thimphu's thin air at 7,600 feet defeat me, I struggled along close behind him, trying to mute the sound of my frantic breathing so that he would not regret having invited someone well past the normal retirement age in Bhutan to work with him.

In the more than ten years Doug and I worked at the college, it grew rapidly from about three hundred to almost 1,400 students, including some from the U.S. and Europe. Both of us had a remarkable variety of responsibilities

Royal Thimphu College's (RTC) first faculty and management committee members gather in front of a traditionally painted entryway.

RTC's architecture combines traditional and modern elements, and its campus abounds with trees, bushes, and flowers.

there in addition to serving on the five-person management committee. We got involved in a potpourri of activities assisting government ministries and other educational and environmental organizations, including teaching English to monks on weekends at a remote monastery, which added importantly to our sense of excitement and accomplishment.

Our personal lives changed even more than our professional ones. Instead of residing in a four-bedroom home in suburban Pittsburgh, we lived in a modest apartment on the college's campus. Its kitchen came with a basic two-ring gas burner for cooking, a water boiler, and a water filter as essential appliances. A "three-minute" soft-boiled egg required seven minutes to cook there because water boils at only about 198°F at the campus's altitude of about eight thousand feet. In our early years there, electricity was so

After Royal Thimphu College's first graduation ceremony, a rainbow shone over its main building.

Somewhat more than half of Royal Thimphu College students are female, which is unusual in Bhutan.

undependable that we kept headlamps on a readily accessible table. Once, a defect in the wiring resulted in a light bulb shooting out from its sconce with such force that it shattered when it hit the wall on the far side of our living room.

On weekends, instead of attending plays and concerts as we did at the university where I taught in the U.S., we encountered yaks, monkeys, leeches, and even a wild boar while hiking. We drank salty butter tea sitting cross-legged on the planked floors of village farmhouses, with snow leopards, mythical animals, and ribbon-bedecked penises painted on white-washed rammed-earth walls. We joined the birthday parties, weddings, and house warmings of Bhutanese colleagues and friends, all fascinating in the ways they differed from similar celebrations in the U.S. Sometimes we just drove down twisting, rutted roads we had never travelled before in search of adventures—of which we had many.

Unfortunately, living in Bhutan made us miss many important family events in the U.S., including our youngest daughter's graduation at the top of her class at Yale. To keep in touch to the greatest possible extent, we travelled back home annually during Royal Thimphu College's two-and-a-half-month winter break. Generally, we also squeezed additional travel or short work experiences in other countries into that time. In fact, we were in North Macedonia, where I had a six-week Fulbright project, with airline tickets to return to the college when Bhutan abruptly closed its doors to foreigners in early 2020 to protect itself from COVID-19. Hence, our unexpected and prolonged return to the U.S., which led to the writing of this book. I hope that the unfortunate turn of events that locked us out of Bhutan will provide you an opportunity to explore this remarkable country through our memories. Please enjoy the journey.

Chapter 1

I Went to Educate and Treasure What I Learned

You may not believe much of what you read in this book. I wouldn't either if I hadn't experienced it myself. I went to Bhutan for a year and stayed for more than a decade. Some people call it the Last Shangri-La, but others have called it the Dark Southland, the Dragon Country of Four Approaches, the Hermit Kingdom, or the Land of the Thunder Dragon. More prosaically, in 2020 *Lonely Planet* named it the "Best Country to Visit." It's a land where gods live on mountain tops, mermaids live in lakes, and spirits inhabit rocks, cliffs, and trees. Where there are over eight hundred species of butterflies, seven hundred species birds, and more than four hundred species of orchids. Where a sick tiger wandered into a suburb of the capital city and Buddhist monks lit butter lamps as they prayed for it. Where forest rangers helped a python that bit off more than it could chew when it tried to swallow a young deer. It's a land where I was adopted by a baby yak, became friends with a young man widely believed to be a reincarnated lama, and had brunch with the king and queen. Living and working in Bhutan was an amazing adventure, and I invite you to join me, if only vicariously. I promise there will be many surprises. If you learn a hundredth as much as I did and have even a scant fraction of the fun I had doing it, you will feel your time has been well spent.

Not only does Bhutan have different names. It is also perceived very differently by different people. For those in China and India, it is a tiny neighbor serving as a buffer between their country and a populous and potentially threatening, nuclear-armed neighbor. Westerners who have heard of Bhutan know it as an isolated mountain kingdom of indeterminate location in Asia or as a high-end tourist destination. Central to the image of their country for many Bhutanese, as well as for some others, is this tiny nation's claim to fame as the birthplace of Gross National Happiness (GNH), a holistic perspective suggesting that the measure of a nation's development should include attention to its environment, culture, and government rather than focusing solely on economic productivity as the traditional measure of development, Gross National Product (GNP), does. Many other extraordinarily disparate visions of the country exist: Bhutan as one of the last remaining strongholds of tantric Buddhism, a country responsible for refugee camps in Nepal, a nation blessed with an extraordinarily beloved and enlightened monarchy or, very simply, as home.

After more than a decade living and working in Bhutan, I still see it as a country whose true nature is often obscured from outsiders just as its mountains are shrouded in dense, ever-changing clouds in the monsoon season. Those clouds allow glimpses of verdant rice fields clinging valiantly to thirty-degree slopes, of distant meditation huts perched perilously on cliff edges, and of tangled jungles sheltering majestic Royal Bengal tigers and swarms of tiny leeches that torment those braving their muddy paths. But the blankets of cloud hide a lot as well, including the scars of newly cut roads and distant monasteries from which emanate the raucous, penetrating sounds that can only come from the ten-foot telescopic horns that monks use when they are not using human thigh-bone trumpets and skull drums to accompany religious rituals.

So, I do not claim to completely understand this extraordinary country. But living and working in Bhutan tremendously expanded my understanding of the remarkable extent to which, despite their shared humanity, people residing in the modern West and those living in a country like Bhutan inhabit worlds that are poles apart culturally, psychologically, and technologically. I went to Bhutan in 2009 to enhance its educational system by assisting in the establishment and development of Royal Thimphu College, the country's first private college. Rather ironically, I ended up having experiences that profoundly influenced me and taught me as much about the varieties of the human experience as a PhD in social psychology from Harvard. This learning occurred although I had considerable experience in dramatically different cultures before arriving in Bhutan, having travelled to over one hundred countries, many of which were classified by the UN as "least developed countries," just like Bhutan was when we lived there.

So, this is not the breathless tale of a first-time traveler to Asia overwhelmed by ancient monuments, new vistas, and exotic cuisines. Rather, this book describes a unique and intriguing country and culture as well as many of the unexpected, exciting, and even moving experiences my husband, Doug, and I had there as we grew to feel at home in physical and cultural surroundings that were strikingly different from those we had known.

One foundational aspect of Bhutanese culture is the belief in *tertöns*, or treasure finders, with powers akin to clairvoyance that let them reveal things hidden from others. An Indian tantric master called *Guru Rinpoche* (Precious Teacher) brought Buddhism from Tibet to Bhutan in the eighth and ninth centuries. He is said to have left behind teachings and other treasures in rocks, caves, and lakes for later retrieval. Pema Lingpa, a fifteenth century Bhutanese tertön, is believed to have discovered important treasures in his dreams and visions as well as in a deep pool of water. His descendants include Bhutan's kings as well as a tertön son, who is believed to have discovered a spell to repel a Mongol invasion of Tibet.

As an agnostic Westerner, I have difficulty accepting literally the idea of tertöns. It is, however, hard to describe the experiences I had in Bhutan as anything other than treasures because of the uniqueness and value of so many aspects of the country and its culture. So, in my own way, I found many treasures in Bhutan: its extraordinary landscape, its rich and unique culture, the incredible warmth and hospitality shown to us by illiterate villagers, colleagues, and so many others including members of the royal family, and the striking remnants of Bhutan's feudal past that make the concept of time travel even more real and intriguing than in science fiction. This book shares some of my most fascinating and unexpected treasures with you. I hope you enjoy them as much as I have.

Because so many people are unfamiliar with even the basic facts about Bhutan, I start by providing some such information in the following table. As is evident there, Bhutan's population is very small, less than all but three of the U.S.'s fifty states. Physically, it is also tiny and carved into deep isolated valleys that run vertically from permafrost and glaciers at its mountainous northern border with Tibet to the subtropical southern border with India—not much more than one hundred miles away,

	FAST FACTS	FUN FACTS
Location	Between China in the north and India in the south	In less than 125 miles between these borders, the altitude plunges from 24,836 to only 318 feet.
Size	14,824 square miles	Bhutan is smaller than Switzerland and about the size of the state of Maryland.
Population	800,000	In 1990 the government estimated a population of 1.5 million individuals. Recent figures vary but are much lower.
Government	Constitutional monarchy	The king can be replaced by a two-thirds vote of the Parliament.
Capital City	Thimphu	Characterized by a UN official as "probably the most remote capital city anywhere in the world,"[1] Thimphu is the only capital in the world without a traffic light. One was installed, but public displeasure led to its removal.
Religion	75% Buddhist (*Vajrayāna*, sometime called Tantric) 23% Hindu, 2% Other	The storied penis of a widely admired saint, known as The Divine Madman and The Saint of Five Thousand Woman, is called The Thunderbolt of Flaming Wisdom.
Language (Mother Tongue)	27% Dzongkha (official language) 26 % Nepali (*Lhotshampa*) 23% Tshangla (*Sharchopkha*) 24% More than a dozen others	Schooling is conducted in English, which is commonly used in business and government as well. Some languages are now spoken by only a few hundred people and one by fewer than a dozen.

Currency	Ngultrum, pegged to the Indian rupee	As recently as a decade ago, a barter economy predominated in some especially remote areas.
Per Capita GDP	USD 3,780	This has increased over seven times in current dollars in the last twenty years.
Literacy Rate	Adult Male: 75% Adult Female: 57%	Female literacy increased five-fold in thirty years, while male literacy more than doubled.
Climate	Varies with altitude; tropical with light monsoon to frigid winters and cool summers	Schools and government offices are closed to celebrate the first day of snow each year in the capital city.
Best Time to Visit	March-early June and October-November	The Chief Buddhist Abbot and his retinue process from Thimphu, the capital city, to a winter residence in warmer Punakha in mid-November, bestowing blessing to throngs of devotees on the way. Yak and cattle herders also move with the season.

One of Bhutan's special treasures is the extraordinary variety of its ecosystems. In fact, this region is known as one of fewer than thirty-five biodiversity hotspots in the world. I experienced this remarkable diversity one long afternoon after Doug and I drove east after hiking from above the tree line in western Bhutan to a small, stone meditation hut with stunning views of the mammoth, ice-clad slopes of twenty-four-thousand-foot Mt. Jomolhari. First, the narrow road snaked down from the 13,083-foot Chele La pass, descending more than a full mile in altitude through primeval fir forests festooned with garlands of grey-green moss, and through lush rice paddies and fruit orchards. After winding sinuously along a narrow river valley for another hour, it curved back up over the ten-thousand-foot Dochula pass with its magnificent rhododendron and magnolia trees. Next, we headed down an additional mile in altitude past wild avocado trees to the town of Punakha, where fifteen-foot-tall poinsettia bushes used as live fencing were

These small Buddhist shrines, containing sacred objects, prayers, and offerings, dot the landscape on paths and in fields as well as near crossroads, streams, and mountain passes. Circumambulating one is believed to produce merit for the individual doing so as well as for all other sentient beings.

These verdant fields produce rice, the essential central component of Bhutanese cuisine.

aflame with glorious scarlet blooms. All this is within less than one hundred miles. No wonder tiny Bhutan ranks with massive China and India among the world's top countries in the distance in altitude between its highest and its lowest points.

The almost miraculous variety in Bhutan's landscape, producing habitats well-suited for animals ranging from elephants and rhinoceros to yaks and snow leopards, has also fostered extraordinary cultural diversity. Over many centuries, migrants from Tibet as well as from neighboring parts of India and Myanmar settled into isolated pockets and had little interaction with each other or indigenous peoples due to the extremely steep terrain separating the numerous deep valleys.

Towards the end of the nineteenth century, Nepali migrants settled in the sparsely populated south where they cleared malaria-infested jungles for farming. Many more arrived in the 1960s to help construct a rough road north from India then across Bhutan's east-west axis. Before that, traders slogged south to India on rutted trails with mules and horses laden with blankets, oranges, and walnuts, which they exchanged for spices and cotton cloth. Others struggled north to Tibet over snow-choked mountain passes with yaks loaded with rice, dried chilies, and handmade paper to bring back tea and salt. This road, although rough and dangerous, facilitated such trade as well as east-west travel across forbidding mountain passes that had traditionally kept different groups within the country separate. Nonetheless, longstanding isolation led to a much greater degree of cultural diversity than would be expected in such a small area, another treasure for a social psychologist like me.

Increasing the potential of this mélange of ways of living to provoke deep interest and reflection is the extent to which so many of these cultures are profoundly different from the tide of Westernization and modernization that has recently swept the world. Bhutan has been influenced by such trends, especially in the capital city. There, coffee shops sell lattes with croissants or Black Forest cake to customers tapping away on laptop computers or chatting on smart phones. Hip hop music, John Denver songs, K-pop, and jeans are popular with urban youth, as are Facebook and other social media. But the traditional salty yak butter tea, a concoction that rarely appeals to Western palates, especially as it cools and the butter congeals, is still popular. Also obvious is the absence of international chains such as McDonald's and Starbucks, although a Thimphu convenience store named 8-Eleven obviously modelled itself on the 7-Eleven stores so popular in Thailand and elsewhere.

But, despite some influence from the secular, empirical, independent, and competitive cultural currents that are so strong in much of the West, Bhutan's culture remains fundamentally religious and traditional. The persistence of elements of a pre-Buddhist animist worldview was evident in the widespread belief at the college that a benign spirit lived in a tree in front of the dean's home. That spirit caused no concern, unlike the ghosts reported to be haunting one of the female dormitories, which caused enough anxiety that monks were called in to exorcise them.

The influence of Buddhism, the official state religion, is striking. The most heavily attended guest lectures at Royal Thimphu College were those by prominent Buddhist religious figures. After these, students waited patiently in lengthy lines to receive blessings. The one time in eleven years that I felt really afraid was when I was trapped in an excited crowd that was pushing so eagerly forward to receive a blessing from a highly venerated lama that I feared being trampled—all while trying to protect a baby being inadvertently pressed so hard into his mother's back by the surging throng that I thought he might suffocate.

A longstanding attachment to the monarchy, and for some the belief in the kings' divinity, is another significant feature of Bhutanese culture. Its persistence was evidenced by the looks of awe, almost reverence, on many students' faces when the Fifth King visited the college. The traditional emphasis on obeying elders and taking responsibility for parents as they age was evident in the way students commonly accepted both academic directives from older relatives at odds with their preferences and parental expectations regarding later financial support.

Traditional beliefs and cultural habits emphasizing respect and hierarchy also led students to address me routinely as "madam" and Doug as "sir" and to sometimes cover their mouths while speaking to us. The strength of such hierarchical habits is amusingly illustrated in the memoir of a Canadian primary school teacher in Bhutan who reported the following interchange with a student when he asked his class to stop calling him "sir."

Student: "But what should we call Sir if we don't call Sir Sir, Sir?"
Teacher: "You could call me Ian."
Student: "Yes Sir. Thank you, Sir."[2]

In addition to Bhutan's extraordinary natural environment and its fascinating culture, I treasure the relationships I developed and the experiences I had with a warm and open people who exhibited almost unbelievable levels of hospitality. One illiterate farmer offered to share the only food in her small refrigerator: two gigantic homegrown cucumbers. Another unlocked a dilapidated cabinet and carefully produced a small packet of saltine-like crackers to accompany the tea she served us. Others, occasionally even those we had not previously met, welcomed Doug and me to celebrations of births, birthdays, weddings, and housewarmings as well as to funerals and other religious ceremonies.

The fact that public education in Bhutan has been conducted in English for many decades and that enrollment in school is now typical, although not compulsory, opened many opportunities for ready communication. Just to illustrate, while out hiking one weekend, we encountered a young woman on a narrow path. We greeted each other and I inquired if she was a student. She replied, in virtually unaccented English, "No, I am an uneducated farmer." An interesting conversation followed.

Another treasure Bhutan provided to me was the opportunity to directly experience the vestiges of a medieval feudal society with serfs, hereditary nobility, and a powerful clergy. Describing this situation, a newspaper editorial observed that "Bhutan ... is a nation in transition–from medieval to modern."[3] Or, as one scholar put it, "In fact, fifty years back, except for a minute proportion of the elite, the social structure, value system, and lifestyle of the Bhutanese did not differ very much from that of their ancestors around 1500."[4]

Reminders of that feudal past are ubiquitous. Massive fortresses called *dzongs*, which have housed both spiritual and secular authorities since the 1600s and continue to do so, dominate the landscape at strategic places like high bluffs and the confluence of rivers. They are extraordinarily impressive, especially because many were built without nails or even written plans. Like medieval European cathedrals, they stand as physical monuments to what vision, persistence, artistic talent, and incredibly hard work over long periods of time by people with diverse skills can accomplish using only the most rudimentary technology.

But even more striking to me are the contemporary behavioral remnants of Bhutan's feudal period. Since Ngawang Namgyal, a Tibetan, unified the country in the 1600s, swords have been worn by secular leaders as symbols of honor and authority. Even today, cabinet ministers and parliamentarians wear them as part of their formal dress. In fact, I once heard one of them complain bitterly that he had been required to surrender his sword before boarding an airplane in Europe. Early during my stay in Bhutan, I was rather taken aback when a member of parliament participating in one of my workshops strode in wearing his sword as well as bright, elaborately embroidered, multi-colored traditional boots called *tshoglham*. Doug, who provided financial advice to the board of a Bhutanese nonprofit that included some sword-wearing officials, jested to me that he hoped his advice turned out to be correct, not only because he sincerely wanted to be helpful but because having to deliver bad news to individuals wearing swords would be more than a little intimidating.

In Bhutan it is still possible to converse with people who lived as children under an essentially feudal system. For example, Aum (a widely used honorific for respected females) Kunzang Choden, a writer born in 1952, visited Royal Thimphu College to talk with faculty and students about what Bhutan was like during her childhood. Her family is considered religious nobility, having descended from two renowned tertöns. She and her Swiss husband live in an imposing and beautiful old manor house, *Ogyen Choling*, which has been in her family for twenty generations, although with many changes reflecting changing times. When she was a child, the village right below her home housed the family's serfs along with others who had small landholdings but owed labor obligations to the manor under existing practice.

Kunzang Choden's stories bring the feudal era alive. She tells of taxes that were in kind, e.g., woven textiles, meat, paper, soot, dyes, and even iron, because there was essentially no cash economy when she was young. Taxes required by some local nobility and/or the central government were so high that some individuals became monks, fled over the border to India or relocated to such remote mountain areas that they, in effect, disappeared. Others migrated to live as serfs for noble families whose demands were less extreme than others'. Those living as serfs cultivated grains and vegetables, herded livestock, wove, cooked, or tended the stables. In return, they received rudimentary housing, food, and clothing as well as elaborate religious ceremonies and festivals, which often extended over many days.

In 1958, Bhutan's Third King freed all those in serfdom as well as enslaved people, generally those captured in raids in nearby areas of India. A related program took land for the government and those who had previously been in serfdom or enslaved from the extensive tracts owned by nobles. Some families that had lived in the village below Ogyen Choling for generations before such changes remain there today.

To deal with changed circumstances, Kunzang Choden's family created a lovely guest house as well as a museum displaying household objects from her childhood within the manor house complex. The museum provides a remarkable glimpse of feudal Bhutan, containing material ranging from huge woven baskets for storing grains to effigies used to treat illness, wooden blocks for printing, and military items including arrows, swords, rhinoceros-hide shields, and bullet molds.

Another valuable treasure that emerged from my time in Bhutan was discovering a lot about myself, especially my ability to adjust and flourish in circumstances tremendously different from those I had known for more than sixty years. I learned to live without many comforts to which I had been accustomed. I figured out how to lose a substantial amount of the extra weight that I had carried on my frame for years to get fit enough to enjoy rigorous hikes in Bhutan's precipitous terrain. I learned that with a lot of thought, hours of googling, and considerable consultation with colleagues as well as relevant contacts inside and outside of Bhutan, I could successfully undertake dozens of activities for the college with which I had no direct prior experience. I felt especially fortunate to feel this sense of excitement and accomplishment because I knew that many people in their sixties and seventies, as I was, experience this period as a time of decline and even loss.

A related treasure for me was that this rewarding work provided a much-needed opportunity for more Bhutanese students attain a higher education designed to provide skills and experiences likely to foster their own and their country's development. Given the very short history of secular education in the country, the fact that it appeared reasonable to open a private college in Bhutan in 2009, although there were already ten modest-sized government tertiary education institutions, was remarkable. In 1914, Bhutan's First King set up the country's initial two elementary schools, serving just a few dozen students each. Not until 1968 did the first twenty students complete the tenth grade in Bhutan. A decade later, the first thirty-four students completed twelfth grade in the country. The very first college degree was not awarded there until 1986.

One of the biggest obstacles to education in Bhutan until recently was parents' unwillingness to let their children attend school. Initially when government officials went looking for students to enroll, parents often hid their children in the forests or claimed they were sick. Children played a vital role for families, herding cattle and performing other tasks necessary for survival and paying taxes. Also, most parents had little idea of why education might be useful. Phurpa Tenzin, who was selected to go to school in 1959 when he was seven years old, described his departure for school this way, "I left my home without a shirt inside my *gho* [a traditional robe still commonly worn by males], barefoot. My parents and relatives saw me off as if their son was

Many young children walk long distances to school.

Schooling is in English from the very beginning, although the national language, Dzongkha, is also taught.

going to war." While at school, he lived with a family near it and he recollects, "The meals were never enough."[5]

His experience was far from unique. Indeed, two of my acquaintances sent by the government as youngsters to a missionary school in India at different times in the 1980s both mentioned being constantly hungry there. One even confessed that he and a friend had used hollow reeds to siphon milk from the large vessels in which it was stored inside of a wire cage. To hide the results of this illicit activity, they then refilled the jugs by pouring water back into them through the reeds.

Conditions for many school children remained difficult despite government efforts to improve them. For example, shortly after we arrived in Bhutan, I read about one school in which students lived by themselves or with an older relative in nearby leaky, one-room bamboo huts, because it was too risky to walk the long distances home due to leeches, snakes, and bears. They had no mattresses, bed sheets or blankets, so they covered themselves at night with cardboard or straw. More recently, numerous students in government schools were hospitalized due to malnutrition, with a few even dying from it.

A story, told by one of Bhutan's most prominent businesswomen, Aum Dago Beda, illustrates the extent to which some parents actively resisted education not that long ago. When she was a child, an acquaintance of her father was extremely upset because his son had been selected to go to school. He did not know how to deal with the problem, because it was very difficult to refuse sending a selected child off to school due to hierarchical social norms. So, Dago Beda's father, who was unusually progressive, suggested that they substitute his daughter for the acquaintance's son. The acquaintance agreed enthusiastically, so Dago Beda went to school under the son's name, which, like many Bhutanese names, is not gender specific. She ended up progressing to college and subsequently to being employed in the civil service in the 1970s working in the then nascent tourism sector. In the early 1990s, using that experience, she and two colleagues founded what has become one of Bhutan's oldest and largest travel agencies. As I recall her story, the acquaintance's son toiled in the rice fields his entire working life.

In the last few decades, parents' attitudes toward education have changed dramatically, as the economic and social benefits of education became apparent even to rural householders. Poor villagers started taking educational loans, or even selling livestock and ancestral property, to cover the costs of books and school uniforms for their children. The hope, typically, is that their children will do well enough in school to gain free access to a government college and that after graduating from college they will get a civil service position, which provides a steady income as well as considerable job security and respect. Such hopes are not always realized. But there is no doubt that within a couple of generations, attitudes regarding the value of education evolved 180 degrees.

A final treasure for me was recognition of how unusual an opportunity I had to discover and enjoy Bhutan's remarkable culture. Sometimes called the Hermit Kingdom because of its history of self-imposed isolation, for most of its history Bhutan actively strove to maintain its isolation. Indeed, the legal code inscribed centuries ago in front of the massive Punakha dzong on a panel of black slate, which has been called the country's first constitution, states starkly, "People from foreign countries shall not be welcomed."[6] So Bhutan's contact with the world beyond Tibet and northern India was extremely limited until the advent of the Fourth King's rule in the early 1970s and its reclusive nature changed very slowly even after that.

The first Westerners to visit Bhutan, Portuguese Jesuits Estevao Cacella and Joao Cabral, arrived in 1627. A century and a half later in 1774, George Bogle came with the first British mission from the East India Company. Other British emissaries occasionally followed him before Britain's departure from India in 1947. But when one of them, Ashley Eden, visited Bhutan in 1864 with the goal of getting Bhutan to sign a treaty with the British at a time when Bhutan's ruler was reluctant to receive him, things did not go well. A local official who welcomed him was punished. Much worse from Ashley Eden's perspective, Jigme Namgyal, then Bhutan's ruler, pulled Eden's hair and rubbed his face with a piece of wet dough, much to the Englishman's astonishment and humiliation. In the 1920s, Alexandra David-Neel, a French Buddhist scholar, opera singer, and mystic, became the first European woman to visit Lhasa in Tibet, although it took disguising herself as a beggar to accomplish that. However, she was unable to get permission to visit Bhutan despite her concerted efforts to do so.

By the early and mid-1900s, Western individuals were occasionally invited to enter as guests of the royal family. The first American to visit, Burt Todd, a friend of a member of the royal family, arrived in 1951. But generally, other Westerners were not allowed until 1974 when the first tourists were granted visas to make good use of hotels built to house guests at the

Fourth King's coronation. The limit of two hundred tourist visas a year was lifted in the late 1970s, but tourists were quite few and far between for decades after that. For example, when Doug and I first visited Bhutan for a trek in 1992, we were two of fewer than three thousand tourists that entire year.

Today it is quite straightforward to visit Bhutan, if time, circumstances, and resources allow it. However, all tourists, except for visitors from a few nearby countries, are required to come on a prearranged tour. Reflecting the country's "High Value, Low Volume" tourism policy, the price, as well as the topography, is steep. Travelling with the required guide and driver provides information, convenience, and comfort. But it is not typically conducive to the kinds of in-depth interactions that a foreign national living and working in Bhutan can have, especially with close attention to cultural issues, an adventurous spirit, and a sturdy car.

In recent years, tourism has expanded greatly. But the number of Westerners who have been allowed to reside in Bhutan for a decade or more as we did is extremely small. To the best of my knowledge, there are only about a half dozen other Americans who have lived and worked in Bhutan as long as we did. Other Westerners living and working in Bhutan for that long can be counted using just one's fingers and toes, with a few toes left over. They include a Welsh Buddhist monk, a Canadian woman who ran a program bringing teachers to Bhutan, a French Tibetan scholar, a self-taught French veterinarian and her Dutch husband, a British teacher who came in the 1970s as a tutor for the prince who became the Fourth King, and a Canadian Jesuit priest who arrived in 1963 at the Third King's invitation to start a school, which opened in a cowshed with seven students. Also included in this count

Our weekend hikes often took us us to monasteries or tiny villages high in the mountains.

The household prayer rooms and temples we saw on weekend excursions were extraordinarily beautiful.

are a small number of Westerners married to Bhutanese who commonly have also made valuable contributions to the country in various areas.

I believe that my time living and working in Bhutan has provided experiences and insights that will intrigue, inform, and entertain many readers. Bhutan has begun to produce scholars, writers, and film makers who provide a rich understanding of the country for those not reading local languages. But, as suggested by a parable found in both ancient Buddhist and Hindu texts, "Blind Man and the Elephant," different perspectives on the same topic derived from contrasting experiences can come together to yield a more nuanced and complete vision of an entity than any single perspective alone. So, I hope readers interested in learning about this remarkable but little-known country will find this book an engaging and informative introduction to this fascinating nation and its culture.

Chapter 2

Geography is Destiny

Sigmund Freud, the early twentieth century psychologist, famously asserted in 1912, "Anatomy is destiny."[7] Had he been Bhutanese, he might have said instead, "Geography is destiny." There are a multitude of ways in which the country's history, culture, and even its ability to continue to exist as a sovereign state are strikingly influenced by both its location and its topography.

Diminutive, landlocked Bhutan is squeezed between the world's two most populous nations, China and India, active competitors for territory and power in Asia and beyond. Exacerbating this situation, both neighbors have clearly demonstrated expansionist tendencies. In the 1970s, India absorbed the nearby Buddhist kingdom of Sikkim, whose royalty had earlier intermarried with Bhutanese royalty. Protected by precipitous mountains and malarial jungles, Bhutan was never colonized when the British ruled India. Nonetheless, "some people even mistook Bhutan for an Indian state or considered it a protectorate of India"[8] in the years following India's independence. The two countries remain closely intertwined today, with about 75 percent of India's foreign aid flowing to Bhutan and several Indian Army training posts within the country.

In the 1950s, China absorbed Bhutan's northern neighbor, Tibet, with which Bhutan historically had important trading, cultural, and spiritual relationships. More than twenty rounds of talks between China and Bhutan since then have not resolved their existing border disputes. The border between them remains officially closed, though smugglers still use ancient trade routes to bring in goods ranging from brightly woven rugs to ornately decorated teacups with lids that preserve the tea's warmth in unheated homes and stores. Many exiles that fled Tibet in the 1950s were accepted by Bhutan. The stories I heard of their escaping over snow-covered passes with babies and elders while leaving behind almost all their earthly goods were heartbreaking. Many of their children and grandchildren still live in Bhutan today. So, we often saw Tibetan dances at school and college cultural shows and ate the special New Years' deep-fried pastries called *khapse* that Tibetan-heritage staff and students at Royal Thimphu College shared.

Serious territorial disputes between nuclear-armed India and China have flared up in several places along their borders in the past decade. One fracas between Indian and Chinese soldiers that included rock throwing and chest bumping was precipitated by a Chinese road building project near India on a high plateau called Doklam that Bhutan and China both claim. Although this seventy-three-day standoff was characterized by outside observers as "one of the worst border clashes between the countries in 30 years,"[9] the Bhutanese media were strangely silent about it, perhaps hoping to avoid public alarm. For about two months before things calmed down, I resorted to my online subscription to the *New York Times* to keep track of how events were unfolding in an area only about fifty miles as the crow flies from the college. In 2020, after further serious border classes between China and India in Ladakh, China suddenly announced that an area in eastern Bhutan constituting over 10 percent of Bhutan's total land area was also disputed territory. It also built a permanent village with about two dozen homes in the Doklam area that year. No resolution has yet been reached in these disputes.

Reflecting the sensitivity of border issues in the area, an issue of the *Economist* magazine arrived from India for the Royal Thimphu College library with a blank piece of paper glued so firmly over a map depicting the Indian-Chinese border that removing it destroyed the image printed on the page. Bemused by seeing this, I wondered whether the Indian government employed legions of people to glue those pieces of paper on one by one or whether a censoring machine had been developed to do the job. I never found out.

Bhutan's current border with India is not in dispute. However, after I commented to a Bhutanese friend on how remarkably close it is to where the very mountainous land ends, he told me an amusing story. Back in the

1800s, Bhutan had possession of the rich floodplains called the *duars* at the foot of the mountains to its south. However, after a war with Bhutan, the British annexed that area. To decide on the new dividing line between Bhutanese and British-India territory, the British asked the Bhutanese to select their strongest man. He then stood where the mountains ended and threw a large rock towards the plains. The place where it landed became the border. It seems unlikely that this story is true. But it aptly suggests how little flat area there is along parts of the Bhutan-India border.

The challenges that tiny Bhutan faces when dealing with its huge neighbors on border issues became apparent when Bhutan's first prime minister delivered a talk at the college. A student asked him why a mountain on the northern border that had been pictured on maps of Bhutan when she was younger was no longer shown there. He looked down and hesitated for a long moment. Then he responded, pointing to his rather bare pate, "When I was young, I wasn't bald. Look at me now." As the students burst into laughter, he continued to crescendoing mirth, "Look at your dean. With age, I guess Bhutan is shedding its hair." He then briefly added that the earlier maps were not official documents, concluding flatly, "That land does not belong to Bhutan." Then he quickly called for other questions.

Border issues are far from the only ones posing challenges related to Bhutan's massive neighbors. For example, in 2013, very shortly before Bhutanese went to the polls in an election in which their prime minister was contending for reelection, India doubled the price of cooking gas and kerosene in Bhutan by cutting subsidies it had long provided for them. This caused great distress to many. The previous year, the incumbent prime minister had publicly met with the Chinese premier, an unusual act which an Indian newspaper negatively characterized as "cozying up"[10] to the Chinese. A few weeks after the prime minister's party was defeated, India reinstated the subsidies.

Despite its reclusive tendencies, Bhutan has long been deeply influenced culturally and politically by the countries that encircle it. Buddhism, the state religion, was brought to the country in the eighth century by the Indian mystic whom the Bhutanese call Guru Rinpoche. He is one of the several foundational figures in Bhutan's historical and political history along with Tibetans such as Ngawang Namgyal, who arrived in Bhutan in the 1600s and is considered the country's founder. Some even assert that the current name of the country comes from the Sanskrit word *Bhotant*, meaning "End of Tibet" if not from the word *Bhu-uttan,* meaning "Highland." The British, when controlling India, clearly supported Ugyen Wangchuk, who became Bhutan's first king in 1907. They even knighted him in 1904 in recognition for his assistance with difficult negotiations with the Tibetans.

Another significant impact of Bhutan's geography is that it is located where the Eurasian and Indo-Australian tectonic plates collided about fifty million years ago forcing up the Himalayas, the world's highest mountain range. The latter plate continues to thrust forward, making the area one of the most seismically active zones in the world, with about twenty major earthquakes in the last three centuries. Just a few months after I arrived, an earthquake measuring 6.1 on the Richter scale hit eastern Bhutan which we felt about one hundred miles away in Thimphu. A dozen people were killed and many more were injured. Almost one hundred schools and nearly three hundred monasteries were damaged or destroyed, and about 1 percent of the country's population were left without adequate shelter.

Just a month later, Doug and I represented Royal Thimphu College at the graduation ceremony of the country's very first college, Sherubste College, in Bhutan's far east. This was a very significant event because it was the first time students received diplomas from the Royal University of Bhutan (RUB) rather than from Delhi University in India which had previously handled academic certification for that college. Excitement filled the air as hundreds of chattering graduates in caps and gowns reunited with old friends. Numerous officials, including the minister of education, gathered outside the college auditorium after making a tortuous two-and-one-half-day journey over rough roads from Thimphu. A carefully produced fifty-page program described the order of events scheduled down to the minute (e.g., at 11:37 a.m., degrees were to be conferred). His Majesty the Fifth King was to be welcomed by a bevy of officials at 9:30 a.m.

But something was wrong. A single-page, hastily duplicated, revised program being handed out was causing considerable consternation. It indicated that His Majesty would not arrive until 3:30 p.m., well past the originally scheduled end of the festivities, with much of the ceremony rescheduled accordingly. Word of mouth indicated that His Majesty's trek to remote, earthquake-affected villages had taken longer than anticipated. When the Fifth King finally arrived, he gave a wise and warm speech and then shook hands and posed for an individual photo with every graduate. I overheard one of them declare that this was the best day of his entire life.

Just two years later, another even bigger earthquake, measuring 6.9 on the Richter scale, damaged more than twelve thousand structures in the country. At the time, Doug and I were having dinner in downtown Thimphu with two professors from California. Without warning, the hotel dining room started to shake violently and the lights blinked out, leaving us in total darkness. After what seemed like an interminable time, although later reports said it lasted just thirty to forty seconds, the room's shaking stopped. We had no idea how to get out of the building in the pitch dark because the usual exit was blocked by ongoing renovations. Our server screamed loudly again and again in panic. One of our guests stood up, put her arms around the distraught young woman, and said calmly, "Don't worry. I'm from California. We have earthquakes all the time and we're fine." After we endured another ten minutes of anxious darkness, the electricity came back on. As we left, the server approached us with a tear-stained face to thank our guest repeatedly for helping to calm her.

A month or so later, Doug and I spent a weekend in the Paro valley, about twenty-five miles closer to the epicenter of that earthquake than Thimphu. We visited a village where some young boys had earlier taken us mushroom hunting in the forest. They astonished us by finding mushrooms high up in the crotches of dead trees rather than on the ground, where we had been looking. We crossed a river on a rickety foot bridge and headed along a path bordered by extensive golden rice fields almost ready for harvest. The afternoon was beautifully clear and very sunny, producing hundreds of twinkling sparkles on the river as if someone had thrown a handful of golden glitter on its surface. I regretted that I had forgotten the hat I always wore when hiking to prevent sunburn. We stopped to chat with a boy of about eleven sheltering from the hot sun under a weeping willow. He took one look at my reddening face and reached up to puck several leafy twigs from the tree. He deftly turned them into a verdant circlet, which he presented to me with a smile. I wore it happily on my head, as I had seen Bhutanese do, as we proceeded toward the village.

Once there, we noticed that some of the dozen or so dwellings constituting the village had new cracks in their rammed-mud walls. As we walked by the home of an acquaintance, the owner popped out of his front door to say hello. We chatted for a few minutes and then asked about the earthquake

This woman, heading toward a festival, is wearing a red embroidered strip of cloth called a *rachu* that is required on many occasions, including visits to temples, dzongs and other government offices.

Rural men, women, and children wear leafy hats to protect them from the intense sun.

damage the village had suffered. He somberly replied he was beginning to dismantle his family's house due to such damage and invited us in to see it and talk further over tea.

We followed him inside and then up a steep staircase to the second floor. On the walls of a large room, which had been completely emptied in preparation for demolition, were three lovely paintings. Two large ones, about eight feet high by three feet across, had been painted on rough cloth which had then been glued to the wall. The smaller one had been painted directly on the wall itself. One of the big paintings had a major rip in it. I asked how that had happened. Our host replied he didn't know, but that it didn't matter because the paintings were going to be demolished with the walls. The family would get new paintings for the new house.

Our host could see that we were struck by the paintings' beauty. He said that if we could manage to get them off the walls in a condition worth saving, we were welcome to have them. We were a bit taken aback but delighted by this offer. He hurried away, returning with a ladder with bamboo crossrails held onto its rough bamboo legs by thick twisted vines. I doubt it had ever supported someone of Doug's size (six feet three inches tall and over two hundred pounds) before. But Doug is never one to refuse a challenge. So, he gingerly climbed up the quaking ladder and gently tugged along the top edges of the paintings. When they came loose, he slowly pulled each of the big canvases from the wall to which it was glued.

When we returned to the US, we hung the life-sized painting of a Bengal tiger in the front hall of our home in Colorado as if it were guarding the entrance. The golden bird perched in a richly fruiting tree in the other large painting also keeps fond memories of Bhutan fresh. I especially love the dozens of small, gold, 3-D dots on its feathers that remind me of similar ones dappled on the images of dragons that are ubiquitous in Bhutanese temples.

Unfortunately, earthquakes are not the only natural disaster common in Bhutan because of its location and topography. Floods, landslides, and fires are also common. Shortly after I arrived in Thimphu, floods caused by cyclone from Bangladesh killed a dozen Bhutanese, destroyed many bridges, and almost flooded Thimphu's main market. Sadly, we also saw reports of children being swept away by flood waters on their way to or from school in the national newspaper. Monsoon rains even brought flooding to the end of the runway at Bhutan's main airport. The day I wrote this page, four soldiers died working to rescue twenty-one people trapped when a monsoon downpour changed an engorged river's course. Heavy monsoon rain also contributed to a landslide that submerged most of a primary school in central Bhutan—including the principal's office and classrooms, which filled with mud and slush that forced its way in through the windows.

Forest fires too are a serious problem, with an average of over sixty of them a year devastating large swaths of Bhutan's heavily forested mountainous terrain. Every ten degrees of slope roughly doubles the speed of a fire's spread. So, Bhutan's extraordinarily steep topography is conducive to fires racing up the hills at a tremendous pace. I will never forget the first time I saw attempts to control a forest fire on the Bhutan Broadcasting System's evening news. A group of men, sweating heavily, were swatting doggedly at leaping flames with thick leafy branches, hoping to deprive a raging fire of oxygen. I didn't believe I could have even lifted branches of the length they needed to use to avoid being consumed by the flames they fought.

Forest fires have been visible from Royal Thimphu College even though it is just on the outskirts of the capital city. Also, once, while hiking near Thimphu, we were startled to hear children from a village we had passed through about fifteen minutes before, racing up the path shouting, "Stop! Stop!" We immediately halted, hoping we had not inadvertently wandered into the off-limits sacred area of a local deity. It turned out that a few minutes after we had left the village, the radio announced a forest fire in the immediate area. We swiftly made our way back down the rocky path, thanking the children profusely. As we drove back towards our apartment, we saw dark clouds of billowing smoke on the mountain and thought again of the villagers with gratitude.

Bhutan frequently experiences natural disasters like earthquakes, floods, and fires. It is especially vulnerable to severe consequences from these events because it lacks much modern technology and is quite poor. For example, a report on one earthquake concluded that structural damage and injuries were both increased because the mortar between the irregularly shaped stones constituting the homes' walls was nonexistent or of poor quality, etc. Also, many people live two or more hours' walk from the nearest basic health facility, which means that injuries are likely to have more serious consequences than when medical treatment is readily available. For example, an acquaintance told us about a relative who, after falling off his home's roof, had to be carried on a homemade stretcher down a rough path for four hours and then driven another several hours to a hospital before his serious head trauma could be treated.

The well-known scholar Dr. Karma Phuntsho and others have suggested that belief in local gods and spirits is so prevalent because of the many difficult environmental challenges the Bhutanese have faced for centuries. In addition to the natural disasters already mentioned, hailstorms, windstorms, droughts, wild animals, insects, epidemics, and the extraordinarily steep and rugged topography all make life difficult and uncertain for the inhabitants of this region, the majority of whom typically survived, often rather precariously, by subsistence farming. A belief in such beings helps to explain the capriciousness of nature because they are seen as being capable both of anger and of protecting humans.

Such beliefs also provide some sense of control, through the development of appeasement and propitiation rituals designed to persuade these entities to protect individuals and their communities. We once witnessed a long, colorful procession of villagers, led by a young maroon-clad monk holding sacred texts, undertaken to persuade the local deities to bring much-needed rain for the rice crop. Also, during the COVID-19 pandemic, Buddhist institutions across the country conducted three-day ceremonies in which offerings were made to Mahakali, a goddess in both the Buddhist and Hindu religions, in the hope that she would banish the disease. The secretary general of Bhutan's Central Monastic Body offered related advice: "We all should give more importance and pray to Palden Lhamo [another name for Mahakali] this year as she is the guardian mother who keeps ... all pandemic diseases at bay."[11]

Bhutan's government has undertaken many efforts to reduce the occurrence of natural disasters as well as to mitigate their consequences. The country has almost seven hundred glaciers and over 2,500 glacial lakes. Rapid glacial melt and/or heavy rain leads such lakes to suddenly burst through the rock walls containing them, killing people and destroying property. After the last such major outburst, an effort was made to reduce the water level of several glacial lakes, so that if they did burst, the resulting flood would be less devastating.

About three hundred farmers, yak herders, and tourist guides hired for this project trudged five days through a frigid landscape, including a pass at over seventeen thousand feet and areas of knee-deep snow. It was so cold that the margarine used to flavor their rice congealed before they finished their meals. With no machinery at all, the workers deepened and widened the lakes' outlets, removing rocks from the icy water by hand. Three died, two from altitude sickness. On the arduous trip back, workers had to burn their blankets and clothes to cook their food.

Bhutan's challenging terrain also has a major impact on what people eat and how it is produced. As one profile of the country explains, "With much of Bhutan too steep, too high or too cold to farm, only 8% of land is cultivable, and most of this is fragmented and scattered in difficult terrain, making farm labor intensive and mechanization difficult."[12] For example, although Japanese aid programs have provided power tillers, many fields are too steep, too small, or too isolated to make them practical. Subsistence farming is still quite common. Until quite recently, most people ate mainly what they—and their neighbors if they had any—could grow. In the lower southern areas, rice and fruit flourish. In temperate areas, wild mushrooms, fiddlehead ferns, and wild peaches are readily found in the forests, and many crops, including various kinds of chilies, can be grown. But in substantial swaths of the country, only cold weather crops like buckwheat, potatoes, broccoli, and spinach can be readily cultivated. Thus, many Bhutanese had little choice but to consume very restricted diets because topography made travel and trade so difficult.

Just how limited these diets are is illustrated by the stories of two foreigners who lived in Bhutan for several decades. Michael Rutland, who came to serve as tutor to Bhutan's crown prince in the early 1970s, told me that even though he then resided in Paro, one of the richest and most fertile parts of Bhutan, the food was so basic and repetitive that he quickly lost a great deal of weight. One day, in response to this, a member of the royal family brought him a large, beautifully illustrated cookbook, printed in English, as a gift. He thanked the donor graciously but wondered what in the world he would do with the cookbook, given that most of the ingredients mentioned in it were unavailable. He discovered, however, that if he propped the book in front of him and concentrated on delicious recipes while he ate, he consumed more than he had been able to otherwise, thus halting his weight loss. Francoise Pommaret, a French scholar who has resided in Bhutan for many years, recalls that in the 1980s, "The diet was extremely limited. Radishes were very, very common, and if you wanted to eat something else you had to grow it."[13] She also washed her hair with ashes because shampoo was not available.

The traditional practice of eating much the same thing every day may help to explain a phenomenon that never ceased to surprise me. Many Bhutanese are so fond of the national dish, *ema datsi*, that they are happy to eat it for breakfast, lunch, and dinner day after day. This dish, featuring chilies so hot that they often bring tears, and a sauce made from a local cottage cheese, is typically eaten with a huge pile of rice. Chilies are so essential to the Bhutanese diet that newspaper headlines announce their impending arrival in the market when the harvest starts. When COVID-19 disrupted the chili supply, vegetable vendors "yelled and hurled themselves at the bags of fresh chilies and then at each other" when a truckload of them arrived because "chili is indispensable to the Bhutanese. Therefore, the absence or shortage of it creates panic."[14]

Even today, with improved roads, more urban centers, and the beginning of limited commercial farming, food production and sale is complicated.

In the fall, bright red hot chilies add intense color to the landscape, drying in fields and back yards, on rooftops, and even hanging outside of windows.

Chilies dry in front of a temple originally built in the 1400s by a saint called the Iron Bridge Builder whose descendants still live there. Some of the iron links in a bridge he built nearby remain there.

An entrepreneur I met who produces Western style cheese in central Bhutan bemoaned the difficulties he faced getting it to Thimphu, in the west, the main market for his product. He transported his cheese by bus because he did not want to spend two days or more on the tortuous drive to the capital city and back. So, he would load one or two large wheels of cheese on the roof of the appropriate bus with the luggage, hoping that it would not disappear in transit at one of the bus's several stops. He had to avoid transport on especially warm days because sitting in the intense Himalayan sun for many hours sometimes spoiled the cheese. If the person hired to receive it at the Thimphu bus station was not punctual, the cheese might go onward with the bus or could disappear from the bus station while waiting for the pickup. In addition, when the bus was delayed by landslides or other problems, the person picking it up had to be paid extra to wait for it. Such events reduced profit and created an erratic supply which inconvenienced vendors and their customers alike.

An imbalance between supply and demand for many food items was not unusual. For example, when we worked in downtown Thimphu before the college campus was completed, one of my colleagues always ducked out for around fifteen minutes in the late morning to get fresh milk, which was sold in used water bottles that the vendor refilled with milk. By lunch time, the fresh milk was gone and customers had to make do with the long-life milk imported from India. Yogurt had recently become available in a couple of grocery stores when we first moved to Bhutan. But it ran out so routinely that I kept a reserve supply in our refrigerator to use as starter which produced a rather watery home-made yogurt in our rice-cooker when necessary. At one point, the country ran out of mozzarella cheese so completely that the pizza shops in Thimphu had to close for over three months. At another time, the price of salt sky-rocketed based on rumors of a price hike which quickly completely cleared stores' shelves of it.

Occasionally, creativity solved the supply/demand issues. For several years, an American of Bhutanese-Chinese heritage who worked at a school in Thimphu and his wife hosted a Thanksgiving celebration at their home for all the Americans in the city. Everyone brought a dish. The hosts did a remarkable job of turning the potluck meal into a traditional Thanksgiving feast. Of course, this required turkey, and none of us had ever seen turkey in Bhutan. Luckily, the husband was friends with someone who was close to the country's then prime minister. One year he persuaded this individual to arrange the import of a large frozen turkey inside what must have been a very cold and bulging diplomatic pouch. Another year the turkey arrived from the U.S. almost completely defrosted in a Styrofoam cooler after a long trip in the baggage compartments of three different airplanes. We too sometimes had unusual items in our baggage, as we often returned to Bhutan from breaks with one hundred pounds of luggage including books and IT equipment for the college as well as other favorite items that were otherwise unavailable in Bhutan.

Although the country's topography creates many challenges, Bhutanese are aware and proud of the opportunities it also provides. For example, about 25 percent of the government's revenue comes from selling to India the hydropower generated by fast-flowing rivers coming out of the high mountains, especially in the summer when monsoon rains swell them. Also, Bhutan's status as a biodiversity hot spot provides great potential for international aid and tourism dollars. For example, the World Wildlife Fund has many projects there and tourists come for bird watching, white water rafting, and trekking in the country's amazing mountains.

Practical considerations, combined with Buddhist and pre-Buddhist animist beliefs, have led Bhutan to undertake remarkable efforts to protect the environment. Prominent among these was officially declaring over 50 percent of its land protected areas. Narrow strips of protected land connecting the larger ones promote both gene flow and adjustment to climate change for many species. Perhaps even more striking is the environmentally friendly nature of the country's constitution. Adopted in 2008, it requires retaining at least 60 percent forest cover in the country. It also states, "It is the fundamental duty of every citizen to contribute to the protection of the natural environment, conservation of the rich biodiversity of Bhutan and prevention of all forms of ecological degradation."[15]

Such policies often come at a substantial cost to villagers. For example, having so much protected land means that many farmers live near areas teaming with wildlife that eats their crops. Small thatch-covered platforms teetering precariously on bamboo legs in the middle of fields growing grains, potatoes, chilies, or other vegetables are commonplace in the countryside. Farmers sleep in these fragile huts to protect their crops from wild animals, sometimes for four or five months in a row. Except for the pleasures of occasional romantic trysts facilitated by this practice, villagers find sleeping in them very wearisome. When wild boars, monkeys, deer, porcupines, or other animals come, those on guard shout, bang vigorously on metal pans, or even light fires. But often such efforts do not suffice. In 2020, farmers in one area in western Bhutan lost 40 percent of their potato crop to wild boars despite such practices. The government has subsidized nonlethal electric fencing in some areas, which helps to protect the crops. But elsewhere farmers rig up their own makeshift fences, sometimes with serious consequences. For example, eight villagers were killed by illegal electric fencing in a couple of villages in one district.

Those living in Bhutan's southern areas are seriously impacted when elephants trample their crops, destroy their homes in search of the salt or grain inside, and even kill villagers encountered during their depredations. Unfortunately, being intelligent animals, the elephants prefer Bhutanese farms to nearby Indian ones, presumably because the Bhutanese do not normally use guns and firecrackers to protect themselves as the Indians commonly do. A herd of elephants even delayed the opening of a domestic airport in Bhutan's south when it trampled needed communication equipment; subsequently, elephants destroyed large quantities of salt, rice, cooking oil, and animal feed after breaking through the shutters of two grocery stores at night.

In other areas, tigers pose problems. One village lost almost a quarter of its yaks, mainly to tigers, in just two years. Near Trongsa, in central Bhutan, tigers killed six hundred cattle in just a year. Sadly, they also killed a villager there who was looking for a missing cow near the only east-west road in the country. A few months before that, we had planned to take a hike not far from there with one of our daughters, who was visiting. A local man saw us heading down a jungle path and, clearly extremely concerned, excitedly motioned for us not to proceed. We gathered from his rudimentary English that he was warning us about vipers, which are occasionally spotted in Bhutan. So, we turned around. Later, after hearing about the tigers in that area, we concluded that he was more likely warning us about them.

Doug and I encountered human-wildlife conflict in person as we hiked through tangled jungle near a village just outside of Thimphu. As evening began to fall, we were startled to hear increasingly loud, utterly bizarre sounds emanating from the dense vegetation on our left. The frightening noise was getting louder and louder, suggesting its source was getting nearer and nearer. It was unclear whether the racket was produced by a human in a panicked frenzy or psychotic episode or by a wild animal we could not name.

We stopped moving, whispering urgently about whether we should turn back and flee toward the village or quickly move forward on the smoother path immediately ahead of us. In the darkening afternoon, we decided to turn back. Suddenly, we saw movement in the branches of large, gnarled trees about one hundred feet away. A large troop of monkeys leaped agilely from bobbing limb to limb. A wildly vocalizing villager was in hot pursuit, protecting his nearby apple orchard. He had obviously frightened the troop as well as us, but this did not entirely put an end to their depredations. More than two dozen hungry monkeys destroyed about half of the apple crop in that valley.

Bears also love to feast on apples and are a more serious kind of threat, especially in the fall when they are fattening for hibernation. Unfortunately, it is not uncommon for villagers to be mauled or even killed by them, because bears are often found near human habitations. For example, the college set up a bee colony in the nearby forest to produce honey to be used as small gifts for guests. Using a basic, hand-cranked centrifuge to spin the honey out of the honeycombs for bottling in recycled glass jam jars bedecked with homemade Royal Thimphu College labels was great fun. But after tufts of bear fur were found in a fence surrounding the hives, a sign warning of danger from bears was put up, as was a barrier across the path going to the hives that we and students had often used. And, when Doug and I started on a one-hour walk along a forest path from Tango Monastery just outside of Thimphu to another nearby monastery, a young monk protectively insisted on joining us, saying he knew how to sight the bears that wandered in the area and, besides, he wanted to practice speaking English.

Having encountered the use of bells to minimize encounters with bears in the U.S. and Japan, early during our stay in Bhutan I purchased two small brass discs connected by a thin leather strap at a religious equipment store. These were meant to provide melodious accompaniment to monastic rituals when they encountered each other and rang. But I thought they would help us avoid a less harmonious kind of encounter with bears, so I frequently carried them when hiking. One day, Doug, who never had much faith in the bells' efficacy, returned from a solo hike and informed me that he had met a bear who said there was no need for the bells because we were too old and tough to be appetizing. Nonetheless, I continued to use them in deep forests, hoping that Bhutanese bears understood their ringing was not that of a dinner bell.

Wildlife protection policies sometimes cause very substantial hardship to others in addition to farmers. For example, fishing is severely restricted in Bhutan for environmental as well as religious reasons. For centuries, a small community of Oleps, who are believed to be some of the earliest inhabitants of Bhutan, had survived by hunting, fishing, and gathering in what became a protected area. When fishing there was officially restricted in the 1960s, they appealed to the Third King under a remarkable and still prevailing custom that allows any Bhutanese citizen to approach the king with a request. He issued a Royal Kasho (a written edit) permitting them to fish.

Unfortunately, as time passed this precious document was somehow misplaced, and the Ministry of Agriculture would not issue fishing permits without it. Consequently, this community became extremely poor. In 2005, the Ministry constructed and stocked a fishing pond for them because fishing is allowed in such places. But much of the land the Oleps used belonged to a religious figure who they believed would disapprove of fishing, even in a pond constructed for that purpose. So, the Oleps fished illegally in the river at night, employing a less sustainable method than had previously been used for their daytime fishing, and poverty remained common. Finally, in 2010, the village became the first in the country to be allowed to fish for one river species, snow trout. They are monitored by National Park officials and not allowed to fish on auspicious days or months in the Buddhist calendar. Enforcing fishing regulations in that community and elsewhere is not easy. Indeed, in 2019, over five hundred fishing related offenses were recorded in Bhutanese wildlife crime statistics.

Recently, illegal timber extraction has been the most frequent wildlife offense. Here again, protecting the environment requires sacrifices. Bhutan's Buddhists have customarily erected white prayer flags in high spots to memorialize the death of a loved one. The more flags that are hoisted, the more the deceased is believed to benefit. Traditionally, each flag is hung vertically on a single tall pole cut from bamboo, blue pine, or other trees, and 108 of them is considered an auspicious number. However, forest officials are loath to give permits for cutting so many trees for a single death. So, younger Bhutanese have begun to use metal poles, to string 108 flags on one tree, or to place new flags on existing wooden poles with disintegrated flags. But many elders have a hard time accepting such practices.

The work of harvesting, carrying, planting, and hoisting memorial flag poles in the customary manner provides a tangible way for family and friends to jointly express their regard for the deceased, as we saw one day when we encountered a group of about twenty-five men planting dozens of flags as

Old and young participate in raising white prayer flags on vertiginous mountainsides for the recently deceased.

Prayer flags in colors representing the sky, earth, water, fire, and air adorn mountain passes where the wind blows the prayers printed on them throughout the world.

we hiked high up a precipitous slope. Some were dragging heavy ten-foot bamboo poles toward the appointed place. Others were digging holes in the hard-packed earth. Still others were struggling to raise the poles or steady them upright while companions tamped down dirt around the poles' bases.

As we passed, a short, middle-aged man missing several teeth trotted rapidly toward us, urging us to have a seat on the grassy slope and join them for lunch. Soon the others trouped over, opening large thermoses of hot tea and bottles of fiery local liquor. They dug hungrily into round metal containers for rice and Bhutan's ubiquitous, stunningly hot red chilies mixed with vegetables and generously heaped our plates high. Then they reached into the pouches formed by loose cloth above the tight belts at the waists of their knee-length robes called ghos to retrieve small cups for their drinks. (I have seen everything from the knives used to cut through jungle vines to snacks, cell phones, and once, to my great surprise, a baby emerging from such pouches.) A fully loaded pouch makes even the slimmest man look as if he has made a habit of overindulging in Bhutan's delicious red rice.

The sun caught on the brightly painted wooden swords that topped each flagpole, symbolizing cutting through ignorance, as the group reminisced about the deceased, an elderly man. The first flags planted whipped in the wind as if transmitting a message with each gust. We were told that these flags help the deceased when the Lord of Death weighs his deeds to decide his fate. This daylong expedition to remember and assist a loved one in his new life was clearly an important event for those close to him and involved them all in a way that stringing one pole with dozens of prayer flags would not have.

As I tried to hold back the tears that the spicy mixture on my plate made nearly inevitable, I looked out quietly at the wondrous view. In the distance, a cottony blanket of clouds rested serenely on the ridge line of massive mountains. Between it and us was a verdant valley dotted with fields of pink cosmos and golden patches of rice almost ready for harvest. But what made the scenery so typically Bhutanese was the remarkable imprint of Buddhism on the land before us, not only the nearby prayer flags and their compatriots on distant hills, but the monasteries and temples spread throughout the landscape. We were fortunate to not only be able to see such scenes but also, very unexpectedly, to become both teachers of and friends with the residents of one such monastery, from the abbot to a youngster believed to be a reincarnated lama. I turn to this story and others about the monks we encountered next.

Trees and flowers grow abundantly around the large traditional homes occupied by farmers in temperate rural areas.

Even in Thimphu, by far Bhutan's largest city, flowers grace the landscape and many residents grow vegetables in their backyards.

Chapter 3

Meet the Monks

To encounter religion in the U.S. or Europe, individuals typically go to a place of worship like a church, synagogue, temple, or mosque. In Bhutan, religion is omnipresent. It comes to you through sight, sound, and smell whether you seek it out or not. The ubiquity of Buddhism was obvious there even before my airplane landed. Several red-robed monks with shaved heads speaking Bhutan's national language, Dzongkha, were fellow passengers on my flight from Bangkok and the plane's landing pattern took us past a legendary monastery, Tiger's Nest, as well as another large monastery in the Paro dzong. Still more monks milled around outside the airport arrivals hall and others walked in groups of two or three along the roadside as we started the sixty-minute drive into Thimphu.

Early in that trip, we saw an astonishing sight—a monk making his way about six or seven feet at a time by prostration in the left lane of the roughly thirty-mile road from Paro to Thimphu. Again and again, he lay down full-length in the roadway, then got up, put his feet where the protective wooden paddles on his outstretched hands had last touched the pavement, and lay down again full-length from that point to inch ahead the same way once more. When the Head of the Central Monastic Body in Bhutan accompanied by a member of the royal family and five civil servants prostrated this same route a few years later, it took fifteen days. It also took a tremendous amount of faith, given that this stretch of road is the most heavily travelled part of the country's east-west highway. A Bhutanese tour guide earned the nickname Chagsel Lama (Master of Prostration) by prostrating over three million times as he made his way for more than two thousand miles throughout Bhutan, India, and Nepal.

Soon after passing the prostrator, I was again reminded of religion when two cars stopped so their occupants could collect holy water from a roadside waterspout. Next, we passed the Tamchhog *lhakhang*, a Buddhist temple still maintained by descendants of the fifteenth century Tibetan called the Iron Bridge Builder, who is reputed to have built 108 bridges in Bhutan and Tibet. The story goes that, due to his wild appearance, a ferryman once threw him into the water when he refused to disembark, laying the foundation for his passion for bridge building.

As the valley widened a bit to allow extensive rice and vegetable fields on one or both sides, we passed other reminders of Buddhism, including small white structures for burning juniper to produce scented smoke offerings and brightly colored, rectangular prayer flags fluttering on trees, bridges, and mountainsides. Some of these graced a high, steep slope to the left of the road, where an imposing, ten-story tall, gilded Buddha statue gazing out across the city from the top of a three-story building filled with 125 thousand smaller statues was soon to be constructed.

Shortly before reaching downtown Thimphu, we saw the first mani-wall, elongated stone walls that devotees circumambulate while fingering their prayer beads and murmuring prayers. Mani-walls commonly have dozens of small metal prayer wheels lining their sides that believers spin as they walk past to send prayers into the world. Finally, when I arrived at the college's office in central Thimphu, hundreds of people were streaming past it towards a nearby temple for an annual masked dance festival. Drowning out the buzz of their conversations was the deep-throated resonance of monks' long telescoping horns called *dungchenps* and the rhythmic throbbing of temple drums. Many of the celebrants carried mats for sleeping on the temple grounds during this multi-day event.

Bhutan's constitution guarantees freedom of religion, but it also states, "Buddhism is the spiritual heritage of Bhutan" and, "It shall be the responsibility of religious institutions and personalities to promote the spiritual heritage of the country."[16] Historically, Buddhist lamas and monks have played an important role in governing, often holding high administrative positions in both religious and secular organizations. Thus, it is not surprising that the nation's 2008 constitution, adopted when the country became a constitutional monarchy rather than an absolute one, assumes the king to be Buddhist. It also declares that religion must be kept "separate from politics" and "that religious institutions and personalities shall remain above politics."[17] Thus, both monks residing in one of Bhutan's more than two thousand monasteries and lay monks, called *gomchens*, who live elsewhere and can have families, can neither vote nor run for office. One electoral district in Bhutan's far east was even unable to fill a local government position for seven years because such a high proportion of the men there were gomchens, and its women did not step forward to run for the office.

Roughly 75 percent of Bhutan's population practices Vajrayāna Buddhism. This is a form of Mahayana Buddhism that started in northern India in the fifth century and then spread to Tibet in the seventh and eighth centuries. Sometimes known as tantric or Tibetan Buddhism, it emphasizes the importance of ritual and of a guru or lama to guide devotees in its practices, including deity yoga, in which individuals assume the identity of a deity representing valued attributes. Some of its practices, including various sexual ones, are kept secret except from the most advanced practitioners. Its devotees see it as the fastest and most powerful way to reach enlightenment and believe that, with great effort, enlightenment can be reached within one lifetime.

The large majority of those who are not Buddhist, who are typically of Nepali heritage, belong to one of nine branches of the Hindu religion. The country's current king gifted a large and beautiful temple in Thimphu to the Hindu community when he was married in 2011, with government funds paying for the expenses. Some Hindus believe that this king is an embodiment of the god Vishnu, as was the legendary Indian king, Rama. Before the new temple was built, I once visited Thimphu's previous small rather makeshift Hindu temple with a friend who went to celebrate Diwali, a major Hindu holiday. A picture of Jesus hung on the wall along side of pictures of numerous Hindu holy men. Surprised, I asked him why it was there. My companion responded, "Jesus was a *Sadhu* [holy man], so we honor him as well." I was struck by the breadth of outlook this attitude reflected.

The new Hindu temple is the site of many events and celebrations, including an annual nine-day ceremony conducted by the Hindu community for the peace, prosperity, and happiness of His Majesty the King as well as of Bhutan and its people. That event ends the day before Dashain, the only one of Bhutan's roughly two dozen national holidays marking a Hindu celebration. The current king fosters connection with the Hindu community through activities such as praying at Hindu temples on his trips to the south, where the Nepali-heritage population is concentrated. He also offered *tikas*, a red mark Hindus place on the forehead to symbolize blessings and protection, to those celebrating Dashain at the new temple in Thimphu.

Interestingly, an official press release about this temple announced that the *Je Khenpo*, the head of Bhutan's Buddhist Central Monastic Body, had the honor of laying its foundation stone in the presence of many parliamentarians. It also stated, "The temple… will work for assimilation of Buddhist and Hindu culture in the royal kingdom."[18] Doug and I enjoyed a wonderfully warm welcome and a delicious lunch when we attended the temple's official consecration in 2020. The many buildings in the temple complex were draped with hundreds of feet of garlands made from thousands of bright orange marigold blossoms, which are customarily offered to honor Hindu gods.

Located on a mountainside overlooking Thimphu that can be seen from many places in the capital city, this temple is now an important symbol of the Hindu population in Bhutan. In contrast, Hindu temples, festivals, and the like are generally not highly visible in most of the country. During our first year in Bhutan, however, one sunny morning in mid-September, we noticed that several small huts serving as temporary temples had almost magically appeared overnight on the college's campus. In addition, many of the cars arriving at the college were decked with brightly colored balloons, ribbons, and garlands of artificial flowers. Scurrying out to explore, we discovered that the construction workers from India, who were building additional classrooms and dormitories to accommodate the coming year's cohort of students, were celebrating a day in honor of Lord Vishwakarma, the chief architect in the Hindu pantheon. He is, as one of the workers explained to me, "the God of Tools."

The altars in the improvised temples featured hammers and rope as well as butter lamps and pictures of Bhutan's Fifth King. Radios blared loud Indian music. The workers enthusiastically insisted we join them in dancing and enjoying snacks and drinks, including alcoholic ones. Later in the afternoon, the inebriated workers piled into open trucks, hefting large mustachioed idols crafted with bare torsos and four arms. We jumped into our car and followed the raucous revelers down to the river, where the idols were being tossed into the turgid water as additional truckloads of boisterous Indian workers arrived, shouting and beating drums. This annual festival brings color and joy to Thimphu, although there were so many complaints about throwing the nonbiodegradable idols into the river that this practice has been forbidden.

When I returned from the riverside to my office, I discovered that my computer, the main tool I used in my work, would not operate properly. As I contacted the college's IT support office, I wondered briefly if I should have paid appropriate homage to it on this special day by decorating it when others were festooning their vehicles with colorful garlands and putting their tools in places of honor on flower-strewn altars.

Doug and I greatly enjoyed this annual festival. The main market in Thimphu was filled with brightly hued idols that brought back wonderful memories of the color and vitality of festivals we had delighted in on trips to India. Once on this holiday, we had a flat tire, our eleventh in the country due to Bhutan's rough roads as well as to the nails and other sharp objects encountered on the campus road in the early years when so much construction was underway. So, we went to get the tire repaired.

Usually, I found the auto repair shop area on the outskirts of Thimphu rather depressing. Indian workmen labor there for long hours in dozens of noisy, small, dark, oil-stained garages squeezed together along muddy lanes so rutted that some speculate they are kept that way intentionally to increase the repair shops' profits. However, that day it was full of music and lively celebration. Indian songs blasted out from huge speakers, loud enough to almost cover the thudding and banging emerging from garages where some workers were still on the job. But others had already started celebrating, chatting animatedly in small groups around festively set tables loaded with drinks and spicy fried snacks. A nearby group in the holiday spirit (whose members had clearly already imbibed the other kind of holiday spirits) warmly invited us to join them for tea and crispy samosas filled with spiced potato and onion. We did so with pleasure, which turned a rather tedious errand into a warm and memorable experience.

Although there are a substantial number of Bhutanese Hindus in addition to tens of thousands of Hindu Indian workers in Bhutan, Buddhism is the religion that is inextricably woven into the fabric of Bhutan's history as well as its contemporary culture. There are about 7,500 Buddhist monks in the country, roughly one for every fifty Bhutanese males, as well as many lay monks and about four hundred monastic schools. Doug and I got to know some young monks quite well after we volunteered in 2010 to teach English at Nalanda Buddhist Institute on weekends. The *khenpo*, or abbot, of this monastery was a very progressive individual who wanted his monks to learn to speak English, even though at that time it was not yet part of the official curriculum developed by the Bhutanese Central Monastic Body.

The first time we went this monastery we got lost, because there are very few road signs in Bhutan and we were driving in the dark, high up on a mountain where we had never been before. When we stopped to ask for directions in a small village, we found almost the entire community in a courtyard at a birthday party for a teenage girl. They generously insisted we join in the celebratory buffet dinner and drinks, which were flowing with great abandon as is common in Bhutan. While chatting with several of the villagers, we sampled the dishes, virtually all of which were full of chilies that brought tears to our eyes and sweat to our foreheads. After a while, a schoolteacher, who was quite drunk, jumped up and started banging on a metal pan to get the group's attention. Waving his hands wildly, he pointed at me again and again, shouting, "Speech. Speech." As others joined in his entreaties, I stood up, embarrassed since I knew neither the birthday girl nor her family. I briefly thanked the villagers for their incredible hospitality and wished the celebrant a "Happy Birthday."

But we still had to get to the monastery, and it was not clear how that was going to be accomplished. Happily, before too much longer, two roughly twenty-year-old monks arrived, saying a villager had called the khenpo who then had sent them to fetch us. We stood up ready to go. But the monks knew a good thing when they saw it. They helped themselves generously to the many enticing dishes still arrayed on the buffet and enthusiastically socialized for almost an hour—including with some of the prettiest girls there—before leading us back to the monastery.

Upon arrival, we were served tea and saltine-like crackers sprinkled with sugar in the monastery's well-appointed reception room. We had a fascinating conversation with the khenpo, whose English was impeccable, about a wide range of topics until it was time for us to go to bed. But instead, our beds came to us as two young monks brought in thin mats which they placed on the floor of the reception room along with blankets and pillows. As the khenpo departed, he pointed out a rudimentary bathroom we could use far across a stone courtyard. He added that we should be careful of a dog which was extremely territorial about that courtyard, especially with strangers.

At 4 a.m., a bell rang loudly to awaken the monks for morning prayers. So, by the time English classes started at 9 a.m., our students (and we) had been up almost half a day. Doug taught the mostly teenage monks who already knew enough English from secular primary schools to carry on at least a simple conversation. I taught those newer to English, who ranged in age from about six to eleven.

Monastic education for those at the early levels has typically included the alphabet, spelling, and reading in Choekey (classical Tibetan), in which most sacred Buddhist texts in Bhutan are written. Memorization of prayers and chants also consumes hours a day. Older students move on to grammar, poetry, philosophy, meditation, and codes of conduct. Considerable attention is also given to learning ritual skills as well as arts and crafts, including religious painting, embroidery, tailoring, astrology, masked dance, and the use of ritual instruments such as horns and drums. Monks also learn the distinctive, extraordinarily deep and resonant throat singing that is a sure sign of their presence. Recently, the Central Monastic Body has changed the curriculum to include more of the material taught in secular schools.

The observance of monastic rules is also stressed, and discipline can be harsh. Indeed, a high monastic official averred, "The cane, the whip and the rosary represent the Bodhisattvas [enlightened beings] who personify wisdom, compassion and power, which are needed to discipline."[19] At the monastery in the Paro dzong, I saw the *kudrung* (disciple master) waving a long whip menacingly as the bell signaling the beginning of morning lessons rang through the courtyard and young monks scurried past him into their class. I was told by individuals who had witnessed it that closed fists and sticks are still sometimes used in monastic discipline, although official endorsement of corporal punishment of monks has ceased.

I decided to take a positive approach with my young charges. Since basic vocabulary seemed a good place to start in teaching them English, we played games like Simon Says, which provided physical activity and fun as well as learning. Using pictures, I also had students name their favorite animals and foods. I had to change the latter to a question about their favorite fruit or vegetable, because otherwise the answer "rice" was given way too often to build vocabulary as this activity was intended to do.

Many of those in Doug's class were initially hesitant to speak, fearing mistakes and subsequent embarrassment or punishment. So, he experimented with various approaches to encouraging participation. One of his more successful techniques was to have one of the less reticent monks start a story with a single sentence, with each classmate subsequently adding a sentence to build the story and then eventually bring it to a conclusion. One of the most memorable stories, given that it came from monks who are expected to promote the welfare of all sentient beings, started with, "One morning Sonam went to the market." By the time a dozen teenage monks had added to this opening, Sonam had met a beautiful girl, fallen in love, discovered a handsome rival for her attentions and promptly killed him, bringing not only the rival but the story to an unanticipated end.

Doug and I returned to this monastery again and again during several years, drawn by fascinating conversations with its khenpo, its serene location overlooking a lush river valley and the chance to teach and to learn from the monks, some of whom we began to get to know as young friends. One of these monks was about ten years old when we first met him. He already quite fluent in English, was a *tulku*, which means that he had been identified as the reincarnated manifestation of a deceased spiritual master who has made the sacrifice of returning to earth for the good of others. Tulkus are often identified at age three or four by highly respected religious figures based on dreams, visions, tests, or prior instructions from a deceased tulku. Tulkus typically leave their homes to receive special training in a monastery. In one monastery, we found in residence not only a three-year-old tulku but his mother as well.

It was intriguing to watch the tulku at Nalanda develop from a bright and energetic child into a thoughtful and curious young man with a broad face and slightly protruding ears who proudly showed us an album of nature photos he had taken with his cell phone. In his later teens, he asked us to bring him a basic science text, implying that we should get it to him discreetly because science was not part of his mandated studies. We did that, figuring that his reading the book could be seen as part of his continuing education in English, and, in any event, it was more likely to increase his understanding of the world than to do him harm.

We went to Nalanda on weekends as often as we could manage, given our other obligations. On one of these trips, after we arrived late Friday night in very bad weather—which made the trip long and quite treacherous—one of the monks asked me why we continued to make the effort to come. I replied that we both enjoyed interacting with the monks and that we wanted to be helpful to them. He looked at me thoughtfully for a moment before replying quietly, "You must be building a lot of good karma."

This reminded me of a variety of actions that Bhutanese have told me they have undertaken to build good karma, which include praying, taking pilgrimages, and attending religious festivals. I was surprised to learn that actions performed on some special days are thought to generate much more karma than the same ones performed on ordinary days. For example, some Bhutanese believe that on one special religious holiday in November the karma generated by a good deed will be multiplied ten million times and that one good deed offsets millions of bad ones.

Sometimes we helped at Nalanda in ways other than teaching English. Once we arrived to find the electric rice cookers not working and over one hundred hungry monks wondering if rice for their dinner could be prepared over an open fire. Doug, who is handy at that kind of thing, figured out how to fix the wiring, and dinner was on. Another time we brought a friend with IT expertise to repair three of the monastery's four computers, some of which had not been working for want of things as basic as a fuse.

Once, we visited Nalanda at the invitation of a monk friend to celebrate the end of a forty-five-day period called Yarney, during which the monks never leave the monastery. Yarney developed to avoid inadvertently killing insects when walking outside during the summer rains, when they are especially active. You can imagine the excitement of the boys and young men cooped up inside of the monastic compound for six weeks when the end of

These butter and flour sculptures called *tormas* come in many sizes and shapes. They typically share the altar with devotees' gifts of food and money.

Monks at Nalanda Buddhist Institute celebrate the end of Yarney, when they stay on monastery grounds for six weeks to protect the well-being of insects active in the early summer.

Yarney approaches. Its last three days are marked with activities including dramatic theological debates, special rituals, and prayers which were fascinating to see.

When we entered the monastery's temple, we saw several three-foot-tall remarkably intricate, brightly colored sculptures called *torma*, which the monks had made using butter and barley flour. Tormas, which are omnipresent in Bhutan's Buddhist temples, differ in size and shape depending on their purpose. Typically, there is an elongated central cone that hosts flat discs containing complex, three-dimensional, multi-colored paintings of flowers, animals, or geometric designs. Many of these discs are true works of art, so I was surprised to learn that torma are often kept on the altar for only a short time before being discarded. It is both appropriate and rather amusing that they are fed to local cows, a unique example of recycling one of the tormas' core ingredients: butter. When I asked why the torma were so quickly discarded after the hours of painstaking work it took to create them, I was told it was to reinforce two fundamental Buddhist beliefs. First, that attachment is unwise because it causes suffering. Second, that accepting impermanence is essential for happiness.

The emphasis on impermanence is extremely strong in the tantric Buddhism practiced in Bhutan. Many especially sacred areas in temples are decorated with depictions of human skulls, which serve as a concrete, if rather macabre, reminder of impermanence. Some temples even have skulls fashioned into drums or featured in display cases and trumpets made from human thigh bones. A monk told me that one must be special to have one's bones used for these purposes. Not only should one be tall enough to have a thigh bone of considerable length, which is essential to get the desired deep, rather eerie sound desired from a trumpet. One should also be a very well-regarded person. Interestingly though, there was a report in the newspaper a year or two after we arrived in Bhutan that numerous graves had been desecrated by thieves taking thigh bones and skulls, presumably for such purposes.

Although we greatly enjoyed teaching at Nalanda on weekends, it was clear that the monks would make more progress learning English with a full-time instructor. So, I agreed to try to locate one. The individual's pay was to be nearly nonexistent due to financial constraints. Also, when recruiting potential teachers, I had to admit that it was necessary to be ready for some less than inspiring experiences. For example, one night when sleeping at the monastery, Doug had the rather disconcerting experience of waking up because he felt something nibbling on his fingers. It wasn't me in a playful mood. Rather, it was a large, beady-eyed rat looking for a snack which thought that Doug looked tasty. Luckily, the rat had barely started his midnight snack when Doug awoke and scared him off. A subsequent call to the college's dean, a biologist, assured us that rats in Bhutan are not known to carry rabies, although some dogs do.

Another potential problem was the dog the khenpo had warned us about. It was fierce enough that I sometimes lay on my thin mattress wondering whether it was better to remain awake with a very full bladder or to try to make it to the bathroom in the face of the fierce growls emanating from his throat whenever he saw me. Looking at his mouth led me to fully understand why humans' sharpest and longest teeth are called canines.

Dealing with that snarling dog always reminded me of how Doug and I were essentially held prisoner by dogs in Thimphu. Shortly after we arrived in Bhutan, our youngest daughter was going to graduate from Yale and we very much wanted to watch the ceremony, which was streamed live starting just after midnight, Thimphu time. Because we did not have internet access at our apartment, we got permission to use the founding director's office, which had a relatively good internet connection. But friends told us it would be unsafe to walk back to our apartment in the middle of the night due to the packs of stray dogs that roam the city's dark streets. We took these warnings seriously because we had often heard bands of them howling ferociously at night after they slept most of the day. So, we took sleeping bags to the office. The founding director was surprised to find us stretched out on his couch and floor when he arrived at work early the next morning. He knew that we worked very hard and there was a lot to be done, but he did not expect us to be pulling all-nighters.

The ubiquitous stray dogs roaming everywhere in Bhutan are tolerated, and even fed and cared for, although almost two thousand dog bites were treated in Thimphu's hospital in one five-month period. This is due partly to religious beliefs. Specifically, Buddhists believe in reincarnation, a return to life after death for individuals who have not achieved full enlightenment, which would remove them from the cycle of rebirths. The form in which individuals are reincarnated depends on how they have lived their previous lives. Those who build good karma by living well are believed to be rewarded by returning as a fortunate human, perhaps wealthy, good-looking, and happy. Those who live poorly, and hence accumulate bad karma, are thought to come back as a lower species and then must work their way back up in later re-births. Dogs are understood to be just slightly below humans. I once heard a Bhutanese man say to another who was shouting and shaking a stick at a mangy mongrel who wanted to share his meager lunch, "Don't do that. That dog could be your mother."

Despite the challenges it was likely to entail, I believed teaching full-time at Nalanda would be a remarkable and rewarding experience for the right person. After much emailing and numerous calls via Skype, I found a suitable young American who was willing to come to teach English for a year at Nalanda. It looked like everything was set. But a problem arose. He was newly married and, understandably, he wanted his wife to accompany him. She was a Buddhist and a nurse, willing to provide much needed health services at the monastery and in nearby communities. If required, she was even willing to shave her head as Buddhist monks and nuns do. However, the Central Monastic Body would not request a visa for her even though that was essential for her to avoid paying the very substantial daily fee charged to most foreign visitors. So, ultimately, the couple decided not to come. A few years later, English was added to the formal curriculum for monks and Nalanda was able to hire a full-time teacher.

One of the things that surprised me most about Bhutan's monks was how many of them were so young, often no more than six years old or so. I later learned that in addition to training youth who chose to become monks or nuns, monasteries and nunneries serve another important function. They take in orphans and children from families unable to raise them due to poverty or other difficulties.

There are fewer than a sixth as many nuns as monks in Bhutan. This may be partly because historically nuns have had much lower social status than monks. Nunneries were customarily supervised by a monastery, although that is changing now. Also, because the government historically supported many monasteries but not nunneries, living conditions and educational opportunities for nuns were substantially more restricted than for monks. In addition, private support for nunneries has traditionally been less forthcoming as well. Recently, the nuns' situation has improved significantly due to the Bhutan Nuns Foundation established by a Bhutanese graduate of Mount Holyoke College in the U.S., However, full equality has not yet been achieved. I never learned what happens to many young girls in situations

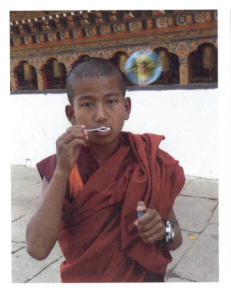

Monks too young to perform in festivals often attend them, purchasing treats ranging from bubble gum to plastic guns.

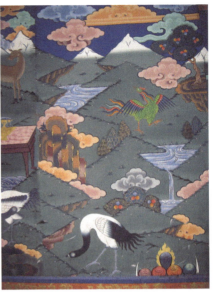

Temples' entryways, walls and ceilings are covered with beautiful and elaborate paintings produced by the monks trained in Buddhist iconography.

that would have led to living in a monastery if they were male. However, numerous households in Thimphu have young female relatives living with them to help with childcare or other domestic duties. Such arrangements most likely absorb many of them.

Clearly then, life circumstances lead many youngsters to become monks or nuns without any particular spiritual calling. Indeed, traditionally in Bhutan, Buddhist parents gave their most promising son to a monastery, which was believed to produce good karma. The current high level of youth unemployment leads at least some young monks and nuns to stay on as they mature, at least partly because of the absence of attractive alternatives. Others choose to leave when they reach adulthood, sometimes to get married. But many remain although expectations are substantial. Celibacy is expected. In addition, lengthy retreats that last three years, three months, and three days in remote hermitages under difficult conditions are considered an important addition to the education provided for monks and nuns progressing past their teenage years into adulthood. The young monks or nuns who stand out sometimes get to further their Buddhist studies in India or elsewhere outside of Bhutan.

Given that so many monks are teenagers and young men, it is hardly surprising to see them stream into Thimphu or smaller towns close to their monasteries on weekends. They visit with family, chat with friends, and stroll the streets looking for shops where they can buy everything from bubble gum to soda to shoes in a color matching their robes. Some go to the movies if they are available, which traditionalists find upsetting. Soccer games on playing fields near their monasteries are also very popular, if such fields are feasible on the mountain tops where many monks live. Those who are adolescents or older all seem to have cell phones and to use them frequently. In fact, at Royal Thimphu College's opening ceremony there were, as is normal in Bhutan for important occasions, several monks on the stage. I was amused to notice that one who was in his early twenties appeared to be dozing off, with his head leaning forward and his eyelids lowered, while an eminent person delivered a lengthy speech. I was somewhat disconcerted when I realized he was wide awake but texting surreptitiously on his cell phone.

The khenpo of a monastery told us that sometimes monks delay coming back from their homes after a break because the attractions of village or city life, including alcohol and young women, are so alluring. This is no wonder, if they model their behavior on one of Bhutan's most renowned and iconic religious figures, the fifteenth century Tibetan, Drukpa Kuenley. This tantric yogi taught Buddhism in extremely unconventional ways, typically involving copious amounts of both alcohol and sex. Arriving in Bhutan in the late 1400s, he is known for having used his "Thunderbolt of Flaming Wisdom" (i.e., his penis) to subdue a demoness as well as to enjoy many women. He is often quoted as having said, "The best wine lies at the bottom of the pail and happiness lies below the navel."[20]

Known as the "Divine Madman," Drukpa Kuenley founded a famous fertility temple, Chimi lhakhang, not far from where Nalanda Buddhist Institute is located. It is home to a ten-inch ivory, bone, and wooden phallus. Monks use it to bless women hoping to conceive a child and couples sometimes spend the night in the vicinity hoping to facilitate conception through proximity to the temple. Two small nearby villages have started booming tourist businesses selling an astonishing variety of penis-themed knickknacks in every imaginable hue and size. Some appear happy, others angry.

Traditional Bhutanese homes are large to provide room for livestock and grain storage as well as for the family. Most also have striking paintings including animals, flowers, complex geometric designs, and even ribbon-bedecked penises.

Many have eyes and even prominent teeth. Some are decorated with colorful ribbons. This is a reference to the belief that after being given a holy string to put around his neck, still a common practice in Bhutan, Drukpa Kuenley put it on his penis, saying irreverently that he hoped it would bring him luck with women.

But gaily painted images of the male organ are not just a way to separate susceptible tourists from their money. They are a ubiquitous and authentic part of Bhutanese culture. As Sonam Kinga, who later became Chairperson of Bhutan's National Council, wrote, "Phalluses are everywhere."[21] Such images are frequently painted on rural homes, hung under buildings' eaves, and posted over doorways. I have seen paintings or carvings of them in an extraordinary number of other everyday places as well: hanging on children's necklaces and from taxi cabs' mirrors, installed in granaries or in fields, sitting on altars in temples, painted on the sides of homes, featured on stamps, and even serving as waterspouts from which thirsty travelers drink.

Images of the phallus also figure prominently in many local festivals at which monks perform masked dances. *Atsaras* (jesters at these religious festivals) commonly carry a carved wooden phallus which they thrust toward female attendees of all ages, including visitors such as myself. They typically wear bright red masks, with a large red cloth phallus attached to the top that flops around as the atsara engages in bawdy antics. During the Lhabon, or the "calling the gods" festival, villagers use a ladder with edges carved in a shape of a phallus. They believe that deities will come down a rope tied to the ladder to bless them. For the three-day Kharam festival in a different part of the country, villagers carve multiple wooden phallic images every year. By the festival's end, the entire village is dotted with these sculptures in front of homes, cattle sheds, and fields. Offerings of alcohol, milk, rice, meat, or vegetables are placed in front of many of them to bring prosperity.

At a tiny village festival, I had my own unanticipated experience related to the continuing veneration of Drukpa Kuenley's phallus. A middle-aged man clad in traditional clothing circulated around the performance ground with a long pole decked with multicolored cloth and ribbons while elaborately dressed masked dancers twirled and gyrated in the center. Occasionally, the man paused, lowered the pole to gently touch a female villager's head and then moved on. When he got to where I was sitting, he softly tapped me on the head with the beautifully decorated pole and intoned, "Blessings from the phallus of Drukpa Kuenley." I felt blessed to have participated in such a memorable festival. But, at age seventy-one, I sincerely hoped that the consequence of this blessing would not be what devotees at Drukpa Kuenley's fertility temple wish for so fervently.

One weekend, we welcomed two young adult monks from Nalanda to our apartment for lunch. They were not looking for alcohol or young women. Nonetheless, it became apparent that one of them had something quite daring in mind. He announced that he had long wanted to learn how to drive. He looked pleadingly at Doug, imploring him to provide a driving lesson. After some discussion, Doug consented if our young friend promised to remember that one lesson does not a driver make. The monk solemnly agreed and off we went to a large open field where we had seen others learning to drive.

The patches of mud and the deep potholes there made it a good approximation of many Bhutanese roads. I watched as our manual-shift car initially stalled and bucked. It reminded me of my own first driving lessons at the age of sixteen, when I had been very disconcerted to see another car in the rear-view mirror after having had two earlier lessons in a deserted area. The young monk was soon remarkably adept. He emerged from the car beaming like a child on his first trip to Disneyland and with our car's clutch only slightly the worse for the wear.

The next year, the khenpo of Nalanda Buddhist Institute planned to retire and a new khenpo was going to be installed. Late the afternoon before the formal ceremony marking of these events, we got an excited call from one of the Nalanda monks inviting us to attend. The celebration was to start in Thimphu, with the Head of the Central Monk Body, the Je Khenpo himself, officiating. Then, it would progress two-and-one-half hours east to Nalanda for further festivities. We were delighted to be invited. But foreigners in Bhutan need a road permit whenever they travel anywhere much east of Thimphu. So, we immediately started that process, which often takes a couple of days. We explained the situation and were told that a permit would be issued first thing the following morning.

The investiture started very early the next day at the Thimphu dzong, which houses both government and monastic offices. Its name translates as "The Fortress of Glorious Religion," aptly suggesting the degree to which secular and religious powers have been intertwined historically in Bhutan. This dzong, which was originally built in 1641, is so massive that it took ninety men to carry just one of the beams used during its reconstruction in the early 1960s. The plan for the investiture was for the large group travelling from Thimphu to the Nalanda Buddhist Institute to stop for breakfast part way along the route. We had been told we could pick up our permit at the appropriate government office before setting out. When we phoned to let the relevant official know we were coming, we were told that the permit had been approved. Unfortunately, however, it had not yet been printed. Furthermore, it would take some undetermined amount of time before it would be ready to be picked up.

As the celebratory caravan of about twenty vehicles prepared to set out, we had to make a quick decision. Given our years of connection with the retiring khenpo as well as many of the monks, we really wanted to attend the full retirement and investiture event. If we waited in Thimphu for the permit to be printed, we would surely miss most of it. However, it was far from sure the checkpoint personnel along the route would let us pass without a printed copy of the already approved permit.

With pleading and ingenuity, two or three of our monk friends tipped the scales regarding how to proceed. They insisted there was no problem with our joining the caravan. Only cars with foreigners are expected to stop at the checkpoints. Others just drive right by. So, just before reaching the checkpoint, we could take the places of two monks in a vehicle driven by other monks. It had tinted windows with thick red curtains providing privacy from prying eyes. Then, the two displaced monks could drive our car past the checkpoint. After the checkpoint, we could exchange vehicles again and proceed. The same approach could be used on the return trip. We were very reluctant to cause a possible problem for the college by going past the checkpoint without a printed permit. But since it had been approved, we figured the repercussions would not be serious, especially since we were coming and going from Thimphu in one day rather than continuing further east. The plan worked as intended, with no harm done.

The celebration was an event to remember. After the impressive ceremony at the dzong, the caravan proceeded to a convivial breakfast at the top of Dochula pass, from which we could see the majestic peaks constituting Bhutan's border with Tibet. Then, further on, it stopped at a sloping field where villagers had set up colorful beach umbrellas and makeshift tables. They welcomed the new and retiring khenpos and the entire procession with a second breakfast. After that, the caravan proceeded to the institute for hours of further celebration full of earnest prayers and colorful rituals.

Our closest and most long-term relationships with monks were with those at Nalanda. But we had many other memorable experiences with monks and monasteries as well. Often on weekends, we hiked to the iconic Taktsang Monastery (Tiger's Nest). It hangs on the edge of a cliff high above the Paro valley on a rocky escarpment near a lovely waterfall. Guru Rinpoche, the patron saint of Bhutan, is believed to have meditated in a cave there after arriving there on the back of his consort, who had assumed the form of a flying tigress.

The hike to Taktsang takes several hours each way. It requires gaining about 1,800 feet of altitude and both mounting and descending a total of over seven hundred, steep, roughhewn steps on rudimentary stone staircases. Nonetheless, it is a popular pilgrimage destination, Bhutan's most well-known tourist attraction, and an extraordinarily beautiful sight. Thus, whenever friends or family members visited us, we hiked the increasingly familiar trail up to it. On our ninth excursion there, the man who takes charge of visitors' cameras and cell phones while they are in the monastery looked at us with a perplexed expression. He exclaimed in a surprised voice, "You again?" since virtually all Westerners visiting the temple are tourists who make the arduous trek up there only once.

Another very different hike led to an unexpected encounter with a monk in the midst of a lengthy retreat. One morning we drove west from Thimphu past the international airport in Paro and far up a steep mountainside through a deep pine forest filled with intensely scarlet blossoms on rhododendron trees thirty to forty feet high. We stopped at Chele La pass, which at over thirteen thousand feet is the highest point on any motorable road in Bhutan. From there we hiked for the first time up through hundreds of prayer flags whipping in the wind, past families picnicking on precipitous slopes and then past a tall microwave tower. We kept going for a couple of hours up grassy inclines above the tree line at close to fifteen thousand feet, taking care when possible to avoid stepping on tiny yellow and blue alpine flowers. To the right, across the Paro valley, we saw Tiger's Nest monastery and snow-capped Jomalhari, one of the highest mountains in Bhutan. To the left lay the deep Haa valley, with the contested Doklam area just beyond it, where Chinese and Indian soldiers faced off for weeks when China tried to build a road through this area that China and Bhutan both claim.

Finally, we approached our goal, a thirty-foot high rocky outcropping which provided a heart-stopping view of a long series of Himalayan peaks thrusting impassive icy fingers into the cloudless azure sky. After climbing hand-over-hand to its top, we reached a small, grassy knoll on which was perched a windowless, slightly lopsided, one-room hut with walls barely six feet high made from flat grey stones. At first, we assumed it was deserted, because it was in a high and windy place far from any source of food or water. However, we unexpectedly heard the faint sound of clinking metal coming from inside and concluded that this must be a meditation hut used for monks' retreats.

Knowing that such retreats are supposed to be solitary experiences, we decided we should not disturb whoever was inside. But our voices must have carried as we quietly discussed whether to scramble down the way we had climbed up or to try a newly visible, easier route just beyond the hut. Before we decided, a short, thin man of about fifty, clothed in a monk's robe and pink plastic sandals, emerged from the hut. He stepped toward us, welcoming us with beckoning arms. Then he turned and led us to a rocky spot just outside the hut's entrance. He pantomimed pouring tea, and quickly disappeared inside.

After several minutes, he emerged with plastic mugs of lukewarm tea clutched in his veined, weather-beaten hands. We took them gratefully and sipped as we unpacked a set of photographs that we carried with us on hikes to facilitate communication when language difficulties obstructed it. We showed him pictures of our daughters, our home in the U.S. after a two-foot snowstorm, the city where we had previously lived, and more. As he disappeared inside to get more tea, we could see that there was no furniture there except for one beat-up plank which served as a table propped up against a wall. The dirt floor was covered with flattened cardboard boxes to protect against the cold and damp. When the monk returned, we all sat

These youngsters at Nalanda Buddhist Institute eagerly learned English on weekend mornings.

Many monks meditate for three years, three months and three days in lonely places as part of their education.

in companionable silence absorbing the glorious view, the only sound the flapping of the many prayer flags strung between two tall wooden poles a few feet away.

As we prepared to hike back down to our car, Doug and I pulled from our knapsacks hard-boiled eggs, tomatoes, and crackers that we had brought for a picnic lunch. We gave them to the monk as thanks for his hospitality. It was hard to imagine how he survived in this spectacular but incredibly lonely spot. Where had he come from? How did he spend his time? Did the weathered cooking oil jugs by his door now store his water? Wasn't he terribly cold at night on the hard floor with the wind pushing its icy tentacles through the chinks between the rocks in the walls? Speaking very slowly, I asked in a couple of different ways, "How long have you lived here?" Gazing calmly at me, he said quietly, "Too long." I have wondered many times since then whether that was what he meant, or whether those words were his way of saying in his very rudimentary English, "A long time."

Several months later, when Doug and I hiked back up to this same spot, the monk was gone, and the meditation hut was empty. However, as we climbed up to the flat space on top of the rock outcropping where the hut was perched, we were shocked to see the naked corpse of a six- or seven-year-old boy. He was lying on his back with pale ribbons tying his pitifully skinny outstretched arms to pegs in the ground. Carefully laid out at equal intervals surrounding his body were pineapples, grapes, and other pieces of fruit. I was grateful the body had not been chopped into pieces as it sometimes is to make it easier for birds and other animals to gain sustenance from it.

We had heard that another lower spot on the hike was a sky burial site, where the bodies of infants and children under eight are sometimes brought instead of being cremated, as is the custom for older Bhutanese. But we had never encountered a corpse there and had no reason to expect one at the meditation hut. We left the frail body behind quickly, partly because the sight was so overwhelmingly sad and partly because it did not seem right for strangers to intrude on what must have been such a tragedy for his family.

Hiking to this meditation hut was one of our favorite excursions, because the views were so extraordinary. Also, the hillsides near it were often covered with bright red dwarf rhododendron or tiny blue wildflowers hugging the rocky earth, depending on the season. So, we returned often, frequently in the sun but once as snowflakes began to swirl down from a threatening leaden sky. Sadly, we often noticed small shirts or other evidence of additional sky burials under the scrubby foliage near the hut, including one heart-breaking discovery: a tiny, empty coffin. Another time when we returned to this spot, four huge yaks were grazing up by the hut on the rocky promontory that was our destination. When they saw us, they gathered near the point where we usually climbed up, their dark eyes watchful in heavy heads with massive horns. We turned back and left them in peace, figuring they were a lot bigger than we, as well as being a much more integral part of that almost celestially beautiful landscape.

Monks, monasteries, meditation huts, and prayer wheels powered by hand, wind, or water are visible manifestations of Buddhist spiritual beliefs that have been a fundamental part of the Himalayan culture and landscape for centuries. In fact, when the British wanted to learn more about closed areas in the Himalayas as they vied with Russia in the "Great Game" in the 1800s, they hired Indians masquerading as monks to map the terrain with surveying instruments disguised as prayer wheels, begging bowls, and rosaries. Monks are so completely accepted and respected as an everyday part of the environment that thieves in Thimphu dressed themselves as monks to avoid suspicion before burgling a craft shop. But even the striking ubiquity of evidence of Buddhism does not adequately suggest the importance of spiritual matters in the everyday life of most Bhutanese. Over many centuries, Buddhist and pre-Buddhist beliefs have merged to create a culture in which a plethora of invisible spiritual forces, from local deities to spirits residing in lakes, cliffs, and trees, are believed to strongly impact individuals' lives. The next chapter turns to discussing these and other unseen forces that fundamentally shape many aspects of Bhutanese life.

Karma is such a fundamental concept in Buddhism that advertisements like this invoke avoiding bad karma as a reason for abstaining from undesirable behaviors.

Doug and the tulku who participated in his English classes stand near the stairway leading to the temple at Nalanda Buddhist Institute.

During a three-year retreat, an essential qualification for becoming a lama, monks are expected to mediate and reflect and to avoid speaking.

Chapter 4

Unseen Forces at Work: Local Deities, Ghosts, and Astrology

The respected Bhutanese writer, Aum Kunzang Choden, has observed, "The supernatural is an accepted phenomenon in Bhutan."[22] But the supernatural is more than accepted, it is virtually omnipresent. As a Bhutanese journalist put it, "Almost everything people do in my village is associated with the need to keep the deity happy, be it for good health, harvest or weather."[23] A wide variety of unseen spiritual forces are believed to affect almost all important matters in life. Even in tiny villages, lay monks conduct the rituals necessary to placate such forces. Shamans, local healers, and other kinds of traditional practitioners also intercede with the spirit world when troubles arise.

Over many centuries, Buddhism in Bhutan has been strongly influenced by pre-Buddhist animist beliefs and associated shamanistic practices connected to the Bon religion. Consistent with this, it is common to see statues of local deities in Buddhist temples along with traditional Buddhist iconography. And, Buddhist lamas, monks, or gomchens (lay monks) may be called upon to perform rituals intended to influence various local gods or spirits.

The local deities are believed to vary greatly in power and temperament. Some are seen as controlling large territories. Others, under them, control smaller things, such as lakes, rocks, trees, or even homes. Some deities are characterized as much more patient and mild-tempered than others. However, it is generally understood that they do not like to be disturbed, and they are upset if resources are taken from their domains. Therefore, villagers are careful to avoid the places deities are believed to inhabit, fearing negative consequences should they impact the deities' homes in any way. Consequently, many natural features, such as trees and springs, are left in their pristine state. On the road between the current capital of Bhutan and its former capital, Punakha, a substantial boulder sits stolidly in the middle of the road, which splits to go around it. Every time we drove that route, I enjoyed the experience of yielding a bit to nature rather than riding roughshod over it with dynamite, as is generally done in building roads in the U.S.

Local deities are seen as helping or hindering peoples' everyday lives. So, a common first response to many kinds of misfortune is to try to propitiate the deity believed to be causing it. For example, a thirty-two-year-old woman suffering from joint pain first consulted a shaman who told her that she needed to appease angry deities. So, she hired another shaman, a Bon practitioner and some monks to conduct the prescribed rituals. When the pain persisted, she went to a *nejom* (a woman known to communicate well with deities) who said that a water spirit living near the woman's home should be propitiated. When that did not work, the still-aching women concluded, "I think I couldn't appease the right deity."[24]

Such approaches can cost a lot. For example, the first year we lived in Bhutan, ten children and young adults from one family who were enrolled in several different schools all came down with a strange illness that included headaches, stomach pains, and convulsions. In just three months, the worried parents spent almost USD 1,500 on multiple rituals, more than half the average annual income in Bhutan that year.

A particularly interesting approach to dealing with a malevolent spirit is called *kago*, giving order. To accomplish this, a lama mentally assumes the form of a wrathful Buddha. He recites a mantra and orders the spirit to cease its harmful behavior. He threatens to make the spirit's head splinter into a hundred pieces, recites other terrifying chants, and throws mustard seeds toward the person the spirit is afflicting. Finally, he visualizes a fence around the spirit's victim to prevent further harm. More peaceful means of dealing with troublesome spirits are preferred, but they are not always considered effective. In keeping with the strong emphasis of tantric Buddhism on compassion, the kago ceremony should be conducted partly to keep the nasty spirit causing the problem from building negative karma for itself through its harmful behavior.

Angry deities are believed to cause mental as well as physical problems. I learned about this firsthand when, serving briefly as the college's counselor in addition to my other responsibilities, I sought out Dr. Chencho Dorji for advice about that work. For years he was Bhutan's first and only trained psychiatrist. Towards the end of an extended conversation, he told me how he came to that profession. The story is as illuminating as it was painful.

Chencho Dorji was one of eight children born to his father and his father's two wives. His eldest brother, Damchoy, joined a monastery as a young teenager and was initially highly regarded there. But after a while, he was sent home unexpectedly, and it became clear there was a serious problem. Damchoy's behavior was so erratic and aggressive that the family had to lock him in a storage room for their own and the community's safety. For more than ten years, they pushed his meals through a hole in a door, fearing to let him out. Since they believed he was possessed by deities, appropriate rituals were performed.

Damchoy remained seriously afflicted, so the family consulted an astrologer who said a female deity who had seduced him was to blame. But appeasing her did not help. Thinking some antiques might be angering various spirits, the family gave away many treasured heirlooms. This too did not work. Then one day, Chencho, who was a doctor by that time but had not had any contact with psychiatry, met an Indian psychiatrist. He decided to take Damchoy and a woman with similar behaviors to him for a consultation. The antipsychotic medication the consultant provided did wonders for the woman. Over time, it helped Damchoy greatly as well.

Seeing the remarkable impact of this treatment, Dr. Chencho decided he should become a psychiatrist. But he, like all other doctors in Bhutan at that time, was a civil servant. So, he needed to get permission to do this. The country had no psychiatrists, but officials did not believe training one was a good use of scarce government resources. So, five different officials denied his request. One of them threw a recommendation letter from the Indian consultant in the garbage to boot. After five years of extraordinary perseverance, Dr. Chencho was able to realize his dream of going to Sri Lanka and then to Australia for psychiatric training. It was not until four years after he returned to Bhutan that he was able to practice his specialty full time after the country's first psychiatry ward was set up in the capital city in 1999.

A few years after that, another Bhutanese citizen was trained as a psychiatrist, and later a Burmese psychiatrist joined the hospital in Thimphu as well. But ensuring that those who can benefit from psychiatric treatment get it remains a significant problem. Dr. Chencho has worked tirelessly to try to spread knowledge regarding the kinds of problems such treatment can help. Nonetheless, villagers still tend to turn to monks, shamans, and local healers first, and sometimes exclusively. Consistent with this, an exhibit at the Institute of Traditional Medicine's museum contains a medication the label says is used for treating patients with "common cold and evil spirits."

Misfortunes such as illness or bad weather are seen to be caused by many beings in addition to angry deities, including spirits, demons, ghosts, and mermaids. Eight boys are believed to have been drowned by a mermaid over the course of many years in a hot region of the country, in revenge for a local man catching her daughter, who was in the form of a fish. A popular hiking route to a mountain lake was temporarily closed in the spring of 2020. The closure's announcement in the newspaper cited concern that crowding and litter were upsetting spirits who were consequently causing hail and heavy rain harmful to crops, as well as fear that hikers might spread COVID-19. Other activities that I have been told upset lake spirits enough to invite their retribution include smoking and eating garlic or onions near them.

Unseasonable storms and the unexpected illness and death of livestock followed after mountaineers were first allowed to try to summit some of Bhutan's extraordinary peaks in 1983. Many yak herders believed that such problems arose because the climbers had displeased the mountain god, Mahakala. This contributed to the government changing its policy and forbidding such activity. As a result, Bhutan is still home to the world's highest unclimbed mountain, Gangkhar Puemsum (Home of the Three Spiritual Brothers). Several expeditions tried without success to surmount this giant when climbing was allowed. Ironically, one of them failed because the climbers could not even find the almost twenty-five-thousand-foot peak on Bhutan's remote northern border.

Because annoying deities is believed to bring misfortune, people often seriously inconvenience themselves to avoid doing so. For example, Doug and I attended a festival at a temple high up on a mountainside in an area reputed to have a particularly powerful local deity. We were glad to finally arrive there because it took three tries to get our car to the top of two particularly steep and rough stretches of the pitted dirt road leading to it. We noticed a U.S.-educated Bhutanese friend, whom we had seen at the festival the previous year, join the crowd watching the whirling, masked monks performing sacred dances. But when we searched for him to say hello shortly thereafter, he had already left. This surprised us, because the trip up to the monastery was so difficult and such festivals are always at least day-long events. Later we discovered that our friend had been sick that day. He had come to the festival nonetheless because it is well known that if you attend this festival once you have to come every year thereafter to avoid the local deity's wrath. A mutual acquaintance remarked that even if our friend might not be completely convinced of this, his elderly relatives would have been so worried about the repercussions of this failure to attend that coming was the right thing for him to do.

The invisible beings that influence so much of life in Bhutan are not only believed to react when actively annoyed. They enjoy offerings and prostrations, and failure to pay them their dues can result in problems. Thus, villagers perform annual rituals to please them, typically involving offerings such as food, alcohol, or money, in hopes of good health and prosperity. For example, those living in one small village take an annual eight-hour hike up a steep route to reach a monastery housing a powerful protective deity. On the way, they stop three times to prostrate and leave offerings of rice and dried meat. The route goes through forest thick enough that one of the men must use his knife to cut through the clinging vegetation while the others shout to ward off bears and wild boars. Their goal is a high peak on which sits a monastery containing a statue of their local deity, which only monks are allowed to view. After arriving, they rest briefly before turning around and heading back down.

The extent to which spiritual activities typically permeate life in Bhutanese households is hard for most Westerners to imagine. It can be illustrated by describing the construction of a traditional rural home. On a day determined by astrologers, a ritual is conducted to get the earth spirit's permission to build. Another ritual determines where the construction should start. The door of the house is constructed with a low lintel as well as a board that must be stepped over at its base. This is done to keep malicious spirits out because it is believed they can neither step high nor bend their necks.

The best room in the house is the altar room. Every morning, seven bowls of fresh water are placed on the altar, which is typically the only elaborately painted and carved piece of furniture in the home. When the construction of the house is complete, or even when each floor has been finished, monks lead a cleansing ritual. If the home's occupants have enough money, this ritual will include many monks with trumpets and drums as well as bare-armed, bare-legged men dancing with flaming torches to chase evil spirits away. Friends and family will parade around the home with offerings before raising one carved wooden phallus to hang from each corner of the roof to ward off problems.

Doug and I participated in a much simpler version of a home cleansing ceremony when we were the first occupants of faculty and staff housing at the college. An imposing, crimson-robed monk preceded us through the doorway to our apartment which had a white scarf draped above it as a gesture of welcome. He then circulated slowly through each room chanting in a deep vibrant voice and throwing grains of rice gracefully into the air as he proceeded. This may have prevented evil spirits from bothering us, but it did not prevent me from being shocked, in both meanings of that word, when I leaned against our living room wall and felt a surge of electricity run through my body due to faulty wiring, although the college was renowned for the excellence of its construction.

Once a new home is occupied, residents annually propitiate the local spirits and hoist a fresh white flag to show this has been accomplished. If a baby is born, monks will name her and perform a purification ritual. When that child heads off to school, she will be sure to get home before dark for fear of ghosts or evil spirits. Her father will invoke deities to promote his team's success in village archery matches. Her mother may well head to a fertility temple if she has not conceived another child as soon as desired. Or, if the mother conceives a male child when her husband is away and that boy grows up to be especially strong, he may be considered the son of a deity.

If grandparents are not residing with the family, they are likely to be living at a monastery or temple to focus on spiritual pursuits. In any event, elders often spend time in both the morning and the evening chanting prayers to help them achieve their wishes, avoid misfortunes, live longer lives, build merit for a better rebirth, and assist them in reaching enlightenment more quickly. The date for beginning the family's planting of rice will be determined by an astrologer. During the harvest, ashes may be dropped around the fields in a ritual to keep wild animals and other pests away. Before threshing the product of their hard work, family members will burn incense and make offerings to the local deities.

Archery, Bhutan's national sport, is very popular. It is often accompanied by considerable drinking and female spectators sometimes cheer on the teams with bawdy songs from the sidelines.

Elderly Buddhists in Bhutan commonly spend much of their time in religious pursuits.

This farmer graciously invited us into his home for tea. As is common, the living area had little furniture.

In Western countries, with increasing levels of education, urbanization, and globalization, many time-honored religious beliefs and practices have waned markedly. As a tourist in Europe, I have been saddened to visit magnificent cathedrals that feel more like tourist attractions than houses of worship. Similarly, there is no doubt that changing levels of development and increased contact with the outside world have impacted beliefs and practices in Bhutan, but only to a limited extent so far. For example, almost two-thirds of trained health workers surveyed reported that patients bitten by snakes typically go to a local healer before seeking treatment at a hospital. Treatments used by such healers include applying honey and rubbing the affected area with a black stone called *jhhar mauro*, which is believed to absorb snake venom. Sadly, such approaches can delay administration of antivenom serum long enough that people die from the bites of cobras, pit vipers, and kraits.

A colleague at the college told me about how the family of a friend decided whether to use allopathic (Western) medicine or traditional healing to treat her mother's serious cancer. They had a monk conduct a divination by throwing dice to decide. Since my colleague's friend had a Master's degree in a scientific field from an international university, I was quite surprised by this. But, upon reflection, it seemed that neither approach to treatment was guaranteed to work. So perhaps this approach reduced the potential for conflict and stress within a family facing an excruciatingly difficult decision about which they might have sharply contrasting views.

Although traditional beliefs are generally most pervasive among the elderly in rural areas, they also strongly impact the lives of younger urban individuals. Royal Thimphu College students commonly listen to Western music and wear blue jeans and t-shirts when relaxing. The college had to cut off access to Facebook during work hours because students' almost obsessive use of it consumed precious bandwidth needed by faculty and staff for their work.

Yet, at the student government's request, the college instituted an annual *rimdo*, an event consisting of rituals and ceremonies undertaken to achieve purposes such as successfully completing projects and overcoming hindrances. Students also have taken responsibility for tending an altar room at the college and they started a meditation club. When a *rinpoche* (an honorific meaning "precious one" used for especially respected Buddhist figures) initially declined to give individual blessings after a lecture, the students' disappointment was so palpable that he reluctantly reversed his decision. Many waited patiently in line twenty minutes or more to receive theirs. A student told me that when smoking marijuana he had a vision of Guru Rinpoche, the yogi who brought Buddhism to Bhutan in the eighth century.

As a teacher, I was disappointed to run into one of my students at a temple festival on a day set aside for study immediately before midterm exams. She explained she had come to the sacred place to pray for success, as many students do. The front page of Bhutan's main newspaper featured a picture of the crowd at that temple with the caption, "Thousands of devotees including students visited the Dechenphug lhakang to celebrate Lord

Buddha's Parinirvana and to receive blessings for the upcoming midterm examinations."[25] When I saw the outcome of my student's exam, I wished she had spent the time reviewing class notes and readings. A final rather ironic piece of evidence of students' interest in religion was the discovery that books on Buddhism were the most common type of material stolen from the college's library.

Both the Buddhist and Hindu religions include the concept of ghosts. It is therefore not surprising that an official at the college, who had been a schoolteacher and principal for many years, told me, "There is probably not a single school in Bhutan that is not haunted." At the college there were reports, almost always from female students, that the forest surrounding the college was haunted by a crying baby. A very bright and mature student told me she was worried that a ghost would steal her soul, and a young teenager, whom my husband and I met in a small village, said she never went out at night because of ghosts.

When the contents of the college's suggestion boxes were reviewed in the very first management meeting after the college opened, all seven notes found there were complaints about the haunting of a female residence hall. The appropriate preconstruction ceremony for the earth spirits and the later cleansing ceremony for the newly constructed residence halls had been conducted before the students' arrival. Despite this, another very public ritual was arranged which mitigated, but did not permanently end, complaints about the haunting. A couple of times when walking not far from the college, I came across initially mystifying multicolored items made of yarn that was threaded around a bamboo core to produce a small, semi-enclosed box. It turned out that these were ghost-catchers that were thrown away when they had served their purpose of ensnaring a ghost or other pesky spirit.

Ghosts not only haunt schools. Spirits of the deceased are believed to be able to take possession of another's body. For example, a final year student at Royal Thimphu College was believed to be possessed by the spirit of a peer who had died the previous year. Students said she spoke with a voice that was just like that of the deceased young woman and she appeared to know the deceased friends, although she herself was not well-acquainted with them. The event caused considerable commotion on campus and things only calmed down when her family came to take her home.

Another of our students, a mature and intelligent young woman, told me that such possessions are very common. She described two of them that she had seen, one involving her own family. Not long after this student's sister died, another young woman in the village started talking in the sister's voice and discussing things that the deceased sister knew, but which the possessed individual was unlikely to know. It seemed clear to everyone in the village that the sister's spirit was in this young woman's body. The possession lasted less than a full day and afterwards the individual experiencing it had no recollection of it. A Bhutanese faculty member explained to me that for about seven weeks after people die, they are in limbo, between their old life and their new one. During that time, their spirit looks for a body to possess.

The belief in possession is so strong that testimony from two individuals, believed to be possessed by the spirit of a murdered secondary school student, in which they identified the killers of the student and his grandmother, was accepted by the court during the double-murder trial. A student possessed by the same spirit confirmed the accusation. The legal officer prosecuting the case argued that "the repeated spirit possessions indicate Kado [the accused] murdered the victims."[26] The court accepted what the three possessed individuals asserted as circumstantial corroborative evidence when handing down a guilty verdict.

Black magic, sorcerers, poisoners, witches, and headhunters often cause concern, especially in rural areas. For example, two men were sentenced to prison after murdering a third. They claimed that the murdered man had been creating trouble in their village through black magic. They alleged that when one of them consulted an astrologer to discover the cause of his mother's serious illness, that man's face appeared in the astrologer's mirror. "If the astrologer did not show the image, I would not have murdered Sangay Tshering," one of the men said in explanation.[27] In another case, a farmer recruited some young women to work in his fields and then kept them there without pay for months by threatening to practice black magic on them if they left.

Older rural women are sometimes believed to be *dug-bekhan*, or poison-givers. This can be an inherited status, as in the case of a woman whose daughter and mother were also seen as poison-givers. When the Fifth King visited this woman's village, he drank some locally brewed liquor she gave him to demonstrate that it was safe. Unfortunately, most people still refused to eat or drink anything she offered. Many continued to ostracize her, even though she visited many religious sites and performed rituals trying to win acceptance. She told newspaper reporters, "The villagers ignore me as if I am invisible."[28]

Khekpas, or headhunters, are believed to kidnap children and cut off their heads to put under dams and bridges to strengthen such structures. I first heard about khekpas from a teacher at a rural school near Nalanda Buddhist Institute who invited us into her classroom so her students could practice their English. On one of several later visits to the school, we asked why there were many fewer students than usual. The teacher explained that a dam was being built nearby and parents had heard there was a khekpa in the area. So, many were keeping their children at home. Those children who came to school were being escorted by adults for safety's sake. A few years later, there was a rumor further east about khekpas that was passed on to parents and teachers through WeChat by a local official. He explained, "It was just a precautionary measure that I took as a member of the community for the safety of the children."[29] Schools were dismissed early so the students could go home. The police investigated, but to no avail. In another area, police arrested and interrogated a monk suspected of being a khekpa. He was released after it was determined he was mentally disturbed.

Both of Bhutan's major religions commonly use astrology, in which the future is predicted based on the movements of faraway celestial objects. Evidence of astrology's importance was quite apparent at Royal Thimphu College. Indeed, when I asked a student what he and his peers used astrology for, he replied simply, "Everything." When I asked for examples, he mentioned activities ranging from determining a good time to get a haircut, to performing charitable acts, to approaching authorities with a request.

Faculty and staff use astrology for a wide variety of purposes as well. For example, a colleague told me that her house back in her village had been burglarized while she was in Thimphu. She consulted a village astrologer to get the name of the thief, although she was quite suspicious of a particular individual. The astrologer was not able to provide the thief's identity, but he did prescribe some rather expensive rituals to prevent future thefts. My colleague said she almost regretted the consultation, because her initial loss was compounded by the substantial additional expenditures these rituals entailed.

Astrology is also used to set the dates for important occasions. Indeed, the celebration of the one hundredth year of the monarchy was postponed from 2007 to 2008 so that it could be held in an astrologically more favorable year. The date of the Fifth King's coronation and his wedding were set by royal astrologers. Astrological considerations even delayed mass vaccination for COVID-19 from late January until mid-March 2021. A mini crisis arose at Royal Thimphu College when the College Management Committee initially neglected to consult an astrologer about the date for the college's first graduation ceremony. This event was especially important because precedents and traditions would be set and the college's public image would be significantly impacted by how well things went, given how many highly respected and influential individuals would be attending.

A very important decision for any major occasion in Bhutan, such as a graduation, is who will be the chief guest. I thought that former U.S. Vice President Al Gore would be perfect for this role at the college's first graduation. His path-breaking work on environmental issues and his experience with democracy meshed extraordinarily well both with programs offered at the college and with Bhutan's priorities. After consulting with other members of the College Management Committee, I invited him through his speech booking service, recognizing it was a very long shot. Unfortunately, the booking service lost interest when informed that the college could not provide a fee. (I have always believed that if the request had gotten through to the former vice president, he might have accepted out of interest in Bhutan's unique environmental policies.) Perhaps more realistically, the college next decided to aim high within the country and to invite Bhutan's prime minister as chief guest. We were absolutely delighted when he accepted.

But then, a faculty member inquired whether an astrologer had been consulted before setting the graduation's date. Somehow the management committee had overlooked this, and it was clear it had to be done. If the date we had already selected was inauspicious and anything went wrong, it would be disastrous. However, changing the date might well mean that the prime minister would not be available, and even if he could come on a different date, it would be embarrassing to change the date for him. We almost literally held our breaths as an astrologer was consulted. The answer was not good. Our emissary to the astrologer was told it was a bad day for making predictions, so no clear information about the suitability of our chosen date could be provided. A subsequent visit to the astrologer led to the conclusion that the day we had selected was adequate, although not especially auspicious. With a collective sigh of relief, we resumed planning. As things turned out, the graduation was a great success. All went well and at the very end of the festivities, a rainbow, considered an extremely auspicious sign in Bhutan, appeared, suggesting the astrologer had been unduly pessimistic about the date.

As the above exemplifies, sometimes what is convenient may not be consistent with astrological considerations. Also, some have more faith in astrology than others, which may be why we ran into the problem just described. A Bhutanese friend told me how he sometimes handles astrological predictions that seriously interfere with a desired behavior. When he needs to go someplace on a day the astrologer has indicated is inauspicious for starting a journey, he selects an astrologically acceptable day as soon as possible before it. On that day he sets out from the house with a big suitcase and ostentatious farewells to his family. Then he sneaks back into the house and later he leaves very quietly on the day that works for him, hopeful of having tricked the spirits.

Although astrology is still widely used for setting event dates, the Fourth King was very skeptical of it. In contrast, a member of his court, Dasho (an honorific used for respected males) Tsang Tsang, asserted that even the best archer could not hit the target if a powerful astrologer wanted to prevent it. To prove his point, the king organized an archery match. On one team were superb archers from the king's bodyguard. On the other team were His Majesty the Fourth King and several district governors, none of whom were as skilled in the sport. However, they were supported by a highly admired astrologer and his two deputies. One of these individuals was considered so powerful that teams facing rivals that had his astrological assistance sometimes conceded defeat without shooting even one arrow.

The Fourth King instructed the *tsips*, or astrologers, to use all their powers to defeat the bodyguards' team. If the king's team won, all three astrologers were promised cash, and the head astrologer would receive a jeep to boot. However, if it lost, the astrologers would be shamed by having leftover rice water poured on their heads, which symbolizes being useless.

The night before the match, the Fourth King and his team slept together in one room so that the astrologers could conveniently perform rituals to strengthen their performance. In addition, the astrologers pricked clay models of the bodyguards with sharpened bamboo to discomfort them. To undermine the bodyguards' confidence, they also buried these archers' names under the soles of shoes.

Contrary to the expectations of most of the audience, the bodyguards won the match decisively, suggesting that skill outweighed the power of astrology. However, reinforcing belief in astrology, in the following months, four members of the team that disproved the astrologers' power by winning despite the astrologers' best efforts had serious problems, including two who died by suicide or illness. Although Bhutan's National Council banned astrological predictions and rituals during archery matches in 2010, astrologers continue to play an important role in many such matches. They are even hired for soccer and basketball games as well.

Both Buddhist monks and Hindu priests learn astrology as part of their studies. For those who want to specialize in this field, there is a college of astrology at Pangri Zampa Monastery on the outskirts of Thimphu which provides a six-year course of study. One day as Doug and I drove past this monastery, we noticed a large, animated crowd streaming into its courtyard. Intrigued, we followed the throng past one of the biggest trees I have ever seen, which is reputed to have grown from Guru Rinpoche's walking stick. Next, we passed large sign boards proclaiming that the astrologers can provide information about your past, current, and even future lives.

We had happened upon a religious festival, the kind of event that has traditionally been the highlight of the year for many Bhutanese. I describe this one in considerable detail because such festivals are a fundamental part of Bhutanese culture. Typically, those attending don their very best clothes and jewelry, bring picnics, and socialize animatedly with friends and family. Attending a festival is not only a major social occasion providing a prime opportunity for those living in isolated areas to meet potential marital partners. It is also seen as a way to gain religious merit. Indeed, one acquaintance told me that when people die the level at which they are reincarnated is influenced by the extent of their knowledge of festival dances.

The essential elements of these festivals are folk singing and dancing by villagers and dramatic colorful religious dances. The latter are performed by monks wearing masks portraying historical figures and animals such as huge-antlered deer and ferocious tigers, as drums throb and horns bray. At larger festivals, a lively temporary market springs up, selling everything from snacks and drinks to religious items, toy guns and used clothing. Some even provide basic children's rides, like the tiny, hand-cranked Ferris wheel for preschool children we once saw, as well as many games of chance, although gambling is officially illegal.

An atsara (jester) plays with a young boy, dressed in his festival finery, whose mother is photographing them.

Monks at the astrology college festival carefully move one of the many structures build for it into the center of the courtyard, while atsaras, dressed in stripped costumes, observe.

This festival, like most held in monasteries, took place in a large courtyard. About sixty monks in bright orange robes loudly chanted and drummed in an ornately decorated pavilion. Directly across the courtyard on its far edge stood nine life-size effigies, some representing members of the royal family. One, with glassless spectacles perched on its nose, looked distinctly Western. Inexplicably, it was bedecked with a maroon monk's robe and a small grey cap just like the one my anglophile uncle used to sport on occasion. Even more surprisingly, two dozen over-sized safety pins adorned its chest, hanging down vertically like a chain. Behind and above each effigy was a gigantic 3-D ghost-catcher. Each was about ten feet high with yarn woven around the bamboo core in bright geometric patterns. A bystander told me that the loud sound of the monks' horns attracted evil spirits so they could be trapped in these and then banished after the ceremony.

Most of the more than two hundred spectators were jammed together, seated on flat, gray paving stones toward the edges of the courtyard. But some were prostrating in front of the effigies, then tucking money into the folds of the effigies' clothing or placing it on low, elaborately carved tables in front of them. A huge metal pot about nine feet in circumference, filled with glowing coals, emitted a column of smoke that wafted across the courtyard.

Bare-footed masked dancers gyrated in the courtyard's center. These monks' brightly colored full skirts flared out around their bare legs as they spun, at first slowly and then more rapidly to the echoing sounds of horns and drums. One of the monks then picked up a plate of food and twirled it around and around within a white scarf. A Royal Thimphu College student attending the festival told me the food was an offering to local deities and that "every word the monks say and every movement they make has a deep meaning." But when I inquired about these meanings, he did not know. The monks chanted in Choekey, classical Tibetan, which few others understand. This reminded me of the Catholic liturgy in Latin when I was growing up.

A middle-aged woman wearing a lovely handwoven outfit consisting of a silk tailored top and a long, tube-shaped skirt with intricate geometric designs invited me to join the dignitaries sitting in a roofed area. She ushered me into the front row of chairs, covered with bright cloths, to sit next to the head of the college. She said that she had come to the college every day for the last month to cook lunch for the participants while they prepared the effigies and practiced the dances. Soon, we were brought tea and delicious, sweet, saffron-flavored rice garnished with white raisins, a treat reserved for special occasions.

Two atsaras, jesters whose antics amuse festival audiences, took center stage. Wearing bright red masks with oversized noses, they chatted with spectators then theatrically chased and wrestled with each other. One of them pretended to whip the other, occasionally flipping the whip over his own back and between his legs, always just missing actual contact. After that, a dozen local women performed folk dances while singing traditional songs.

Later, a stream of about fifty monks lugged all nine effigies and their ghost catchers out toward the courtyard's center. Audience members filed solemnly past the effigies, placing white scarves and other offerings in front of them. After another ritual involving peacock feathers and an ewer of holy water, the atsaras motioned the audience to be seated. The monks' chanting and instruments swelled to a pounding cacophony as other monks clapped in unison, with the audience joining in. Throughout the ceremony, occasional firecrackers exploded loudly, emitting brilliant flashes of light. One

In Bhutan's first capital city, Punakha, monks perform masked dances in the dzong.

Monks jump and whirl in elaborate costumes as they perform dances based on a variety of traditional Buddhist themes and stories.

produced a perfect ring of smoke about ten inches wide that drifted slowly across the courtyard.

Finally, handfuls of corn and rice were passed out to festival goers and monks alike. They were thrown in the air at intervals for over an hour as the rituals continued. By the end, everyone had corn and rice lodged in the folds of their clothing and nestled in their hair. I found a few remaining grains of rice two days later during a shampoo despite earlier vigorous brushing. The festival's patron told me that some people criticize Bhutanese for throwing food like this, believing it should be given to the poor instead. But, she explained, Bhutanese believe these offerings will be found by the deities and that this will bring good fortune to everyone, including the poor.

The festival just described is the only one of dozens we attended that featured royal effigies. Their presence, although atypical, was not surprising because religious and temporal power have been extremely closely intertwined in Bhutan for centuries, a link that remains strong today. So, in the next chapter, I turn to a discussion of that link and other issues related to the monarchy, including some wonderful experiences Doug and I had with the current king, queen, and other members of the royal family.

Chapter 5

The Dragon King and I

When I envisioned the wise king or the beautiful queen in the fairytales I read as a child, I never guessed that I would end up attending a royal wedding or having brunch with an actual king and queen. The closest anyone in my family had come to such experiences was when my cousin, Eugene, was one of the thirty thousand people the United Kingdom's Queen Elizabeth invited to her summer garden party one year. But much about Bhutan is unexpected, which is one of its great charms.

The country's monarchy is barely more than a century old, having been founded in 1907. But to understand its current role in Bhutan, it is important to briefly go back more than four centuries to 1616, when Ngawang Namgyal came from Tibet and unified the area now known as Bhutan under his rule. Generally referred to as the *Zhabdrung* (The One at Whose Feet We Submit), he was told in a dream that he was destined to bring the Drukpa stream of Buddhism to Bhutan, and he crisscrossed much of its area giving religious teachings. In 1633, after founding a monastery that still stands near Thimphu today, he undertook a three-year retreat during which he made six thousand prostrations a day.

At that time, there was no central authority in the area as well as frequent and disruptive conflict between rival chieftains. After visionary experiences, the Zhabdrung sent out a notice saying, "All gods, humans and spirits of the Lhomonkhazi [the name for this area then] from this day fall under the dominion of the great magician Ngawang Namgyal and everyone must heed his words."[30] Eventually, functioning as both the highest lama and as king, he beat back several Tibetan invasions and quelled numerous internecine conflicts. He also set up a dual system of governance. Under him, and later under his reincarnates, one individual was responsible for ecclesiastical and another for secular affairs. Typically, both were lamas or monks. He promulgated laws, set up a tax system, and built dzongs and temples that reinforced both his religious and political power.

The Zhabdrung was so central in his time that his death was hidden for decades. After his demise, food was still prepared for him and messages purportedly from him were left on a board near the entrance to his supposed religious retreat. During the first two-and-one-half centuries after his death, two crucial changes occurred in Bhutan. First, the preponderance of power in the dual government gradually shifted from its religious to its secular heads with the result that the Zhabdrung reincarnate heading religious affairs became less powerful. Second, recurrent fighting between local power centers re-emerged.

The results of such conflict included high taxes, looting, and forced labor as well as death on the battlefield. In the latter half of the nineteenth century, Jigme Namgyal, a descendant of a famous religious figure, managed to accrue a great deal of power through military success in ongoing conflicts and by appointing relatives to influential posts. After his death due to injuries suffered when falling off a yak, one of his sons, Ugyen Wangchuk, emerged as a widely respected figure and consolidated that power. He ended the remaining conflict by winning a historic battle and building a close relationship with a prominent incarnation of the Zhabdrung. He also assisted the British in difficult negotiations with Tibet, for which he was knighted by the UK, bringing him considerable prestige.

Shortly after that, in 1907, Ugyen Wangchuk was declared hereditary king of Bhutan at a ceremony during which representatives of many sectors of Bhutanese society, including numerous religious leaders, demonstrated their approval by affixing their seals on a parchment. A representative of the British crown also attended. Ugyen Wangchuk brought peace and stability to the country and managed to ward off China's claims of suzerainty over the country. He also strengthened relations with the British and set up the first secular school in the country for fourteen students.

His son, Jigme Wangchuck, assumed the throne in 1927 as Bhutan's second king. One of his important contributions was making the onerous taxation system less complex and burdensome. A typical tax-paying household at that time owed the king about one thousand pounds of rice, sixty pounds of butter, and sixty baskets of bark for paper, not to mention a substantial amount of textiles, straw, dry grass, mustard, dried chilies, and dried pumpkin. Jigme Wangchuk also reduced some of the existing extraordinarily harsh punishments for criminals, their families, and even their villages, and fostered good relations with India as it emerged from the grasp of the British Empire.

Bhutan's third king, Jigme Dorji Wangchuck, reigned from 1952 to 1972. He ended serfdom and undertook related land reform. He also gave citizenship to many Nepali-heritage individuals, who constituted about 20 percent of Bhutan's population at that time. In addition, he took some modest steps toward decentralization and democratization, although the country remained an absolute monarchy.

Bhutan's fourth king, Jigme Singye Wangchuck, took charge in 1972 at the young age of seventeen upon his father's death. At that time, a small number of primary school graduates served as government officials because very few Bhutanese had any education beyond that. During his thirty-four-year reign, households with electricity increased more than sixfold to sixty-five thousand, the number of students in schools rose by more than tenfold to over 150 thousand and the number of heath service centers increased more than twelvefold. He also strongly promoted the Buddhist religion and related aspects of cultural preservation. (More will be said about this in Chapter 6, because this effort also led to an issue which still haunts the country to this day.) His accomplishments were such that the highest Buddhist cleric in the country identified him as a reincarnation of the Zhabdrung. In 2006, *Time* magazine named him as one of the one hundred people "most influencing and transforming our world," and he received the J. Paul Getty Award for Conservation Leadership as well.

Perhaps this king's most remarkable achievement was orchestrating the transformation of the governmental structure from an essentially absolute monarchy to a constitutional monarchy with most of the power concentrated in a parliament. In 2006 at the age of fifty-one, when a new constitution was in strong draft form, he abdicated in favor of his son, Jigme Khesar Namgyel Wangchuck, who was crowned in 2008. The country's new constitution requires kings to retire at age sixty-five. Even more surprisingly, it allows for their impeachment with a two-thirds vote by the members of parliament.

Nonetheless, the position remains fundamental to the country and its sense of identity.

Doug and I were in Bhutan in April of 2007, exploring possible job opportunities. Our visit coincided with the week in which mock elections were conducted in preparation for the first parliamentary elections to be held as part of the transition to a constitutional monarchy. At over eight hundred polling stations, Bhutanese familiarized themselves with the concept and the actual process of voting for members of various political parties. In this practice election, four fictional parties were presented: yellow for "the preservation and promotion of our rich cultural heritage and tradition," red for industrial development, blue for fairness and accountability, and green for the environment. The following month, a runoff election was held between the two parties receiving the most votes. Interestingly, the yellow party ultimately won forty-six of the forty-seven contests, suggesting that maintenance of tradition was strongly desired. The Election Commission was so determined to encourage citizen participation in the subsequent actual parliamentary elections that people in extremely remote areas were paid to vote because, for them, getting to a local ballot box entailed a several-day roundtrip through difficult terrain and a significant amount of time away from work in their fields.

Consistent with the outcome of the mock election, but even more striking, was the general attitude of the citizenry towards the anticipated shift in governance. As the Minister of Economic Affairs put it in a talk at Royal Thimphu College, "At first the people of Bhutan totally rejected democracy."[31] Bumper stickers, placards posted on buildings, and numerous conversations all suggested that the majority of people did not want a shift from the absolute monarchy to a democracy. They were anxious about exchanging a system that had brought so many positive changes since 1907 for one involving politics and politicians. The general feeling seemed to be one of resignation to the Fourth King's wishes combined with an often rather faint hope that democracy would work well since the king obviously thought it was the best course of action.

One incident that strongly reinforced the almost worshipful attitude of many Bhutanese toward the Fourth King was the way he handled a significant threat to the country that arose during the 1990s and persisted into the early part of the following decade. Several Indian militant separatist groups had set up camps in Bhutan's southeastern jungles to wage guerilla war in the bordering Indian states of Assam and West Bengal. Over many years, Bhutan actively encouraged these groups to leave, even offering them money to do so. But they stayed put. With India getting impatient and even suggesting it could enter Bhutan to clean out the camps, in 2003 it was decided that military action was necessary. Doug and I were not in Bhutan when this happened. However, we were both fortunate enough to learn a lot about it from individuals directly involved.

In 2014, I spent a week leading a faculty workshop in Bhutan's southeast at the Jigme Namgyel Polytechnic Institute (now called Jigme Namgyel Engineering College) perched on a ridge above the river valley where some of these militants had camped for years. I talked with many individuals who lived in the area when the militants did, as well as when these intruders were flushed out. When not on raids into India, the insurgents lived quite peaceably with locals, who earned valued income selling them food and other necessities. Sometimes students, wearing their distinctive Bhutanese dress so that Royal Bhutan Army patrols would not mistake them for militants, would hike down the mountainside to play cards with the militants or to swim in the river near their camps.

But things changed. One day in December 2003, the Fourth King arrived and took up residence in the Polytechnic's guest house. He was finalizing plans to dispel the militants by force. Careful advance preparation had been done to increase the chance of success. For example, on earlier visits to some of the militant camps, the king had taken boxes of apples, which his soldiers handed out to the insurgents there. Little did the recipients realize that by subtracting the number of remaining apples from the number originally placed in the baskets, the Bhutanese got a reasonably good count of the insurgents' number.

Clever ruses were also used to hide preparations right before the military action, including holding religious services to explain the inflow of people to the relevant areas, disguising soldiers in religious clothing, and hiding weapons in religious paraphernalia. Stories about exactly what happened next varied. Two people told me that once the fighting started, statues left the temples and joined the battle with their one thousand arms swinging to assist the king and his forces.

At a dinner party at his home in Thimphu, a high official in the Royal Bhutan Army who was part of this mission (and had a picture with the

Fourth King to prove it) described the strategy to Doug. The militants were first lulled into thinking this was just another royal visit to discuss their desired departure. But then, large numbers of armed Bhutanese unexpectedly charged into their camps at daybreak, making disorienting raucous noise to scare them into retreat. The goal was to minimize deaths on both sides while still making sure the insurgents fled into the arms of the Indian soldiers who had been alerted to wait for them just across the border. These military efforts were supplemented by countrywide prayers and rituals asking the protective deities for success.

Whatever the precise details of this event, a few things are clear. The Bhutanese forces, led by the forty-eight-year-old Fourth King himself, were successful in routing about thirty camps containing roughly three thousand militants in just a few days. Bhutanese casualties were very modest in number, with just eleven deaths. Most significantly, a serious problem potentially threatening the country's safety and security had been resolved. Eight years later, after his retirement, I saw the Fourth King at the first annual Druk Wangyel festival, initiated to mark this victory. As described later in this book, it was held at the top of a mountain pass in blowing fog and snow flurries with hundreds of Bhutanese of all ages sitting on the frigid ground. Handsome and dignified, the king walked slowly through the excited crowd, stopping to greet many individuals. He then entered a covered pavilion made

Dignitaries, including the Prime Minister, enjoyed the first Druk Wangyel festival, sheltered from the blowing snow by a tent with dragons featured on its exterior.

At the annual Druk Wangyel festival honoring the Fourth King and the Bhutanese Army for their 2003 victory over Indian militants, most masked dances are performed by members of the army rather than monks.

of white cloth and decorated with brightly colored images of dragons from which he observed the festivities.

Deep public support for the monarchy is no doubt related not only to all that the kings have done to safeguard the country and improve the people's lives of the people. Their unostentatious lifestyles and willingness to mingle with the public are also very conducive to support. For example, the Fourth King lives in what is usually characterized as a log cabin, and he is often seen pedaling his bike along the roads. In 2009, I spoke with a man who claimed that he had repaired the Fourth King's television not many years before, and that it was a 1950s style TV built into a wooden cabinet with doors on the front like the one my family had in second grade. During the COVID-19 pandemic, the Fifth King travelled around the country looking after the welfare of both frontline workers and ordinary citizens, and the queen personally cooked meals for health workers and others. The Fifth King often gives relatively short notice before arriving at various places, at least partly to minimize the elaborateness and expense of preparations for his visits.

More than one prince or princess has come to Royal Thimphu College for activities ranging from serving as the chief guest at a college event to playing basketball with the students. Indeed, there was considerable consternation when one of the more aggressive members of the college's female basketball team fouled a princess, since formal etiquette demands that one neither speak to nor touch a member of the royal family without their initiating the interaction.

Public support for the monarchy has also been greatly reinforced by the fact that many members of the royal family are well-known for their philanthropic activities. Some are strong supporters of religious and cultural institutions and events. Others focus on women's and children's welfare, the environment, education, health, sports, or rural development. One of the Fourth King's sisters, Ashi (Princess) Kesang Wangmo Wangchuck, was cofounder of Royal Thimphu College and provided the land for its campus. Before the college opened, we chatted with her numerous times when she visited the developing campus to plan the planting of a wide variety of flowering trees and shrubs. A lovely magnolia tree near the entrance to the college's main building was transplanted there from her garden.

However, it took a chance meeting with a professor from Berkeley, Dr. Judith Justice, for me to learn about the vital role Ashi Kesang played in virtually eliminating leprosy in Bhutan. After spending some time studying at Berkeley, Ashi Kesang returned to Bhutan in the early 1980s to get involved in a leprosy control project initiated by her mother. Professor Justice joined her in this endeavor at one point. As a man who suffered from this disease explained, "Leprosy was a dreaded disease ... In almost every village it was rampant."[32] Ashi Kesang travelled to remote villages for two years finding people who suffered from leprosy and persuading them to receive treatment. She even lived for a while in an isolated leprosy colony, where she helped to treat and rehabilitate many suffering from this terrible disease. Her interaction with leprosy patients and their families was also crucial in reducing the ostracism and stigma that these patients suffered.

Later, Ashi Kesang became involved in a broad array of other social service activities including supplying temporary housing for patients and their families near hospitals, supporting drug rehabilitation efforts, and donating vital hospital equipment. As in her leprosy eradication work, her involvement has typically been much more personal than just supplying financial resources, however valuable they might be. For example, when she donated metal sheeting to replace leaking banana leaf roofs in a poverty-stricken area, she personally visited the villages involved. I asked one of her family members when she would arrive back in Thimphu from that trip. He replied, "I hope in a few days. But it could be a week or two if she encounters landslides on the road."

Ashi Kesang is remarkably warm and thoughtful as well as philanthropic. Occasionally, she would send a modest gift to us—fresh strawberries, a luxury in Bhutan, or a rug for the ice-cold floor of the bedroom in our apartment. We enjoyed several delightful dinners at her home in the royal enclave in Thimphu. Although her home is referred to as a palace, it is more like the well-appointed residence of an affluent American executive or upscale lawyer than a European palace. She also graciously lent us her home in Paro for a number of weekend excursions. Aside from the stuffed leopard in the foyer and some beautiful Bhutanese artifacts, it too was not unlike an executive class home in the U.S., with one rather amusing exception. Bhutanese are used to sleeping on very hard surfaces, because many people sleep on the floor with thin mats. The first time we stayed at this home, we could not get to sleep because our bed's mattress was so thin. After tossing and turning for quite a while, we decided to use the heavy quilts that had been thoughtfully provided to keep us warm as extra padding underneath us. Then we put our outdoor clothing on over our night clothes, hopped in bed and slept soundly.

On another occasion at that residence, we experienced the Bhutanese tradition of hot stone baths for the first time. The tub, constructed out of tight-fitted wooden planks placed outside near an apple orchard, was spacious enough for two occupants to recline facing each other. Several inches from one end of the tub was a slatted barrier that let water through but protected the bather from the section of the tub into which an assistant dropped large, red-hot stones that had been heating for hours in a crackling fire and then on glowing coals. Every twenty minutes or so, the assistant would inquire whether we needed additional stones to keep the bath at the desired temperature. It was a totally delightful and relaxing experience.

We had previously seen several young children enjoying a hot stone bath in a round metal tub so small they had to stand up in it along a roadside near a frothing river. Woven bamboo fencing around the tub provided a modicum of privacy. Later, we were invited by a monk we met on a hike to enjoy a bath in his rather rickety outdoor tub near a fire pit. But the moonlit, hot stone bath at Ashi's was our absolutely best experience of this lovely custom. I was told that, in some areas of Bhutan, locals bathe only once or twice a year due to the amount of effort involved in gathering the firewood, finding, carrying, and then roasting the stones until they glow and keeping the water at a comfortable temperature. That led me to see the wisdom of Royal Thimphu College supplying hot showers in its faculty apartments and dormitories, even though they were often cranky and difficult to regulate.

Ashi's nephew assumed his responsibilities as Bhutan's Fifth King at the age of twenty-six. "He ... is believed to be the realization of a religious prophesy ... a sacred reincarnation destined to safeguard Bhutan and her pride."[33] A tall, good-looking man with a disarmingly informal manner, he earned the sobriquet "Prince Charming" on a state visit to Thailand. Having studied in Bhutan, the U.S., England, and India, he is educated and cosmopolitan to an extent that would have astonished the founder of the Wangchuck dynasty, who had some training in reading and writing but no formal education. Doug and I were fortunate to have numerous interactions with him at the college, at his wedding, and at his palace in Thimphu.

A banner celebrating the Fourth King's 60th birthday features him and the Fifth King. The smaller banner below it pictures the Fourth King's four wives, the Fifth King with his wife, and the Fifth King's coronation.

Citizens stroll along Thimphu's festively decorated main street past the circular structure from which police usually direct traffic as they celebrate the Fourth King's birthday.

The Fifth King inherited the throne in 2006 at a very challenging time. Not only did he have to navigate the transition to democracy which his father had decreed. He also had to deal with the full force of his father's 1999 decision to finally allow TV and internet into the kingdom at a time when more than half of the population was under twenty years of age, and hence very impressionable. In this extremely traditional society, youth were suddenly exposed to the outside world, with images of gang violence, drug use, suicide, and, for most of them, almost unimaginable wealth and ease.

In addition, by 2006, in a culture that had traditionally emphasized respect for elders, many young people had attained levels of education far beyond that of their village elders and parents, only about half of whom were literate. Nonetheless, many youths were unemployed. Vastly expanded educational opportunities meant that graduation from secondary school or college no longer virtually guaranteed a comfortable life as a civil servant. Compounding this situation, opportunities in the anemic private sector were very limited. So, as will be discussed in Chapter 7, concern about "youth problems" was rampant, and solutions were not at all apparent.

As a result of this, one of the Fifth King's priorities was youth issues. Indeed, in his coronation address, he called youth "our most important citizens" and stated, "The future of our nation depends on the worth, capabilities and motivation of today's youth. Therefore, I will not rest until I have given you the inspiration, knowledge and skills so that you will not only fulfill your own aspirations but be of immense worth to the nation."[34] Thus, it was perhaps not surprising that His Majesty made several visits to Royal Thimphu College and the government colleges to talk with students and faculty. He was well positioned to understand Bhutan's youth, being relatively young himself. His international education, motorcycle riding, and love of Elvis Presley's music helped him to relate to a generation of Bhutanese beginning to be influenced by global youth cultures.

His Majesty's first visit to Royal Thimphu College occurred in the spring of 2011 when he came for five mornings in a row to talk with faculty and students. His questions to the faculty focused mainly on student motivation, preparation for college-level learning, and the like. On another visit a few years later, he began by pointing to Doug and saying, "Keep it up. It's good you participate in the People's Voice," a now defunct public affairs program on Bhutanese television during which Doug, as a member of the usually tiny studio audience, often asked questions or made comments. Students told me that although they were awed by His Majesty's presence, he was friendly and easy to talk with, which was no doubt facilitated by his taking the time to meet them all in small groups.

Later in 2011, the Fifth King married a beautiful and intelligent twenty-three-year-old, Jetsun Pema, who became Bhutan's queen. For months before, the country was alive with excited preparations for that occasion. Colored lights were strung across buildings in downtown Thimphu. Many hundreds of people prepared songs, dances and other entertainment for a national celebration held three days after the wedding in the country's one and only large public stadium. Over three thousand school children from across the country sent in paintings, drawings, poems, and cards. One of the most touching of these was a painting with two panels. The first, portraying the burdens of kingship, showed the king, before the wedding, dragging a map of the country up an incredibly steep and rocky slope. The second showed the queen, after the wedding, lightening his load by joining in his effort to uplift the country. A sixth-grade student from an eastern village sent a card reflecting his rural roots as well as many Bhutanese's deep connection to the monarchy. He wrote simply, "Baby need milk. Cow need grass. But we need Our King and Queen."[35]

Caught up in the country's "Royal Wedding Fever," Doug and I attended the public part of the wedding which was held on the grounds of the dzong in Punakha, Bhutan's original capital. We headed about two and a half hours east from Thimphu to Punakha the night before, wanting to make sure no unanticipated landslides or other road problems would keep us from the festivities. We spent the night at a friend's home in a small village about forty minutes by foot from the dzong.

The next day, we set out mid-morning toward the dzong under bright sun through golden rice fields close to ready for harvesting. After walking for about thirty minutes, we braved crossing one of the world's longest suspension bridges which spans the Po Chhu (Male River) flowing along the eastern side of the dzong. It was an adventure. The rickety bridge swayed in the morning breeze and sagged substantially in the middle of its 520-foot length. A teenager squeezed past us on a motorcycle riding over the bumpy planks clearly intended for horse and foot traffic only, which separated us from the fast-moving river far below.

Another ten minutes' walk brought us to the massive *Pungtang Dechen Photrang* dzong. Appropriately for a wedding celebration, its name translates as "Palace of Great Happiness." Huge crowds in vivid festival finery were gathering around an open field in which graceful folk dancing was already underway. We spied some of our monk friends from Nalanda Buddhist Institute and chatted with them for a while. Suddenly, we noticed a commotion in one section of the festival ground. A surging crowd started to line up along an embankment at the edge of the field filled with dancers. Officials and police began to take up positions there as well. We rushed down to join the hundreds of people standing along the edges of path being cleared and craned our necks to get a view toward one end of it, where the hubbub was reaching a crescendo.

His Majesty the Fifth King himself was there, stopping every few hundred feet to talk briefly with eager onlookers. Shortly before he approached us, he talked briefly with a woman, touching her gently on her arm as they spoke. She was so frail and elderly I wondered how she had managed even to walk to the festival grounds. Later, I learned he had asked her if an injury she had suffered shortly before his visit to her village a few months before had healed well, demonstrating a remarkable memory as well as considerable empathy for his subjects. He then resumed walking past the mob of well-wishers until he saw us. He stopped again, greeted us warmly by name, and chatted for four or five minutes. Doug, who is never shy, congratulated him on his wedding and said, "We wish you a marriage as happy as ours." We saw for ourselves in this encounter why this king is often called the

People's King. In addition to remembering our names, he referred to a conversation we had had several months before at the college.

As His Majesty moved on from us, he turned to an aide and said (or as the Bhutanese would put it "commanded"), "Take the Schofields into the Royal Enclosure for some refreshments." We were promptly escorted under a rope marking the edge of the VIP section, across a grassy field, and into a spacious tent. Refreshments were deep in the interior, with chairs and tables set up on the grass towards its front. Surprisingly, by that time, the tea had run out. There was, however, plenty of *ara*, the local whiskey.

Neither of us is a heavy drinker, especially of ara, which can be quite potent. Also, we recalled a debate at a faculty dinner about whether a used flip-flop is an essential ingredient to flavor ara, as one faculty member insisted it was in his village. As we abstemiously sipped our drinks, one of the king's aides repeatedly encouraged us to have more. We declined, saying that we had to drive back to Thimphu before too long. Taking yet another generous pull on the ara in his glass, he said with a broad smile, "Generally, you shouldn't drink and drive. However, if you must, you should drink a lot, so that there appear to be three roads in front of you. Then, you simply take the middle path." (A Buddhist joke, since Buddha encouraged avoiding the extremes of self-indulgence and self-denial and taking a middle path instead.) We preferred, however, to keep our wits about us, especially since the wedding provided a wonderful opportunity to renew our acquaintance with many interesting and influential individuals.

One of the great pleasures of working and living near the capital city of a tiny country like Bhutan is that during everyday events we encountered individuals with a wide range of fascinating experiences and responsibilities that substantially impacted the entire nation. Never was this clearer to us than as we nursed our ara, chatting with acquaintances including three cabinet ministers, the opposition leader in the parliament, a rinpoche, and numerous others.

As usual at many social gatherings, the celebration of the royal wedding ended with the *tashi lebey*, a dance in which all join hands to repeatedly circle one way and then back again the other. With simple steps and graceful hand gestures, participants sing a well-known tune which helps time the steps. This is sometimes performed at an ever-increasing tempo, which leads the less fit dancers to drop out, gasping and laughing, exhausted by the ever-escalating pace.

As we meandered back across the undulating suspension bridge for an evening meal with our friend, we were buoyed by the memory of the warm camaraderie of several hundred people joyfully dancing the tashi lebey in concentric circles. We thought it would be our last special memory related to this glorious event, but it was not. Early the next morning, our friend took us to visit a friend of hers, a woman who was one of the Indian contract teachers hired for temporary teaching jobs when Bhutanese are not available. After giving us a brief tour of her school, the teacher invited us to breakfast in her lodgings. We were surprised when she opened the door to a supply closet adjoining the chemistry lab to reveal the tiny room where she lived, with a sleeping mat in one corner and basic furnishings. She cooked us a wonderful breakfast, a steamed Indian dish called *idli*, made from a batter of rice and urad, a kind of seed, as we chatted about her experiences as a teacher. As we left the high school to walk back to our car near our friend's home, we were surprised to see a boy of about fifteen sitting high up in the crotch of a large tree near the school's gate, diligently studying for an upcoming exam. Because foreigners—most especially Westerners—were scarce in that neighborhood, he seemed at least as surprised to see us wandering down the path as we were to see him comfortably ensconced in that lofty, leafy bower.

Once back in Thimphu later that morning, we started receiving excited calls from friends asking about our conversation with His Majesty. At first, we were mystified, because we had not yet mentioned that experience to anyone there. But the confusion was soon resolved. Unbeknownst to us,

His Majesty the Fifth King met with Royal Thimphu College's management and faculty, pictured with him here, as well as with all its students in small groups during five mornings in 2011.

Royal Thimphu College's graduation ceremony closes as I and other college faculty and staff join in the traditional tashi lebey, the same dance concluding the royal wedding's festivities.

videographers from the Bhutan Broadcasting Service had been behind the king as we spoke with him. His conversation with us was included in the royal wedding coverage that was beamed to the entire nation on television. We were delighted to be able to catch a "re-run" of it.

Another memorable experience provided the opportunity to meet both the king and queen on a less public and formal occasion. Around 9 p.m. the evening before Thanksgiving in 2013, there was a knock on our apartment door. A colleague announced with great excitement that the college had just received a call from the palace. All Americans and Canadians (even though their Thanksgiving is somewhat earlier) in Thimphu were invited to Thanksgiving brunch the coming morning. After a flurry of checking that appropriate clothing was clean and ironed, the Royal Thimphu College contingent of twenty-six Americans, students, faculty, staff, and their families, was ready for their most remarkable Thanksgiving ever. A college bus took us to the palace grounds, situated near the monumental Thimphu dzong. There we joined another dozen or so guests: the new UN representative and her family, a few American doctors on short-term volunteer assignments, and a smattering of Canadians, mainly teachers in the Bhutan Canada Foundation teacher program.

We followed the chamberlain down a short path into the palace grounds. A huge Bhutanese flag, lit by the intense Himalayan noontime sun, flapped quietly in a gentle breeze, reminding us of where we were and who we were going to share Thanksgiving with—the *Druk Gyalpo,* or Dragon King, and the *Druk Gyaltsuen*, or Dragon Queen. This flag has adjacent triangular fields of yellow, representing the king, and deep orange, symbolizing the flourishing of Buddhist teachings. A large white dragon in the flag's center symbolizes purity, referring to the loyalty, patriotism, and sense of belonging to the kingdom of Bhutan's diverse linguistic and ethnic groups.

To me, the dragon, like kings and queens, is a being of fairy tales and fantasy. But it is totally different for the Bhutanese. The dragon is an integral part of their history and culture, indeed of their very identity. For many, the dragon remains a real entity. In fact, the scholar Dr. Karma Phuntsho has written, "Many Bhutanese ... still believe that there existed a reptilian creature which could fly and roar in the sky to cause thunder."[36] The Bhutanese people call themselves Drukpa, meaning "Dragon people," and the name many use for their country, Drukyul, translates as "The Land of the Thunder Dragon." These names reflect a story about a twelfth century Tibetan

The *Druk* (Thunder Dragon) on Bhutan's flag is a mythological creature so central to Bhutan's identity that the country is often called *Drukyul* (Land of *Druk*), and the King is referred to as the *Druk Gyalpo* (Thunder Dragon King).

tertön, Tsangpa Gyare. Looking for a location suitable for a monastery, he encountered nine dragons that suddenly rose up into the sky, roaring loudly like thunder. Flowers, rather than rain, then fell from the heavens. Interpreting these events as auspicious signs, he built a monastery right there.

Seeing the roaring dragon on the flag reminded me of an event in which still existing beliefs about dragons figured prominently. In July 2009, the twenty-first century's longest total solar eclipse was visible from Bhutan. To see it, we drove up a steep hillside on the outskirts of Thimphu, where a gigantic Buddha was being constructed in an area that provided a clear view of the sky across the valley and over the mountains. As the moon's shadow started to cover the sun, raucous shouts and eerie wails began to emanate from the valley below. They contended for our attention with a cacophony of frenetic drumming on metal pots and pans. Bhutanese friends explained that many people still believe that a solar eclipse is the result of a dragon swallowing the sun. Loud noises are believed to save the sun, and the light and warmth it brings, by scaring the hungry dragon away. Sure enough, the sun returned in its full glory.

A remarkable scene greeted us as my gaze moved from the dragon on the striking flag to further around the palace grounds. Large round tables with patterned white tablecloths stood on manicured green grass studded with jewel-like patches of brightly colored flowers on the lawn adjacent to the *Wang Chhu*, the Thimphu River. White cloth also covered the chairs clustered around the tables, with an enormous golden bow at the back of each seat. Elegant airy white cloth pavilions provided light shade for each table. The lovely garden party ambience was enhanced by gold-rimmed white china at each place setting.

The king and queen emerged from their modest palace to greet guests one by one in a receiving line. After a short period of socializing, guests were asked to be seated. Doug was ushered to a seat at the largest table, near which he had been standing. Shortly after he sat down, the king sat next to him, followed by the queen, who sat next to her husband. The king, officially the chancellor of the Royal University of Bhutan, turned to Doug saying, "How are things at the college," and a lively conversation ensued.

I sat at another table with a doctor with whom I had been conversing. Soon, a parade of retainers emerged from a screened area, providing a varied array of food and drinks that His Majesty had personally selected for the event. First came my favorite Bhutanese dish, *desi* or *dretsi,* teacup-sized bowls of sweet white rice with butter, saffron, and golden raisins, typically reserved for special occasions. After that came numerous drinks and dishes including salty butter tea, juices, vegetable soup, and an unusual stuffed muffin with Chinese flavors. Then, in honor of Thanksgiving, came the Western cuisine, which included waffles and French toast served with something akin to maple syrup.

During the meal, the king circulated to each table, interacting at least briefly with each of the guests. He spent the longest time at a table of students from Wheaton College in the U.S. who were in an award-winning exchange program at Royal Thimphu College. No doubt this reflected the fact that His Majesty studied briefly at Wheaton before heading to England and graduating from Magdalen College at the University of Oxford. Meanwhile, Doug had an extended conversation with the young queen covering many topics related to education, psychology, and youth issues in Bhutan. After that, group photos were taken with the king and queen and we all departed, very thankful indeed for such an enjoyable and memorable Thanksgiving.

Chapter 6

Being Bhutanese

As usual, tea and snacks were being served after a lecture in the spacious auditorium at the Thimphu headquarters of the Royal University of Bhutan. Reflecting neighboring countries' influence on Bhutanese cuisine, I was enjoying both spicy Indian samosas and momos, a mild Tibetan dumpling filled with vegetables. As an extended conversation with a young woman about my many years in Bhutan ended, she said to me with a smile, "Why Madam, you are almost Bhutanese by now." Reflecting her pride in her unique country, it was meant and received as a compliment. But it also raised an interesting question in my mind, "Just what does it mean to be Bhutanese?"

One answer is deceptively simple. You are Bhutanese if you meet the criteria laid out for citizenship in Bhutan's 1985 Citizenship Act. But the young woman's comment suggested that she believed shared values and experiences lead to a distinct national character or identity that even a foreigner can share, at least to some extent.

So, what does it mean to be Bhutanese? This is a question best answered by the Bhutanese themselves rather than an outsider like me. But more than ten years in the country gave me at least an informed outsider's perspective on the question and led me to believe that there are at least five things that are deeply characteristic of many Bhutanese. The first of these is the extent to which religion, most commonly Buddhism influenced by animist beliefs, permeates every aspect of life. For example, although Bhutan has a very low population density and travel is generally difficult, huge crowds almost magically appear at important religious events. My first exposure to this phenomenon occurred within a few weeks of my arrival in 2009. As I returned to the college's downtown Thimphu office from an errand, I was mystified to see block after block lined on both sides by crowds three or four people deep—despite a pelting spring rain that foreshadowed the beginning of the summer monsoon.

I joined the excited throng and soon saw a large black SUV with lilac privacy curtains crawling along the center of the road at about one mile an hour. Protruding from a rolled-down front window was the fleshy arm of the Head of the Central Monastic Body, the Je Khenpo. He was protected from the rain by a large green umbrella held by a young monk in the SUV's back seat, whose wrist sported a large showy watch. The Je Khenpo's hand clutched a thin, orange eighteen-inch wand. He blessed individuals in an unending line by touching its tasseled tip to their heads as they bowed low and covered their mouths in respect. The two following pickup trucks were gaily decorated with white, yellow, red, and green strips of cloth that significantly blocked their drivers' views forward but added a very festive touch. Each truck had perched in its cargo bed a sizable rectangular structure with embossed metal images of clouds and dragons on its walls and an elaborate golden spire on top. I could just barely discern large metal statues inside each. I later learned that this procession was the Central Monastic Body arriving for the summer in Thimphu from much warmer Punakha, where they always spend the winter.

Large public religious gatherings like this are common. For example, when some sacred relics were brought from India to Thimphu, a crowd more than half the size of the total population of the city turned out to view them. Later, in Mongar, a town in the east with about three thousand inhabitants, the line of devotees waiting to see these relics snaked back and forth across the full length of a soccer field nine times. In three other eastern *dzongkhags* (districts), over forty thousand people, a third of their entire population, came to receive blessings from those relics. Similarly, over two hundred thousand people, about a quarter of Bhutan's entire population, attended at least part of a fifteen-day event at which a Buddhist master placed attendees in touch with a tantric deity as an aid to enlightenment.

A second fundamental aspect of Bhutanese identity, the deep respect for and attachment to the monarchy described in the previous chapter, merits further note here. Events featuring the Fourth or Fifth King draw large, enthusiastic crowds similar in size to those at religious functions. Homes and offices are filled with pictures of Bhutan's kings, the queens, and the two young princes born to the current royal couple. This is not the kind of obligatory display commonly found in authoritarian countries, as suggested by the fact that such images also commonly appear in relatively private places, like the desktop picture on computers or phones as well as in more public settings.

Tens of thousands of Bhutanese invested the time and effort in 2016 to plant 108 thousand (108 is a lucky number for Buddhists) saplings to mark the birth of the first child of the Fifth King and his queen. The link between attachment to the monarchy and Bhutanese identity was made explicit in an online post responding to a newspaper article titled, "What Makes Us Bhutanese." A reader, Sonam Jatso, wrote, "I believe it's our deepest gratitude and love for our kings that makes us who we are. It's that special bond between our kings and our people that sets us apart from other countries."[37]

No doubt, the high regard for the monarchy is due, to some extent, to the previously discussed historic connection between religious and political power in Bhutan. Also, the constitution declares the king the embodiment of spiritual authority, consolidating two sources of power and respect, secular and religious authority. Another source of attachment to the monarchy is the institution of *kidu*. Basically, with kidu, the king helps people in need, a system that is extremely useful in a country without most of the social safety nets available in many wealthier countries. So, for example, almost thirty-five thousand people were granted modest amounts of money from the Kidu Fund when COVID-19 resulted in many becoming unemployed.

The granting of kidu is an enactment of the idea of *dramtshig*, a foundational value in Bhutanese society, which posits a sacred commitment in relationships that pairs duty and obligation. So, a master has the duty of ensuring the welfare of a servant, and the servant must serve the master with dedication. A parent must ensure a proper upbringing for a child, and a child must obey and later care for the parent. In granting kidu, the king is living up to his obligation to promote his subjects' welfare—just as they are obligated to serve him and the country for which he stands. Kidu is so central to the relationship between the king and Bhutan's people that when the Civil Society Act was passed in 2007, its preamble stated that "kidu must be held sacrosanct."[38]

Kidu involves many kinds of welfare, including the granting of citizenship, land, college scholarships, and more. Almost 150 thousand people have received land kidu from the Fifth King since 2008. Importantly, kidu is often provided at a very personal level. For example, two days vigorous walk through the forest from the tiny yak-herding settlement of Sakteng in Bhutan's remote east, Doug and I encountered a young man dressed more for the office than for the steep, rocky path on which we walked. He had been sent by the king to isolated villages to locate children who needed kidu to cover the incidental expenses required for enrolling in school, such as school uniforms and notebooks.

As another example, in a village outside of Thimphu, we met a preadolescent girl who was orphaned when both her parents died in a car accident. The king gave her uncle, a subsistence farmer, a stipend to cover the expense of raising her. The uncle and his niece live in a rough, wooden, two-room structure surrounded by an apple orchard and fields in which they grow broccoli, cabbage, and potatoes. One day, the girl offered to show us her schoolbooks. We ducked in through the threshold of their small cabin, past a three-foot pile of potatoes in the cooking area. It was eerily dark and there was little furniture. Entering the home's main room, we were astonished to see that the walls were completely covered with brightly colored, life-sized pictures of the Fifth King's face, taken from the coronation edition of the country's main newspaper that had been published several years earlier. These pictures not only blocked the wind that would otherwise have blown in through the cracks between the log walls. They also brightened the cabin's otherwise dark interior. In addition, they clearly bore testament to the occupants' gratitude for the king's financial assistance.

Royal Thimphu College has often enrolled one or more students funded through kidu. Their stories are often heart-rending. For example, one young woman took on full responsibility for four younger siblings during middle school because her father died from alcoholism when she was three, and her mother died from a brain tumor some years later. One of her younger sisters was unable to walk due to polio, so that child received kidu from the Fifth King. The future Royal Thimphu College student, her polio-afflicted sister, and their uncle attended a nearby event to see and thank the king. He talked with the polio-stricken girl and then casually asked the elder sister where she went to school. She replied that she had hoped to go to college but could not afford to. After further communications with the king's staff, she was informed that she would receive a kidu scholarship at the college, where she did well.

A third striking characteristic of the Bhutanese, no doubt related to the closeness of the country's Tibetan-influenced feudal past, is the degree to which the Bhutanese show respect for hierarchy. It is often said that Bhutanese values are strongly based on the sixteen rules of conduct laid down in the seventh century by the Tibetan king, Songstan Gampo, two of which call for respect for elders and people in high positions. When observing social interactions in Bhutan, I was vividly reminded of Geert Hofsteade's groundbreaking research on cultural differences in values which has led to the conclusion that Bhutan "definitely has a hierarchical society.... people accept a hierarchical order in which everybody has a place and which needs no further justification."[39] On a scale from one to one hundred, Bhutan's score on Hofsteade's measure of hierarchy is ninety-four whereas the U.S. scores only forty and many European countries score lower than that. A score of eighty is considered very high and Bhutan's score is exceeded by fewer than 5 percent of the more than sixty-five countries on which information is available.

The legacy of hierarchy in Bhutan is remarkably strong. According to the laws promulgated in the 1600s by the founding father of Bhutan, Zhabdrung Ngawang Namgyal, theft of monastic property had to be repaid one-hundred-fold, theft of the king's property eighty-fold and theft of a subject's property only eight-fold. Barely more than a century ago, a visiting British representative wrote, "All Bhutanese officials are carried when the road is too steep and bad to ride a mule. ... The orderly ... carries the officer, seated pickaback in a strong cloth firmly knotted on the man's forehead."[40]

Evidence of the continuation of very hierarchical practices since then is legion. For example, Tshering Dorji, nicknamed "the Finance Minister's flogging drum" when he oversaw inventory at the Finance Ministry from around 1967-1971, recalls, "It was normal for at least two or three of us [young clerks] to get his lashings every day."[41] A strong indication of lingering hierarchical traditions is that the individual voting records of members of parliament are not disclosed. Shortly after arriving in Bhutan, I read an editorial critiquing continuing hierarchy that observed, "When a local villager talks to ... [a] senior official it sounds like the weakest student in the class talking to the class bully."[42] Bhutan's 2015 Gross National Happiness Survey contained a question regarding how many days a year individuals were engaged in *woola*, compulsory labor contribution to the community, which includes carrying baggage for officials and preparations for official visits (i.e., arranging red carpets, tents, curtains, etc.) Bhutan's first democratically elected prime minister observed that the country is a democracy only in principle saying, "We have the legal frameworks in place ... we are elected by the people ... but we have only half of what we need as a democratic country. We are yet to establish a democratic culture in the people and this could take years."[43]

But it did not take scholarly research or newspaper articles to bring the continuing importance of hierarchy to my attention. It was obvious in my everyday life. As Doug and I headed east for the Sherubste College graduation ceremony, school children in one village bowed to us as our car passed by. An acquaintance explained that since cabinet ministers were also heading to the graduation and Royal Thimphu College had provided us with a driver and a nice vehicle for the lengthy trip, we had most probably been mistaken for important officials. At that graduation ceremony, when I surreptitiously glanced back at the rest of the audience, I was amazed to see every single one of the students and faculty members with their eyes downcast, as a sign of respect for the king who was delivering a speech on the stage.

Another reminder of the ubiquity of hierarchy was the fact that, like Japanese, Bhutan's national language, Dzongkha, varies depending on the relative status of the individuals conversing. For example, I quickly noticed that the relative status of two individuals can easily be determined by the frequency with which one of them inserts the syllable "la" into a conversation, even when they are speaking English. Also, it is quite common for individuals to characterize themselves as being a "common man," from a "humble family" or the like. Indeed, the day I started writing this chapter, a letter to the editor in the national newspaper contained the words "from my humble common man's understanding ..."[44] In addition, the status of male Bhutanese is made evident to all from a great distance on the very frequent occasions, such as on entering a government office or monastery, when "formal dress" is required. Specifically, the color and design of the large scarf called a *kabney*, which a man must wear, signals which of eight different status levels he occupies from king to commoner.

Indications of the importance of hierarchy in shaping social behavior were legion at Royal Thimphu College. Students who were sitting down when I encountered them at various places on the campus popped up to stand as I passed by, something that had never happened in decades of walking across U.S. campuses. In addition, students commonly insisted on carrying my modest-sized briefcase roughly two hundred feet from a classroom to my office as a mark of respect. When I mentioned to a colleague that I would like to learn to play *khuru*, a traditional game using large metal darts with wooden handles, she suggested that I ask the student government president to make the needed darts for me. Similarly, when I bought a flowering plant for a garden behind our apartment, the vendor advised me to have my students gather manure to put around it to make sure it would flourish. I could only wonder what would have happened if I had asked U.S. students to perform similar personal tasks. It would not have been pretty.

Students and many staff at the college routinely addressed me as "Madam" and male faculty members were always addressed as "Sir," with these honorifics often appearing at the end of nearly every sentence. A thirty-year-old man applying to the college's continuing education program for working adults told me that he wanted a college degree because he was tired of having to say "Sir" when interacting with former high school classmates who had joined the civil service after completing college. A prospective student who had left another college part way through his studies gave the same reason when applying to Royal Thimphu College to complete his degree a few years later. All this did not even begin to prepare me for the time a young Indian faculty member entered my office, kneeled down, and then kissed my foot, but that's another story.

I once heard someone aptly characterize Bhutan as "The Land of Exquisite Politeness." Norms require that anyone asked a question start answering it by thanking the questioner profusely for the query. Even more startling, an expatriate friend told me that when she encountered a thief in her home one evening, he greeted her with, "Good evening, Madam," before turning and fleeing. So, polite behavior in Bhutan is not always a result of deeply felt respect for hierarchy. It is partly a habit. It is also an essential tool for anyone who hopes to interact successfully with government officials or highly respected individuals.

Specifically, there is a formalized set of behavioral expectations contained in traditional Bhutanese etiquette called *driglam namzha* ("system of order or uniformity" or "system of harmony"). This system was originally adopted centuries ago in Zhabdrung Ngawang Namgyal's court, and many still see it as an essential aspect of Bhutanese culture. Driglam namzha prescribes how one bows, sits, eats, walks, talks, greets another, and dresses, with considerable focus on how a subordinate does these things in the presence of an elder or superior. It has aptly been dubbed an "elaborate choreography of deference." It is so important that I could look out my office window each spring through a rapidly growing thicket of bamboo and see students under the tutelage of a faculty member practicing how to bow and properly present a white scarf. Elements of Bhutanese etiquette are also included in the orientation sessions provided for new international faculty.

One evening during our first year in Bhutan, I had my own unanticipated lesson in driglam namzha when a group of those deeply involved in establishing Royal Thimphu College was heading in a college van to the home of one of the college's cofounders, Ashi Kesang Wangmo Wangchuck, the sister of Bhutan's Fourth King. As we approached downtown Thimphu on our way to the royal enclave, one of my colleagues suddenly blurted out in a dismayed tone, "Oh no! We didn't bring *khadars*." These white scarves are presented when greeting a highly respected person, welcoming others, or for similar occasions. A hurried discussion determined that even at the risk of briefly delaying our arrival, we should stop to procure them. Luckily, khadars are so commonly used that they were readily available at a fabric shop. So, although I was not yet aware of the subtleties that differentiate one khadar from another according to the specific occasion, I purchased a scarf before climbing back into the van in a light drizzle.

I had been in Bhutan long enough to realize that you can't just hand a khadar to a member of the royal family and say something like, "This comes with my deep respect and best wishes." Rather, the almost six-foot-long piece of silk must be presented in a specific way which starts with gathering it into many accordion-like folds. It takes luck or considerable practice to unfurl the scarf directly into the waiting hands of the recipient, rather than to have it fall to the ground, embarrassing all concerned. Unfortunately, the back seat of a van was not spacious enough to implement my colleagues' instructions regarding how to do this. So, when we arrived at the palace, they were kind enough to wait in the increasingly heavy drizzle while I practiced the correct moves several times. Ashi Kesang, being who she is, would undoubtedly have received the scarf graciously no matter how askew my throw went. But, to my great relief, the presentation went reasonably well—although it did not quite confirm the adage that "practice makes perfect." The rest of the evening, which included yet another new experience for me, yak teriyaki, was delightful.

Doug and I did our best to become aware of local norms and practices regarding how to interact with those in high positions. It was not always easy to intuit. One such situation arose when our host at a house-warming event seated us next to a former prime minister for lunch and the lengthy folk song and dance performance following it. We enjoyed a lively and fascinating conversation during which the former PM remarked several times that we should drop by sometime for a visit at his nearby home. We were not sure whether it was appropriate to follow up on that invitation, even though it seemed sincere. We tentatively decided to do so, and a few weeks later strolled by the entrance to his home to scope out the situation. However, the sight of armed guards at the entrance to the compound deterred us from trying to enter the grounds.

So, we next approached a Bhutanese friend, explaining the situation and asking what we should do. Her reply was telling. She said that most Bhutanese would not follow up on such an invitation, primarily because they would fear somehow embarrassing themselves or others by not behaving properly in the presence of such a high-ranking figure. She then went on to say, "But you should follow up on it. Everyone knows that foreigners behave differently."

We did follow up on it, and had another very stimulating and enjoyable conversation, this time over tea in the former prime minister's extensive and beautiful garden. Our friend's comment about foreigners behaving differently reminded me of an amusing story told by adventurer Burt Todd, whom Doug met a year or so before we went to Bhutan. Mr. Todd, reputed to be the first American to visit Bhutan, was a guest at a royal wedding there in 1951. Wanting to dress appropriately for such an august occasion, he brought a white tie and tails overland with him when hiking in because there were no roads. As he returned to his quarters after the wedding ceremony, he noticed that one of the other guests appeared to be gossiping with others about him. When he inquired what the problem was, his escort replied, "Oh, personally I think it's fine. But that woman ... thought it rather pathetic that an official guest should appear with such a terrible split in the back of his coat."[45] Not surprisingly, in 1951 there had not had enough contact with the outside world for Bhutanese to recognize the tails he wore as a sartorial attempt to honor a very special occasion.

Rather unexpectedly, our working at Royal Thimphu College was partly a result of the consequences of the hierarchical norms in Bhutan. The college's founding director told us that one of the reasons he invited us to join the college was that he believed we, as Americans, would tell him frankly what we thought and would also be willing to share bad news. Such behavior is especially valuable in Bhutan because it is broadly acknowledged that there is a high level of self-censorship there. As a newspaper editorial put it, in most Bhutanese meetings, getting "feedback from members present is almost as difficult as finding mineral water in the Sahara desert...genuine criticism is seen as being rebellious, quality feedback is minimal due to fear of consequences and even today the words of a bad adviser is [sic] preferred to the truth."[46] Confirming such assertions, an acquaintance who worked as a civil servant told us of the lambasting he had received for daring to differ with his immediate superior after that individual made a statement regarding a crucial matter that was seriously incorrect. The tongue-lashing focused on the inappropriateness of differing with his superior, rather than on the accuracy of their respective statements on which consequential decisions depended.

Even reporting bad news is often avoided because it can be seen as an implicit criticism of leadership. A newspaper article contended, "Physical abuse by superiors is gone for good, but browbeating, indirect punishment and administrative burdens are very much prevalent."[47] Consistent with such observations, after a highly respected religious figure published a controversial article critiquing civil servants for depending too heavily on their positions of power and providing poor service, a newspaper columnist wrote, "In a close-knit and hierarchical society, it takes somebody like a *Rinpoche* to speak out the truth."[48] But it is not only speaking the truth that is limited by hierarchical norms. So is asking questions. A foreign professional working in Bhutan was told by her boss, "If you want to stay in this country as a foreigner you will have to learn that one does not ask questions. It is perceived as being rude."[49] Also, school children report that they don't ask questions because that is the teachers' role, not theirs.

In fact, speaking at all is often constrained, consistent with another one of Songstan Gampo's sixteen rules, which is often translated as, "To be polite and to speak less."[50] Until very recent years, speaking up, making mistakes, or otherwise displeasing one's teachers or other superiors often resulted in corporal punishment. Such punishment was routine in Bhutanese schools until about a decade ago, fostering what one document published by the Ministry of Education characterized as a "culture of fear."[51] For example, a monk in his early twenties with whom we became friends wrote us a letter describing his life saying:

> In fifth grade I had ... to walk two hours to school down to the bottom of the valley and then up to the very top of the mountain and then ... back ... every day even in the monsoon rains. ... I was chosen ... to stay at the ... school dormitory ... because we had to practice late every day for a big culture show. ... Sometimes, when I woke up, my pillow [was] wet with tears because I really missed my family ... Once I ran away ... home, but when I returned my punishment was a whipping with stinging nettles ... and teardrops fell like the summer rain. ... When I became a monk [at age 14] ... everything was different and strange for me. One of the hardest things was that we had only two hours to memorize a page of prayers everyday which we had to recite to the teacher or be beaten with a leather whip.

Sometimes punishment was not only for offenders but for all their classmates. For example, in an extreme incident after corporal punishment had already been officially banned, an elementary school teacher pricked all children as young as second grade with a syringe when one of their classmates broke a school rule by speaking just one word in the local dialect rather than English.

The year Royal Thimphu College opened a newspaper article stated, "Not very long ago, the idea of learning in Bhutan was associated with a teacher brandishing a menacing stick, with which the said educator would attempt to drive what was scrawled across the blackboard into anxious students' heads. ... [This approach is] still perpetuated ... in varying degrees in schools across the kingdom."[52] Consistent with this, Doug and I saw a panel discussion on television in which the teachers asserted that they intended to continue the "necessary practice" of corporal punishment.

Having been introduced to education of this sort in their earlier years, many students at Royal Thimphu College were loath to draw attention to themselves by speaking individually in the classroom. Rather they preferred a choral response, with the teacher asking a question that could be answered by the whole class with obvious one-word answers such as "yes" and "no."

However, group support helped to free students to respond to teachers, so having them report on the outcomes of small group discussions worked quite well in my classroom.

My students were also used to memorizing notes provided by teachers rather than focusing on understanding the ideas they conveyed. A colleague told me about a secondary school teacher who took points off a student's test grade because the youngster had omitted a comma in a definition. Although this did not change the definition's meaning, the teacher insisted that it be included for full marks, saying that such precise memorization was essential for later national exams. Given students' expectations and prior experiences, finding ways to teach them to evaluate arguments and to formulate their own opinions based on evidence was a major challenge. The college undertook serious professional development efforts to assist faculty in this endeavor. But, since most of them had experienced a memory-focused education themselves, many found the change in emphasis unappealing and/or difficult to implement.

A fourth and very important aspect of being Bhutanese is illustrated by my students' responses to a discussion assignment about the core elements of Bhutanese identity. They listed "believing in community rather than individualism" as well as "being truly devoted to Buddhism, respect, and preserving our age-old traditions." Like many of the other behaviors discussed in this chapter, contributing to one's community was one of Songtsan Gampo's rules of good conduct.

Historically, Bhutanese had to depend on their families or local communities for almost everything, because the population was so thinly dispersed across extraordinarily steep and rugged terrain. Many important tasks were most efficiently and effectively accomplished in concert with others. For example, digging irrigation channels or building suspension bridges is extremely arduous work which is greatly lightened if neighbors cooperate. So, a system called *zhabto lemi* was set up to accomplish such tasks. Although it was described as voluntary labor, in most cases, villagers were required to contribute such work without pay. When we first arrived, the zhabto lemi was three months a year in some areas, although it was not supposed to be more than fifteen days. This system was officially abolished in 2009, but the custom of requiring work for community projects has continued in many places.

Royal Thimphu College students illustrated the custom of working together to solve community problems when some of them banded together to attempt to fix several tremendous potholes near the college's entrance that plagued the roughly 50 percent of them who commuted daily. Unfortunately, in this case, community self-reliance proved less powerful than bureaucracy. The students needed permission from the local government to do this work because the road was heavily travelled. But a dispute between different governmental jurisdictions regarding which one had the authority to give such permission bogged the project down for so long that the students abandoned it, and the road remained in serious disrepair for quite a while.

The Bhutanese emphasis on community and interdependence is captured in a popular parable, "The Four Friends." Images of the four—an elephant, a monkey, a rabbit, and a bird—appear in homes, temples, handicraft shops and adorning t-shirts, and note cards. A brightly painted, larger-than-life statue of them is even found in the center of a roundabout on the road leading up to the Royal Thimphu College campus. There are numerous variations of the basic tale. But all emphasize the value of interdependence and cooperation, with some highlighting respect for age as well.

One version of this story says that the four animals are discussing who is the oldest and wisest. The elephant says he can remember when a lofty nearby fruit tree was no taller than him. The monkey claims he fertilized the tree when it was so small that he could hop over it. The rabbit declares he watered the tree when it was just a tiny sapling. Finally, the bird claims that he planted the seed. The four friends are hungry, but the tree has grown so tall that none of them can reach its fruit. To solve this problem, the smaller animals climb on the back of the elephant and form a tower by perching on top of each other. By cooperating, they reach and share the fruit from the tree they each nurtured in their own way.

Individuals' deep embeddedness in their communities has become less essential to survival with the arrival of formal education, rapid urbanization, government-sponsored health care, roads, and the growing availability of tools such as power saws and power tillers. But such social and technological innovations are still limited. They are also recent enough that attitudes and behaviors continue to reflect a strong sense of interdependence and community in many parts of the country. Thus, driving past rice fields at transplantation time, Doug and I often saw groups of bare-foot village women bent over side-by-side in muddy paddy fields, singing while working together to plant acre after acre of slender, bright green seedlings.

Relatively well-off farmers now sometimes hire others for work that would have been done communally in a previous era. But the practice of community members helping each other persists. For example, in 2011 the Fifth King started the DeSuung program, discussed in more detail in Chapter 10, for individuals willing to volunteer to assist others in times of natural disaster or other needs. It has been very successful in mobilizing volunteers to deal with difficult situations including the COVID-19 pandemic. An individual participating in it wrote on the program's Facebook page, "I am proud to be a DeSuup and I think as a DeSuup you will be a complete Bhutanese," explicitly linking being Bhutanese with helping others.[53]

Building a home is an arduous activity that has historically been a community effort in Bhutan, with individuals reciprocating the favor as needed. Traditional homes are large and often three stories: the bottom one for cattle, the middle one for grain storage, and the top one for living space. Typically, there is also an attic for drying and storing agricultural products. Homes are built with thick, rammed-earth walls that preserve heat in the winter and keep the house cool in the summer. Steps are carved into a whole tree trunk to provide access to the upper stories.

Once, hiking in the glacial Phobjikha valley with Doug and a friend, I thought I heard faint singing. My companions teased me, saying my overactive imagination was reacting to the wind rustling in the tall fir trees and the

Neighboring farmers near Paro work together to thresh an abundant rice harvest.

Women in the high Phobjikha valley pound mud to create the walls of a new home for one of them and her family.

eerie atmosphere created by the deep shadows they cast, which Bhutanese say typify deities' homes. As we walked onward, the singing became more distinct, so we veered off the heavily wooded path towards an open field to discover its source.

There, ahead of us, and standing atop a dun-colored mud wall that made up the unfinished first floor of a rammed-earth house, was a group of several middle-aged women. The women sang a lively song as they rhythmically pounded mud into crudely constructed rectangular wooden forms, producing the initial layer for the new home's second-story wall. They wore traditional Bhutanese female garb, called *kiras*. These are long, rectangular, full-length pieces of cloth wrapped around the entire body with a tight, wide, decorative fabric belt at the waist. The part of the cloth covering the chest is pinned to that covering the back with an intricately crafted metal ornament at each shoulder. A long-sleeved blouse is worn under the kira. The long-sleeved jacket often worn over the kira reflects Bhutan's generally cool climate. All the mud-stained women had short very simple haircuts, which a friend told me the Zhabdrung had introduced to differentiate Bhutanese from Tibetan women centuries ago. Four of the women were missing several front teeth. All had the red-toothed smiles that signal frequent chewing of a mild stimulant called *doma*, a widespread pastime in Bhutan.

On the nearby ground, several men were shaping large logs into beams and arched window frames using a plane blade and machete-type knives. An elderly man with skin weathered by a lifetime of sun and wind stood close by, just outside the door of a wooden-shingled bamboo-thatch hut. He held in his arms an infant kept warm by a blue blanket sprinkled with images of white stars and teddy bears. A toddler wearing red rubber galoshes that looked way too big for his feet watched our approach with some apprehension. But everyone else displayed welcoming smiles.

We observed the work with great interest for a while. Then Doug asked if he could take some pictures. The group agreed, but soon began motioning for him to join them on top of the first-floor wall. He climbed right up. As most of the women resumed pounding, one lent her pounding stick to Doug. He went to work enthusiastically, joining in their song as best he could. One of the women then noticed his size-sixteen shoes and, laughing, indicated that he could pound the mud with his feet as well. As rural Bhutanese have begun to move beyond subsistence farming, scenes like the ones we encountered have become less common. But the communal spirit they reveal is far from lost.

Examples of this communal orientation were common at Royal Thimphu College, even though it is a temporary community for most participants and near an urban area rather than a rural one. For example, when a relative of a faculty or staff member died, colleagues provided *semso*, money to assist with death rituals. Similarly, it was not unusual for a coworker to circulate from office to office to share a treat like small candies. If something is not locked up in a cabinet in traditional Bhutanese homes, it is considered available for everyone's use. The difference between this communal orientation and more individualistic Western norms was made clear when Western exchange students, who generally got along well with their Bhutanese roommates, complained about roommates using their clothes or other property without asking permission.

As Linda Leaming, an American woman who married a Bhutanese man and has lived in Bhutan for decades, has observed, "Bhutanese share food, clothing, shelter, cars, time, ideas, laughter, money and jokes—just about anything—with friends, family, and complete strangers ... giving bestows importance on the giver. It's always better to give than to receive.... Giving to those who don't need it or who are ungrateful makes you a bodhisattva [enlightened being]."[54] A colleague at the college told me that when he reprimanded a student about having done a friend's assignment for her, she defended herself by saying she was just helping and that her behavior was "an act of love."

Consistent with the importance of community, social harmony is a widely shared value. What would be considered a very modest critique of another, even a social equal, is likely to be considered impolite or unacceptable. For example, in the national parliamentary election, one candidate was fined by the Election Commission for saying an opponent was, "All talk and no action," an extremely tame critique of an opponent by U. S. or European standards. Similarly, after a first-year student posted a relatively mild complaint about the college on Facebook, other students insisted she apologize to the entire college community in the seven-hundred-person auditorium. I and another staff member intervened, feeling this was an overreaction.

Not long ago, an entrepreneur who wanted to start rainbow trout farming had to wait three years to do so. A rule reflecting the emphasis on social harmony requires that such enterprises must be given clearance by local communities before they can be undertaken. His neighbors, concerned that the local deities would be angered because the fish would be killed for food, refused multiple times to approve his plan. They finally gave their assent after a day-long meeting in which a government official emphasized the economic potential of the farm as both a source of employment and a tourist destination.

Differences of opinion can have serious negative consequences. For example, villagers who favored a political party not supported by others ended up having to use a distant water source rather than the regular and much closer communal water tap. Political disagreements created so much friction during the first parliamentary election that the college and a civil society organization provided students with training in productive discussion of differences of opinion.

Family ties, as well as broader community ties, are strikingly strong in Bhutan. As a well-known Bhutanese journalist, Namgay Zam, said in talk at the college, "In Bhutan, loyalty to family comes above everything. ... [It] is so strong your ability to decide as an individual may be lost. ... We still function as communities, not as individuals."[55] Historically, family in Bhutan has included those well beyond the basic nuclear family. Joint living arrangements were encouraged in the past by the fact that taxes were sometimes levied on households irrespective of their size.

Strong ties with extended family members are evidenced linguistically. For example, relatives that Westerners would refer to as "cousins" are often referred to as "brothers" or "sisters" or "cousin-brothers" and "cousin-sisters." Also, financially well-off individuals commonly assume substantial responsibility for relatives who are less so. For example, a Royal Thimphu College student who was the only one in her family with a college education told me anxiously that thirteen relatives were expecting her to help support them once she graduated. In addition, a successful civil servant mentioned that his household consisted of sixteen people, although he and his wife had only two children. The rest were relatives from rural areas hoping to find work in Thimphu.

The extremely strong influence of the family was very evident in students' choices of college majors, which almost always reflected what a parent or other respected family or community member had selected, even if the student had another preference. Also, one of the most frequently mentioned goals in the college's admission application essays was to make life easier for other family members, especially parents. Statements such as, "The foremost thing on my wish list is to help my parents," and "One of my most important ambitions is to ... keep my mother and father in peace, away from all the works they are doing for my sister and me," were very common. In a different context, another student wrote, "My mother wants me to be a good son ... and she always calls me and reminds me that I should study hard. I am her only son, so I think I have to be accomplished and competent enough to look after her when she is old. ... I will try."[56]

A Western clinical psychologist who worked in Bhutan for several years summed up the situation to me by saying, "The boundary between we and I [in Bhutan] is not as strong as in the West." The lack of emphasis on the individual, relative to the family or community, is also evident in that, until recently, the Bhutanese did not celebrate individuals' birthdays. In fact, most people did not even know their birth date. When formal record keeping increased several decades ago, large numbers of people selected January 1st of the year they were born as a convenient birthday. I saw likely evidence of this practice for myself when a Bhutanese woman I met on an airplane heading to Bangkok opened her wallet to give me a business card. There, on an identity card, her birthday was printed as January 1, 1979.

Consistent with an acceptance of hierarchy and an emphasis on community, highly valued individual characteristics include respect for others, humility, and modesty. In striking contrast, a fifth strong characteristic of many Bhutanese is their obvious pride in their country and their high regard for its values and culture. This is especially striking because "sixty years ago, there was no national language or shared cuisine as the country was deeply divided into numerous valley communities which rarely mixed with one another."[57] But then something happened.

The Fourth King came to believe that Bhutan unique culture was a major asset supporting its sovereignty. Potential threats to independence were great for this tiny nation wedged between two huge countries, both of which had absorbed previously independent neighbors (Tibet and Sikkim) in the preceding few decades. In addition, there were calls in the region for the formation of Gorkhaland, a proposed state in India for the Nepali-speaking Gorkha ethnic group. This created concern because the proposed location of Gorkhaland adjoined areas of Bhutan where Nepali-heritage individuals predominated, and their population continued to increase disproportionately.

Effective strategies to retain sovereignty were limited, although Bhutan's Third King had begun to establish Bhutan's identity as a sovereign nation in the broader world by joining the UN in 1971. Then, under the leadership of the Fourth King in the 1980s, Bhutan joined the International Monetary Fund, the World Health Organization, and UNESCO, and it established diplomatic relations with countries including Switzerland, Nepal, and Japan. Clearly, none of these activities were likely to deter Bhutan's absorption into a neighboring giant should the neighbor decide to claim it. But they did help to establish it as an independent nation with international friends and allies. Unfortunately, these moves also posed the potential threats of Westernization and/or globalization to Bhutan's almost untouched and highly valued culture.

So, under a new "One Nation, One People" policy promulgated by the Fourth King in the late 1980s, a strong effort was made to foster a unified Bhutanese identity based on the religious and cultural legacy of Zhabdrung Ngawang Namgyal. As Dasho (an honorific) Kinley Dorji has pointed out, "In their determination to preserve its [Bhutan's] cultural heritage, the custodians of tradition interpreted culture as being synonymous with Buddhism from where the cultural identity had been drawn."[58]

As part of the process of national identity building, emphasis was put on codifying and implementing driglam namzha. Those of Nepali heritage were no longer allowed to wear their traditional clothing outside of their homes and a new emphasis was placed on the wearing of the traditional clothing from the time of the Zhabdrung, the gho and kira. The feeling was that a nation "of a little more than half a million people living in a region that is home to two fifths of mankind not only had to be different but had to look different to survive."[59] The Dzongkha language was also emphasized as part of identity building. Nepali, which had been one of the country's three official languages, was removed from the curriculum of some southern primary schools where the Nepali-heritage population was concentrated. Only Dzongkha and English were taught in schools after that.

Greatly compounding the dissatisfaction among many Nepali-heritage individuals related to these changes, a census conducted in 1988 classified them as citizens only if there was official proof of their residence in Bhutan as of the end of 1958. Since a reliable system of evidence was not available, many of them, including even those born in Bhutan, were classified as illegal immigrants. Furthermore, the 1985 Citizenship Act laid out many requirements for citizenship, making it difficult for those considered noncitizens to become citizens. These included speaking, reading, and writing Dzongkha proficiently, which even many non-Nepali heritage citizens were unable to do.

Those demonstrating against such changes were classified as "anti-nationals" and individuals related to them were not eligible for citizenship. Violence ensued on the part of both angry southerners and government troops, with advocates of a separate Gorkhaland intensifying the turmoil. Consequently, a very large number of Nepali-heritage individuals were forcibly evicted from the country or fled from the turbulence and danger in Bhutan's southern region.

By 1993, after several years of unrest and conflict, the camps set up in Nepal by the United Nations to receive individuals fleeing from this strife contained about one hundred thousand people. The events of this period are rarely discussed publicly in Bhutan, and many are hesitant to talk about them even in private. Thus, I do not have reliable firsthand information about how this situation impacts the current sense of "being Bhutanese" of the substantial number of Nepali-heritage individuals living in Bhutan. One of them in his twenties told me simply, "There is no discrimination," and named cabinet-level officials and other prominent citizens of Nepali heritage to support his analysis. Others saw the situation differently, pointing out, for example, that many Nepali-heritage individuals related to those deemed anti-nationals because they protested or fled during the upheaval in the late 1980s and early 1990s remain without important citizenship rights more than thirty-five years later.

The Fifth King clearly signaled increased acceptance of diversity when he gave a speech in 2008 emphasizing the importance of social cohesion that included the phrase, "One Nation, One Vision." This was a significant revision of the "One Nation, One People" motto promulgated by his father. Speaking at a graduation ceremony for college students in 2011, the Fifth King specifically urged them to focus on ending economic disparities rather than attending to "useless and irrelevant" regional and religious divisions.[60] By 2022, he had given citizenship kidu to about twenty-five thousand people. Inspection of their names on the lists I have seen suggests that the large majority are of Nepali heritage. There are dozens of posts on His Majesty's Facebook page profusely thanking him for granting citizenship kidu. However, there are also many pointing out that others have been waiting for it a long time in difficult circumstances. Clearly, the consequences of the earlier era still impact the country in numerous ways.

Despite the many questions raised by human rights groups about the events and the later consequences of the conflict in the early 1990s, most Bhutanese do not appear to see them as undermining their feelings of pride in and admiration for their country or its royalty. This may be due in part to Bhutan's relatively young population, since events that seem relatively recent to a person of my age may seem like ancient history to someone much younger. In addition, the sense of pride is reinforced by the fact that Bhutan has begun to be recognized worldwide for its progressive environmental policies and the idea of Gross National Happiness (GNH).

In the same way that foreigners sometimes naively tout Bhutan as the Last Shangri-La, some Bhutanese also offer it fulsome praise. For example, the first paragraph of a college applicant's admissions application essay read, "I am lucky to be born into this land of the Thunder Dragon. ... As everybody says, Bhutan is a piece of heaven on earth." An article about the country in Bhutan Youth stated, "For me there is no difference between heaven and my country ... because here ... everything is perfect ..."[61] Another young person's contribution to a Druk Journal issue on national identity asserted:

> There is a totally different level of pride, perhaps the best kind, that I feel when I call myself Bhutanese. It is a beautiful feeling one gets when one thinks about the best thing in life. It makes us feel most fortunate. I could actually even write an epic about how grateful I am to be born in a paradise like Bhutan, and it still might not suffice...[62]

Others even go so far as to assert that nothing bad will even happen to the country because of the amount of karmic merit that has been accumulated by its populace.

Reacting to such views, an eminent rinpoche caused a huge stir when he wrote in a newspaper article:

> Thinking that we are citizens of Shangri-La nation may be our problem ... When we think we're too special, we become spoiled ... That manifests in a so-called youth unemployment problem, which may have more to do with our young not wanting to do any menial or manual labour while we import thousands of Indian labourers to do our

construction for us ... More subtly, this feeling of specialness manifests in a reliance on exalted words and concepts, and in an antipathy for the kind of trench work and attention to detail required to translate words into actions ... Maybe most importantly, it will help Bhutan a lot if we think a little less that we are so special.[63]

Of course, many Bhutanese do hold positive but more tempered visions of the country than the youths quoted earlier, suggesting that formalized rules of politeness do not guarantee true consideration for others, that excessive attachment to tradition can stifle creativity, and that emphasis on hierarchy produces unemployment since young people will not take available low-status jobs.[64] But generally, Bhutanese seem extremely proud of and attached to their country and its culture. For example, historically, Bhutan has not faced the "brain drain" that plagues many developing countries, although concern has arisen about this issue in the post-pandemic era as emigration rates increased very markedly. Traditionally, those who studied or worked abroad, usually in Australia or the Middle East, have returned even if they lived elsewhere for some years. Such behavior speaks louder than words in confirming the sincerity of individuals' positive feelings about their country.

So, am I truly "almost Bhutanese"? No, I'm not, although I have seen more of the country than many Bhutanese and have also been profoundly influenced by my experiences in Bhutan. I am not religious by nature, although I greatly appreciate many of the values promoted by Buddhism, especially compassion, interdependence, and the acceptance of impermanence. I also see tremendous value in the Bhutanese emphasis on family and community. Coming from a country which strongly fosters individualism, I now more deeply appreciate just how important common ties can be in providing a web of support when problems arise and creating an atmosphere of warmth and care that extends beyond the immediate nuclear family.

I also greatly admire the energy, intelligence, and public-spiritedness of the Fifth King, but do not feel the same kind of deep-seated reverence for royalty that many Bhutanese seem to. In fact, early on I had an experience that showed me just how deeply ingrained my democratic attitudes are. At the opening of the college, I and others in the founding group were presented to a distinguished member of the royal family. When the moment came to bow, my back did not bend as low as I had consciously intended. The bow was clearly sufficient for the occasion. But as I walked away, I pondered the way my body had expressed a relatively democratic ethos even though my conscious intention had been to blend into the Bhutanese context with a deeper bow.

The biggest area of difference arises with regards to hierarchy. Compared to many Bhutanese, I value formal position, seniority, and age, in and of themselves, less and accomplishment more. I tend to say what I think if I believe that will be helpful even when my view differs from what a superior believes, although I always try to be tactful and courteous. Finally, not being Bhutanese myself, I cannot draw a sense of pride from recognizing the many positive attributes of the country. However, I do admire much about it, including the warmth and hospitality of its people, its remarkable environmental policies, and the rapidity with which it has been able to improve its people's the life chances while preserving crucial elements of its heritage.

# Chapter 7

Growing Up, Growing Old

Although at Royal Thimphu College I was something like a Jack (or Jill) of all trades, I am a social psychologist by training. For over thirty-five years before moving to Bhutan, I taught courses relating to gender, adolescence, personality, and social structure, as well as research methods. Thus, I was particularly attuned to trying to understand my experiences in Bhutan related to gender, age, family, and the like. As described in the preceding chapter, being Bhutanese is a fundamental aspect of identity for many in Bhutan. But individuals each have additional attributes that importantly shape their experiences and what is expected of them by others. As in virtually all societies, there are also shared practices that accompany crucial life transitions, like birth, marriage, and death. This chapter focusses on how gender and age impact individuals' life experiences as well as on the ways in which significant life events are marked in Bhutan.

Unlike attitudes in many Asian countries, there is not a strong preference for male children in Bhutan. Typically, a male or female baby is a cause for celebration. A few days after the birth, friends and community members gather at the parents' home to congratulate them and welcome the new arrival with modest gifts including dairy products, rice, baby clothing, or money. One such party we attended got quite boisterous as guests consumed more and more of the customary drink for this occasion—the local whiskey, ara—combined with eggs and butter. A celebratory meal was served, including chilies so hot that the Bhutanese woman sitting next to me began to sweat upon eating them as tears gathered in her eyes. The mounds of chilies consumed at the party reminded me of what a student told me shortly after we arrived: "In Bhutan, chilies are a vegetable, not a spice."

I was surprised at another similar celebration when the parents could not provide an answer to my question, which is so common about newborns in the West: "What's the baby's name?" I was told that a baby is typically not named until some days after its birth when its parents take it to a temple or monastery where it receives one, two, or three names from a monk or other respected religious figure. Bhutanese names often, but not always, have religious meaning. For example, the very popular name "Sonam" means religious merit and "Chime" refers to immortality. Most names do not signal an individual's gender. Despite the fundamental importance of family in Bhutan, typically, no family name is given to the children of Buddhists there. This posed a real challenge for newcomers like Doug and me, because family names cannot be used as a cue for family relationships. However, names do usually signal immediately if someone is of Nepali heritage. Such individuals, usually Hindu, typically have distinctive first names and family names such as Chhetri, Sharma, or Rai. However, such family names, which reflect caste or ethnic group membership, are shared by so many people that they too do not dependably signal common nuclear family membership.

Traditional naming practices sometimes pose problems for the Bhutanese themselves now that the population has grown substantially, and they are increasing likely to interact with the outside world. In very sparsely populated areas, like most of Bhutan, relatively few names are needed to distinguish one person from another, so there are only about fifty names that are commonly used. But with an expanding population and more urbanization, the chances of individuals being mistaken for each other because they have precisely the same name have increased dramatically.

This was brought home to me by several experiences during Royal Thimphu College's first year when we had only about three hundred students in the entering cohort. The first of these occasions was when the college held a practice run for the first student cohort's arrival. Banking services were limited at that time and students were coming from nineteen of Bhutan's twenty districts, including very rural ones. So, we knew many students would arrive with large stacks of cash to pay their first semester fees. To test the planned procedures, staff who would be receiving the students' payments sat behind tables in a designated area. A bevy of other staff took on the role of the arriving students. As the first set of staff members enacted registering the mock students and accepting stacks of money, one of them suddenly exclaimed, "Oh no!" It turned out that both the founding director and Doug had chosen the name, Sonam Dorji, and the system being tested had no way of handling identically named students.

Another consequence of the modest number of names was apparent on the roster listing the forty students in a class that I taught during the college's first year: There were six Sonams and five Tsherings. This certainly helped me in remembering names. But I found that learning individual student's names in Bhutan was more difficult than it typically was in the U.S. This is because I could not generally start by determining whether the name suggested a male or female and then looking first at those for whom it was most likely to be, as I had often done.

The fact that individuals may not be given more than one name in Bhutan also now causes previously uncommon problems. For example, an acquaintance named simply Sonam was initially unable to book an airline ticket because he had no first and last name to use in filling out required fields of an international airline's online booking form. He ended up entering, "Sonam Sonam." However, he was concerned because the name on his passport did not exactly match the name on his ticket, which could cause problems when boarding the plane or going through immigration formalities.

Although most Bhutanese names are not gender specific, gender does typically make a significant difference in life chances and experiences in Bhutan. A national survey concluded that although 55 percent of men can be considered "happy" or "extremely happy," the same is true of only 44 percent of women. Broad gender gap indices created by UN and World Economic Forum suggest that overall, Bhutan has a greater gap between males and females in various important areas than about three-quarters of the other ranked countries.

Although the gender ratio in Bhutanese schools was as lopsided as fifty males to each female in the 1970s, currently, there is rough gender parity in schooling. This change over time was highlighted for me when a male student told me that his parents had just decided his youngest sister should go to college, although previously only the boys in his family had been given that opportunity. Historically, men were also more likely to engage in tasks that required long treks through steep terrain, such as trading with India or Tibet. This may explain why males who have the large-muscled calves useful for the speedy completion of such excursions have traditionally been considered

Children too young to wander outside by themselves keep track of what is happening in their village by peeking out the windows, which traditionally have no glass in them.

Rural boys have fun on the way home from school, near lumber for a home under construction.

particularly desirable husbands in rural Bhutan. The knee-length ghos men wear make the size of their calves readily apparent to all, although that attribute probably receives less attention in urban than rural contexts because it has less relationship to economic success there.

There is a saying that "women are nine births lower than men" in the cycle of rebirths in which Buddhists believe one moves up or down according to the way one has lived the previous life. Almost 40 percent of Bhutanese women agreed with that adage in a 2017 survey. As recently as a couple of years before we moved to Bhutan, a committee of the National Assembly produced a report that contained words that translate as "stupid, ignorant woman," and in some rural areas, women are still referred to as *aumsu mo rem* (helpless women), whereas men are called *kep phoja* (superior male). Consistent with that heritage, women hold only about 40 percent of the positions in Bhutan's employer of choice, the civil service. Men also greatly outnumber women in elected and appointed positions. In fact, only four of the forty-seven individuals elected to the first National Assembly in 2008 were female. In the 2024 election, that number decreased to two. At Royal Thimphu College, it took about a decade for the first female to be elected student government president, although the student body was consistently slightly over 50 percent female.

The changing position of women in Bhutan was highlighted when it was realized that there was no female equivalent for the impressive sword that males receive as a symbol of authority when assuming a high-level office. It took a while, but by 2016, a modest-sized brooch called a *gyentag* was designed. The first of these was given by the king to female ministers, parliamentarians, and others that year. When I first saw one, I was struck by how much less obvious they are than the long swords that unmistakably proclaim an important male's status the minute he enters a room.

The 2008 Bhutanese constitution guarantees men and women equal rights. Property is passed down through the female line in much of western and central Bhutan, giving women considerable power and ownership of the fundamental resource in an agrarian society: land. This has turned out to be something of a double-edged sword though, as it also tends to keep women tied to rural areas where economic opportunities are generally fewer than in urban ones. In spite of the dearth of women in positions of power and responsibility, class discussions at Royal Thimphu College suggested that most students did not perceive gender discrimination in the country. Consistent with that, a relatively recent study suggested that two out of three Bhutanese women agree that "there is gender equality in Bhutan."

Yet domestic violence directed against women and girls is a concern. A 2010 survey found that 68 percent of Bhutanese women thought a husband was justified in beating his wife for one or more behaviors such as going out without telling him, arguing with him, or neglecting the children. Almost one-quarter thought a beating was justified if the wife burned food. The proportion of women accepting such behaviors was lower in a later survey. Nonetheless, over half of the women and girls felt that a husband was justified in hitting his wife for one or more reasons such as the wife not completing housework, disobeying him, or not taking care of the children. No wonder that one of my first-year students wrote in a journal entry that she did not want to get married because "a husband might beat me if I don't listen to him." Consistent with this, many of my students used the word "hot-tempered" when listing common male personality characteristics. This term was never applied to females, who were commonly characterized as being warm and gentle in this class exercise.

Courting behaviors provide a window into gender roles and assumptions. As in many other parts of the world, in Bhutan, males typically take the initiative in courtship. One of the most striking examples of this is *bomena*, a time-honored practice in rural central and eastern The Bhutanese writer, Sonam Chuki, describes bomena as "a form of flirtation and courtship that was intended to lead to marriage. That it did not always do so was accepted, more for men than for women."[65] In this nighttime practice, a male surreptitiously sneaks into the home of a female through a window or a door, which typically cannot be locked from the inside in traditional homes. The female can refuse the attentions of a suitor arriving in this manner. If the courtship proceeds, the male may return repeatedly over many months. But if he is ever still with her in the morning, the couple is generally considered married. Although bomena was traditionally intended to lead to marriage, it sometimes led to rape and/or children born without the woman having a male partner to share parental responsibilities. This practice has waned in recent years, due to factors ranging from the increased prevalence of electric lighting and household locks to changing social mores, but it continues to some extent in rural areas.

The informality of many marriages makes it easy for one partner to leave the union. The troubles that this can cause were brought home to us one rainy afternoon when we gave a ride to a woman in her mid-twenties and three young children who were trudging despondently along the edge of a narrow road outside of Thimphu. With tears in her eyes, the woman told us of her desperate situation. Her husband had left the family a few weeks before and they had no other means of support because she was a homemaker and had not been employed before her marriage. She had no idea where the children's father had disappeared to and did not expect to hear from him again. We dropped the despondent group off near the small and unprepossessing home of a friend of hers. As they disappeared in our rearview mirror, I hoped they would find at least temporary respite there.

Marriage between one man and one woman is now clearly the norm in Bhutan. There is no provision for gay marriage, and homosexual acts were outlawed until 2020, although the legal prohibition was rarely if ever enforced. A woman can have only one legal husband, but in some highland areas custom allows her to have two or more, commonly brothers. This practice has some practical advantages in a harsh environment with limited resources. It tends to reduce population growth and to keep land holdings consolidated. In addition, it provides more male labor per household than a monogamous arrangement. Having two husbands can also be useful in rugged terrain where one family member typically needs to head off on extended journeys with yaks or mules to barter or sell goods while others are needed for arduous work connected to livestock production. Nonetheless, this practice is waning. Early arranged marriage, involving girls as young as ten or twelve, was common in some highland areas as well. However, as education has become more highly valued, such early marriage has become unusual.

The law allows a man to have as many as three wives simultaneously. In a wide-ranging interview, the cabinet secretary to the first democratically elected government in Bhutan commented, "Had my elder wife conceived in time, I wonder whether I would have ever married her younger sister. ...The entire credit for my happy family and life goes to my two wives. ...Today, the love and affection of my wives and children continue to be the everlasting strength and encouragement of my life."[66] The social acceptability of polygamous marriages is evidenced by the fact that the highly respected Fourth King has four wives, four of five sisters from a prominent family descended from Zhabdrung Ngawang Namgyal. Pictures of him and his four queens together are common in Bhutanese homes. Reflecting the Bhutanese lack of emphasis on formal public marriage ceremonies, they jointly had eight children before their public marriages in 1988. I was interested to hear from friends that the Fourth King had decided that the son who was his successor should have only one wife. However, since even the Bhutanese characterize their countrymen as fond of gossiping, I cannot attest to the truth of this assertion.

Today, well-off urbanites often have formal wedding receptions. One we attended was held in a spacious hall with chairs placed around its edges and a large central area for mingling. Servers offered generous amounts of food and drink as guests in their best clothes chatted with each other for two or three hours. A few months before attending this event, I read in the newspaper that it was no longer legal to eat wasps, which are considered a delicacy appropriate for wedding celebrations. Fortunately, from my perspective, wasps were not on the nonetheless impressive menu.

Another wedding reception we attended was held in a lovely hotel with a sizable dining room. The bride and groom sat in an alcove off to the side, individually receiving well over one hundred guests who presented them with white scarves and gifts that were then piled high beside them. An excellent luncheon, including numerous chili-laden dishes, was served at large round tables in the hotel's restaurant. Interestingly, a member of the royal family who attended this event due to a long association with the family hosting it was seated in a separate room immediately adjacent to the restaurant. She then invited a half dozen people, including Doug and me, to join her there for lunch and an engaging conversation.

Both age and gender are important in Bhutan, even though the Bhutanese have only recently begun to celebrate birthdays. Doug and I had a very memorable time at the birthday party of a thirteen-year-old we met in a village about an hour outside of Thimphu. Sometimes on weekends we would select a road to explore, not knowing where it went but anticipating the pleasure of discovering previously unseen views and new villages. After driving along an extremely rough potholed road beside a frothing stream for half an hour and managing to progress no more than about five miles, we came to a rather basic looking village surrounding the first prison we had encountered in Bhutan. We decided to press on. After a few more miles the road got so rough we were afraid we would damage our car or end up stuck in the mud. So, we parked and strolled further along the rutted road, unexpectedly encountering a good-sized school where someone we knew taught. As we stood at its gate wondering if we could appropriately wander in, a preadolescent girl approached us and asked if she could show us around. We were delighted and she escorted us through the grounds, explaining what we saw.

Having finished the school tour, we decided to wander further down the road. Our self-appointed guide asked if she and a couple of friends could join us. As we strolled along together, she chatted volubly about the area, including warning us to be careful because a bear had recently been spotted nearby and they sometimes attacked villagers. Then our new friend, whom I will call Dechen, invited us to her home for tea. We gratefully accepted and met her mother in their sunny living room. It contained two simple couches, a small coffee table, and a glass-fronted cabinet displaying an array of mugs, Bhutanese and Western teacups, and beautiful hand-carved wooden bowls made from burls. A very large, generously stuffed, orange teddy bear relaxed on top of a cabinet next to a small lamp as we sipped sweet milk tea.

Dechen told us excitedly that she was going to have a birthday party in about six weeks. Looking expectantly at us she inquired, "Will you come?"

We agreed and I gave her my phone number so that she could be in touch. Roughly each week thereafter until her birthday, she called me in the evening. She would inquire about what I was doing and then share news about her schoolwork, her friends, or her family. The call would end with her reminding me of the upcoming birthday party and a renewed invitation to attend.

On the appointed Saturday afternoon, Doug and I arrived for the party. We climbed up the steep steps to Dechen's house and into the living room where several pink and blue balloons had been put up in honor of the occasion. The birthday girl was already in the living room with her much younger sister and several friends. Dechen and a few of her friends were wearing the beautiful, full length, hand-woven kiras women wear to *tshechus* (religious festivals), the equivalent of their "Sunday best." A few other friends wore everyday kiras or casual Western clothing like sweatshirts, leggings, and outdoor jackets. Dechen's mother, working on preparing a meal in the kitchen, came out briefly to say hello before returning to chopping onions and tomatoes. Soon, an Australian, who was one of Dechen's teachers, arrived with his wife, a faculty member at Royal Thimphu College. Then, several boys arrived in casual clothing, some wearing jeans or bright orange and yellow t-shirts emblazoned with the words "Qatar Foundation."

Dechen's father, a taxi driver, proudly brought out the family's present to her: a substantial cake with white icing and pale blue decoration, clearly purchased from a Thimphu bakery. We were surprised, because Western baked goods like birthday cakes were quite an unusual and expensive luxury at that time in Bhutan. He carefully placed the cake on the table next to some paper plates and a butter lamp, which he lit. He then cut the cake and passed it around while everyone socialized and dug into the very special treat. The teacher read a story to some of the younger guests. Then, a meal with mountains of rice and the ubiquitous chilies was served.

Next, everyone seemed to know it was time to do something to entertain the group. The teacher and three boys sang a song while the rest of us clapped in time to its rhythm. Different combinations of girls performed folk dances and songs in the small open space in the center of the living room. One of the boys read a short excerpt from a book. Then it was my turn. I had no idea what to do that would be fun for such a varied group. But I felt I had to join in the spirit of the event. I explained the idea of a song that can be sung as a round, and I introduced the group to "Row, Row, Row Your

Boat." I led the first group. Doug led the second, and we were merrily off down the stream. I later realized that this particular round was not an ideal choice, because I had never seen a boat on Bhutan's many rivers, lakes, and streams. Despite that, all joined in with gusto. The warm camaraderie at the party, as everyone contributed something to the occasion, is a feeling that I will never forget. As evening approached and the party came to an end, Dechen slowly walked us to our car, reluctant to see us leave.

On her thirteenth birthday, Dechen was entering the period which national policy in Bhutan defines as "youth," between thirteen and twenty-four years old. Unfortunately, in Bhutan, the term "youth" most typically seems to be followed by the word "problems" or "unemployment." Of course, concern about, and often disapproval of, youth is common in many societies. Indeed, I recall writing a paper in middle school that started with a quote from ancient Egypt lamenting the state of its youth. But such concerns are likely to be especially common in countries like Bhutan, which are undergoing change so rapid change that elders must deal with the emergence of unfamiliar values and behavior inconsistent with tradition.

Because TV and the internet were not allowed in Bhutan until 1999, those at the upper end of the youth cohort today are the first to have had such purveyors of external influence available their entire lives. That same period has also seen substantial improvement in the roads between Bhutan and India with an accompanying huge increase in the importation of goods, including cigarettes and prescription drugs, from the outside. Both changes have contributed to commonly cited youth problems in Bhutan.

Many older Bhutanese express serious concerns about some youths' lack of dedication to maintaining Bhutan's unique culture, which is seen as linked to the nation's very survival, as well as to respect for cherished customs. Many youths clearly prefer Western dress to traditional clothing. I have seen Bhutanese teenagers in jeans and t-shirts open backpacks to change quickly into the required gho or kira before entering a monastery and changing back again as soon as they leave it. Similarly, most Royal Thimphu College students expeditiously swap their ghos and kiras, which are required during classes, for informal Western garb when their classes are over. A wealthy student even ordered a striking prom gown from France. It was lovely, but seeing her wear it made me a bit sad because the Bhutanese weave some of the most beautiful fabrics in the world. Some youths also question whether the emphasis on driglam namzha is appropriate in a democracy, since many of the behaviors it entails can be seen as reinforcing the gap between those of higher and lower social status. Others complain that it focuses attention too much on superficial behavior rather than moral values.

Tobacco use by youth is another issue of serious concern. Until the pandemic brought about a policy change to reduce the cross-border traffic created by the smuggling of tobacco from India, Bhutan was the only country in the world to completely ban the sale and production of tobacco products. Its efforts to control tobacco go back centuries. The country's very first legal code, promulgated in the 1600s, forbade the use of tobacco in government and religious buildings. By 2003, eighteen of Bhutan's twenty districts had outlawed tobacco use more generally. Indeed, on one weekend trip, I saw a sign indicating that we were entering a tobacco-free dzongkhag where the fine for smoking was at least two days' wages for an unskilled worker.

Access to the outside world through TV, DVDs, and the internet popularized smoking, especially among urban youth. With tobacco sales banned in most of the country, smuggling became rife. By 2008 government statistics suggested that 10 percent of Bhutanese men and 7 percent of Bhutanese women used tobacco. Consistent with concerns about tobacco use by youth, 18 percent of male youth under eighteen and 6 percent of their female peers also used tobacco at that time. In 2009, the world's strictest anti-tobacco law, the Tobacco Control Act, was passed. It completely prohibited the sale of tobacco products in Bhutan, banned smoking in most public places, and required smokers to produce tax receipts for tobacco purchased outside of the country on demand.

But youth tobacco use increased nonetheless. Indeed, by 2018, Bhutan had the highest rate of adolescent smoking out of ten South Asian countries—and tobacco use started early. The first person arrested under the 2009 act was a youth, a twenty-three-year-old monk, Sonam Tshering, caught with less than seven ounces of chewing tobacco and no tax receipt. After he was sentenced to a three-year prison term, popular opinion led to reducing the law's draconian penalties. But it still banned the sale of tobacco within the country and its use in many places.

A survey I conducted at Royal Thimphu College in 2010 found that 20 percent of male and 9 percent of female students usually smoked every day, although the law prohibited smoking on the grounds of educational institutions. Even practices such as having staff members patrol the bathrooms in the academic areas and fining students caught smoking were unable keep the smell of tobacco smoke from routinely wafting into nearby classrooms. So, the college decided to try a different approach by mobilizing the campus around the theme "Living Free Without Tobacco or Drugs."

As one part of this campaign, I customized an American Cancer Society smoking cessation program for the Bhutanese context and offered it in weekly meetings I conducted for interested students. Several participants thought Nicorette would help them quit, so I tried to locate some. One shopkeeper told me it had not been approved for import by Bhutan's Drug Regulatory Authority, as all medications must be to be legally sold, asserting I would not be able to find it. But I kept searching and finally located a store with about fifteen packets of it. I bought them all and handed out a free one-week supply to each of the students who wanted to try it. I gave additional free packets to those who found it helpful, along with information on where it was available.

Always results-oriented, the college's founding director wanted to assess whether the Living Free campaign had any impact. As a social psychologist who greatly enjoys research, I volunteered to carry out a study of this issue. So, both before the campaign started and after it had been underway for most of the semester, student assistants unobtrusively counted the number of cigarette butts found every day at secluded spots around campus where students frequently hung out to smoke. In addition, staff members who were not otherwise involved in the campaign estimated daily for three months how strong the smell of cigarette smoke was in indoor locations where it was typically present. We were pleased to find substantial decreases in both indicators. Three years later, at the eightieth birthday party for the United Kingdom's Honorary Counsel in Bhutan, one of the former smoking cessation program participants greeted me. As we enjoyed the delicious chocolate cake the Fifth King had sent in honor of this occasion, this young man proudly volunteered that he had not had a cigarette since completing the sessions.

Even more concerning to many than tobacco use is the drug use that is now common, especially among young urban males. Wild marijuana grows profusely in much of Bhutan. In earlier times, it was used to fatten pigs and was essentially never used by humans. Now, however, marijuana is used by over 20 percent of Bhutanese male adolescents and 4 percent of their female peers, the highest rate in South Asia. Pain medicine and sedatives smuggled in from India are also ingested for recreational purposes by some youth as well.

Doug and I became friends with Lama Shenphen, a Welsh Buddhist monk who has spent almost twenty years working with young addicts in Thimphu, typically young men from families stressed by divorce, desertion, alcohol, or other problems. He told me this work can be discouraging, but there have been notable successes as well. For example, I recall sitting with him as he encouraged a promising young recovering addict to start a coffee house, envisioning how it would be furnished and what could be served. Fifteen years later, this young man and his wife run a thriving business in Thimphu serving coffees, teas, pastries, and light meals that are especially popular with foreign students and expatriate professionals.

Excessive alcohol use is also a serious youth problem in Bhutan, as it is for the older population. Alcohol is so deeply embedded in Bhutan's culture that alcohol-related problems are the primary cause of admission to Bhutan's hospitals and the most common cause of death.[67] Alcohol is used to welcome guests, to wash down food, to freshen the mouth after a meal, to drink with food and after tea, to begin and end rituals, to celebrate, to honor guests, to mark arrivals and departures, to give to a guest going on a journey to carry with them, and many other occasions. Each of these uses and others, including night-caps and wake-up drinks for guests, has its own specific name. No wonder there is a bar for every fifty-six adults in Bhutan, although home brewing of alcoholic drinks also consumes a noticeable portion of the grain production in some areas.

Heavy drinking is common even at a relatively early age. A study at one of the government colleges found over 20 percent of students scored above the "chronic" to "alcoholic" levels of consumption on a Western alcoholism screening test. A full quarter of students reported missing classes or turning in assignments late due to drinking. Especially in the eastern part of Bhutan, consuming alcohol was traditionally common even for young children, although in the last decade or two that has become less socially accepted. When I asked the docent at the Folk Heritage Museum in Thimphu about the purpose of a strikingly large, covered vessel, she replied casually, "It was for storing wine. Women had to work in the fields, so they would wine-up the babies and young children to quiet them."

When I served briefly as a counselor at Royal Thimphu College, I worked with numerous students whose drinking led to behaviors resulting in disciplinary actions. Jam sessions, a popular event at the college, were discontinued mainly because of excessive drinking, despite extensive monitoring by college staff. A small group of students at the college who were addicted to drugs or alcohol set up a group called RTC Survivors using Narcotics and Alcoholics Anonymous as a model. I helped them with logistics and admired their attempt to turn their lives around. Several years later, I was delighted when one of them sent me an upbeat email saying he had at a good job in India.

Another youth problem in Thimphu, Bhutan's only city of any significant size, was gangs. These have waxed and waned markedly during the last couple of decades. After a long period in which they were very quiet, gangs, with names like "the MB Boys" (MB for mass beating), "Bacteria," and "Virus" emerged as a frequent topic of concern shortly after we arrived in Bhutan in 2009. Most were formed by teenage males, although there were a few female gangs as well. They engaged in fights over turf and other issues, sometimes using knives and knuckle-dusters. Many were involved with drugs and alcohol as well.

The police took a novel approach to this issue. The chief of police called a meeting which over fifty gang members attended, including the leaders of two of the most notorious gangs. There he asked them to sign a pledge to dissolve the gangs. He also promised to provide gang members with

Royal Thimphu College students' outfits at a prom reflect many Bhutanese youths' penchant for Western clothing on formal as well as informal occasions.

An adolescent monk shares a pleasant moment with a policeman near the entrance to a dzong.

concrete assistance in charting a more productive future, including working with the government to set up counseling as well as an employment program. The leader of the MB Boys apologized for inflicting "unnecessary shame, pain and damage to the society" and promised to "shun gangs and gang violence."[68] The chief of police then appointed the meeting attendees as goodwill ambassadors for the police and gave them responsibility for advising others not to join gangs. The police strategy included numerous follow-ups. These included visits with parents and schools to discourage gang membership and required community service for gang members who were not responsive to police requests. These efforts were apparently useful, because the public clamor about gang activities virtually disappeared after a while.

Yet another major youth problem is unemployment. Having risen sharply in recent years to almost 16 percent, it is much higher than the general Bhutanese unemployment rate, which is around 6 percent. It is a serious issue itself, and it contributes to many of the other problems just mentioned as well. Youth unemployment impacts a relatively large percentage of the population because Bhutan has a relatively low median age of twenty-eight, a full decade lower than the median age in the U.S. and roughly twenty years lower than those in Germany and Japan. Many factors contribute to high youth unemployment including a mismatch between the education young people receive and job requirements, youths' strong preference for living in a few urban areas, and competition from inexpensive foreign labor which keeps wages for many kinds of unskilled or semiskilled work very low. In addition, Bhutan has a small, relatively weak private sector due to challenges including lack of credit, difficult transportation, complex bureaucratic regulations, and a small market as well as competition from over two dozen state-owned enterprises.

The attitudes of college-educated youth, the group most likely to be currently unemployed, are another very important factor in increasing youth unemployment. As Sangay Tenzin Tshering, a 2019 Royal Thimphu College graduate put it, "Bhutanese have this stereotypical view of thinking that government jobs are the best and any others are just not good."[69] A study of the college's students' aspirations concluded, "The allure of a government job ... is such that even as some students ... deep down ... would prefer a career outside the government ... they would readily forego this for the prospects and perks of government employment. ... Becoming a government servant is also what their parents wish."[70] College graduates, including those from business programs, commonly do not look for jobs in the private sector unless and until it is clear they will not get one with the government or a state-owned corporation.

Until quite recently, a college education was a virtual guarantee of lifelong government employment, which brought with it respect, security, and even opportunities for further study outside the country. Back in 1974, a college education was so rare and precious that the National Council spent time discussing in what positions the three graduates available that year should be placed. But now, things are different. Roughly 18 percent of all Bhutanese between nineteen and twenty-three years old are enrolled in higher education. Thousands graduate each year, but the civil service typically has jobs for only about a quarter of them. This creates a major problem, especially since Bhutan's private sector is so limited.

Similarly, graduates of Bhutan's technical and vocational education system face employment hurdles. This is to some extent due to widely acknowledged deficiencies in the training offered. A newspaper editorial explained, "A common complaint from ... graduates is not being able to apply their skills in the job market. An institute uses machines made in the 1960s to train its mechanical students when vehicles that flash by the institute are half computerized."[71] But just as fundamental are young peoples' attitudes towards blue-collar jobs. An official at the Ministry of Labour and Human Resources explained, "Job seekers prefer to remain jobless than to take jobs that are available. Most Bhutanese are least interested in manual jobs."[72] Consistent with, and contributing to such attitudes, when the government began to explore overseas employment opportunities for youth, it decided not to send workers for domestic help, construction work, or agricultural work such as kiwi picking in New Zealand.

As a result of such attitudes, Bhutan's booming construction industry depends on tens of thousands of Indians, not only as unskilled laborers, but also as plumbers, electricians, carpenters, masons, and the like. Many of these workers are quite skilled. But you cannot depend on it. Royal Thimphu College is widely acknowledged to be one of the best constructed projects in Bhutan. Recall that when I leaned against one of the walls in our living room as we were moving into our apartment, an electric shock ran through my entire body.

Similarly, auto repair shops depend almost entirely on Indian labor. Indeed, the foreman of a Thimphu auto repair shop told me that in his fourteen years of work there, he had never seen a Bhutanese graduate of the auto mechanics technical training program take a job in one of the dozens of the auto repair shops clustered nearby. Rather, they tried to get jobs as drivers, but relatively few have been successful in that.

Since youth problems are so salient, any discussion of what it means to be a young person in Bhutan requires attention to such issues. But that can leave the wrong impression. These problems are found in many countries, and often in more severe forms. Interacting with students at the college as well as many younger students we got to know gave me a close-up view of some of the challenges Bhutanese youth face in a rapidly changing society. It also highlighted several characteristics that I came to greatly respect. Some of these, like their dedication to assisting other family members and their desire to make their parents proud, have already been discussed. Other positive attributes were quite evident as well.

Many Bhutanese young people are remarkably open, gracious, and warm. On our weekend hikes in rural areas, it was extremely common for secondary school students to welcome us in a variety of ways. When we walked past a private high school in the Paro valley, an eleventh-grade boy emerged to chat with us. He spent the entire afternoon hiking with us, and then translated when a farmer who did not speak English invited us in for tea. The next time we returned to that area, he joined us again. On another walk in a village called Namseling we met a secondary school student who invited us into his home for tea. He kept in touch with us by phone and nearly two years after we first met, he called to invite us to his village's tshechu, a lovely event with about seventy people present. He introduced us to the local area's *gup*, or mayor, who invited us to have lunch at his home during the festival's noon break. The men enjoyed lunch while the women scurried around preparing and delivering it to them and to us as we sat with them as guests of the gup.

In the village of Ura, in central Bhutan, a teenage girl asked if we would like to see the local temple. When we said yes, she ran to get the keys to open it up for us and then stayed with us during our exploration of the entire village. And then there was the middle-school student whom I will call Kinley. We first met her when walking near her village outside of Thimphu. She chatted with us for a while. Then she took us home to meet her parents.

We met her again several more times because her family's apartment was in an area we enjoyed exploring.

A few years after we first met her, Kinley enrolled in secondary school in Paro, about an hour's drive from where we lived. She kept in touch by phone and invited us to visit her at her new school. On one such visit, she unexpectedly gave me a beautiful necklace made from silvery polished seeds that her grandmother had given to her. At first, I refused to accept it. But Kinley was so crestfallen by this that I finally agreed. When her family later moved to Thimphu, she invited us for dinner, during which we had a fascinating conversation with her father, a high school teacher and principal. I had never really felt comfortable accepting Kinley's necklace, because it was a family heirloom. So later when we visited her at school in Paro again, I returned it. Initially, she refused to take it back. I finally convinced her to do so by saying that it would now be a lasting reminder for her of both me and her grandmother since we had both worn and treasured it.

I was also touched by the way some students showed their appreciation for the teaching and mentoring I did. For example, one young man emailed me occasionally for several years after he graduated. He signed his notes, "Your student forever," which I found very sweet, even moving. Another student I mentored as he and some classmates prepared for a regional competition was in touch two years after he had graduated to let me know he was successfully turning the business plan they had developed for the competition into an actual business. He wrote, "I would not be who I am today without your motivation and support. Thank you, madam." Yet another student to whom Doug and I gave a short lift in our car—although we had not met him previously—showed up at our apartment several days later with two jars of homemade wild strawberry jam, which his family in central Bhutan had made earlier from a secret patch of berries they had discovered that spring. These students, like the female graduate who brought me a bag of avocados, a luxury in Bhutan, from her family's farm, clearly expected nothing in return.

In addition to greatly admiring the openness and generosity of so many Bhutanese youth, I also respected the courage and spirit many Royal Thimphu College students showed in participating in exchange programs the college set up with universities in the U.S., Europe, and Japan. Of course, students from countless countries do a similar thing. But many of our students grew up in tiny communities with extraordinarily limited exposure to the outside world. In addition, they understood that the academic backgrounds of many of their new classmates would be both stronger and better aligned with the demands of tertiary education elsewhere than theirs was. The students eagerly applying for these opportunities knew they would be facing substantial personal and academic challenges, often halfway around the world from their friends and family. Reflecting similar courage, thousands of Bhutanese youths have begun to take jobs in the Middle East and Australia due to the lack of employment within it.

The very substantial challenges Bhutanese youth face when going abroad now are not as great as they were just one generation ago. It is hard to fully recognize just how daunting these were, even quite recently. For example, a middle-aged Bhutanese acquaintance who studied at a college in England told us that he was terrified when he first arrived in the London airport because he saw people getting into a large box and then disappearing before the box's door opened again. He had never seen an elevator before. Another, who had never seen automatic doors, told us about trying to leave the London airport after his first arrival there. He had watched other people exit and assumed that an operator observing from somewhere above had opened the doors for them. When the doors did not open for him, he did not realize he was standing too far away to activate the trigger mechanism. Rather, with a sinking feeling in his chest, he thought he was being blocked from entry to this unfamiliar land after his long journey.

Even today's generation encounters some such challenges. For example, when we arrived in Bhutan there was not a single escalator in the entire country. We happened to be at a modest-size shopping mall shortly after the first one was installed. People of all ages were loath to step onto the moving staircase and did so with great trepidation, although a few adventurous youngsters got quite a thrill out of riding the escalators up and down repeatedly.

My admiration for those Bhutanese youth who go abroad for study or work is also enhanced by the fact that most have not had experience with the degree of independence that many Western students who make a similar choice have had. The Bhutanese consistently refer to college students as children, and they are commonly treated as children as well, although a great many are in their twenties due to late enrollment in elementary school. For example, as mentioned previously, students almost unanimously reported following the wishes of a parent, uncle, or guardian when selecting a major, even when they had some other preference. Even more tellingly, when one of our students was having academic difficulties because he often missed morning classes, a parent requested that college staff go to his room to wake him every morning. A female student who lived off campus complained to me that she had to be home immediately after the end of classes and that she was not even allowed to join her friends on weekends for short shopping, lunch, or hiking excursions.

Although Western exchange students were generally extremely positive about their experiences at the college, one theme that emerged consistently in their feedback was that they felt too restricted by college rules. Royal Thimphu College allowed its students an unusual amount of freedom compared to Bhutan's other colleges, believing that this would help them mature into responsible adults. However, especially in the college's early years, parents and Bhutanese students themselves often suggested that its rules should be stricter.

Bhutanese youths' relative lack of autonomy primarily reflects cultural norms promoting respect for all kinds of seniority, including age. Degrees of seniority that would seem relatively minor in the Western world are much more important in Bhutan. For example, some students at Royal Thimphu College had part-time jobs as Resident Assistants (RAs) in the dormitories. Despite the various sanctioning powers associated with that position, RAs in one entering cohort often had a very hard time enforcing rules on students even just a year ahead of them. This was a sufficiently common problem that interviews of candidates for the coveted RA positions routinely included questions about how such a situation would be handled. Reflecting the same emphasis on seniority, in the college's first and second years the students elected their student government president from the small number of older students who were taking time off from government employment to earn a college degree.

The importance of seniority in Bhutanese culture was highlighted in 2006 when a new position classification system was implemented in the civil service. A seniority system based almost entirely on longevity had been the cornerstone of the civil service up to that point. To give more weight to merit in promotions in the new system, applicants from both one and two levels below an open position could apply for it rather than just those in the level immediately below it. The newspaper explained that this created serious problems because "when a civil servant from two positions below happened to be selected, the civil servants only one position below were psychologically affected" and upset because someone with a year's less seniority had bested them.[73] Four years later, the Royal Civil Service Commission retreated from this change.

Just as those like college students on the cusp of adulthood are seen differently in Bhutan than in the West, so too are those entering their later years. When we first arrived in Bhutan to work at Royal Thimphu College, civil service retirement there for many positions was at age fifty-five. We were in our mid-sixties. The difference in expectations about retirement age most likely reflected historical differences in longevity. For example, the average lifespan in Bhutan only a decade before that was just under sixty years compared to over seventy-six in the U.S.

Regardless of the age at which individuals are considered elderly, what it means to be elderly in the two countries is very different. In Bhutan, elders are shown great respect just for being elders. Indeed, in the Tsa Yig, the basic rules laid down in the 1600's by Zhabdrung Ngawang Namgyal, Bhutanese were directed to treat elders with reverence. A newspaper article titled "Old Is Gold" discussed opinions on the relationship between age and fitness for political leadership. One individual was quoted as saying, "At this juncture, young leaders cannot take the country ahead no matter how qualified and wise he/she may be." Another, after mentioning that government ministers sometimes have had difficulty with civil servants who have more years of seniority, said, "Imagine what will happen if a young

Farm work is taxing, especially given Bhutan's steep topography. But many elders continue to contribute to their family's livelihood if they are physically able.

Elders especially enjoy religious festivals, where they socialize with friends and family as well as pray and watch the masked dances.

MP ... becomes Minister or the Prime Minister," clearly envisioning major problems.[74]

The respect for elders still evident in Bhutan was brought home to us explicitly when a middle-aged gentleman came to our apartment for advice because he was considering starting a college and he wanted to learn about our experiences at Royal Thimphu College. When leaving, he presented us with four large fresh mangos and said gravely, "I want to thank two such elderly people for giving me so much of your time." His reference to our age was an extremely polite and respectful one. However, I must admit, I said amusedly to Doug once our guest had departed, "It sounds like he doesn't think we have very much time left."

This positive attitude toward elders was also very evident in an essay titled "All About Me" in which one of my students wrote, "I like to enjoy nature and I find joy in small things. ... There is no happiness which can compare to the joy you get from making others happy. I spend most of my time with old people, because my mother says that if we help old people they will always bless us." The difference in attitudes toward the elderly in Bhutan and the U.S. was underscored for me when the roughly sixty-five-year-old, grey-haired wife of an American staff member said to me, "I am so glad to be back in Bhutan. I felt invisible in the U.S. because of my age."

Until very recently, Bhutan was a relatively static traditional society with little formal education outside of the monasteries, so the main source of knowledge and wisdom for most people was life experience, which elders have in abundance. The difference between traditional knowledge and book learning was highlighted for me when some boys in a small village took Doug and me mushroom hunting. As we wandered through the forest, Doug and I carefully surveyed the ground, hoping to be the first to spot a potentially edible mushroom. We were astonished to hear a shout of triumph as a twelve-year-old shimmied up the rough trunk of a tree and pulled several large mushrooms out of a leaf-filled crotch between two ancient branches. The nearly twenty years of formal schooling that Doug and I both have were worth less than the boys' few years of experience in the forest in supplying their family's dinner.

Formal education, shifting employment opportunities, and urbanization are changing the kind of knowledge that brings economic benefits and social respect in Bhutan. Elders' knowledge and experiences are becoming outdated or irrelevant in many contexts compared to the knowledge gained through formal education. Accompanying this is a shift in beliefs on the part of some about the role youth should play in decision-making. As Bhutan has modernized and become a democracy, some youths have begun to openly complain about not being heard by elders. For example, a twenty-one-year-old male expressed his frustration by saying in a focus group discussion, "At a gathering of the elderly people ... if we pop in ... the elderly people will ask you to get out of their meeting ... Just ignoring us. That culture is there."[75]

Family dynamics involving elders and those younger seem likely to change along with broader societal changes. When Doug and I were invited into a farmhouse in the Paro valley for tea, an illiterate mother asked us to look at her third-grade daughter's schoolwork. She clearly knew much more than her daughter about farming. But she had no idea what the child was learning or how well her daughter was doing in school. I wondered what would happen to their relationship as the daughter grew older and recognized more and more clearly the limitations of her mother's knowledge in a society where elders themselves still expect to control most everything.

As another example, when my white-haired, seventy-two-year-old sister visited us, an intelligent, curious, but uneducated driver asked her if she had ever encountered a dinosaur. She, taken aback by the question, managed to reply politely, "No, unfortunately they were before my time." He then continued, "Well, did you ever meet Jesus?" These queries are a striking illustration of the extent to which even many middle-aged Bhutanese are just beginning to learn about the outside world. But it seems likely that youths with enough formal education to know that dinosaurs became extinct millions of years ago might be less willing to follow parental advice or dictates when interactions like this reveal their parents' lack of the kind of general knowledge that is increasingly available to and valued by the younger generation.

Chapter 8

The Long and Winding Road

Roads may sound like a boring topic. But they are never boring in Bhutan. When we emerged from our car to see why the road we were on in a well-off part of Thimphu was blocked, we discovered the Fire and Rescue Service struggling to rescue two bulls that had fallen into an open road drain. And, in the eastern part of the country, twenty volunteers including a cabinet minister in his formal office clothing took only nine hours to construct a temporary replacement for a forty-foot bridge that washed out during the monsoon rains. Roads illuminate a great deal about Bhutan's culture as well as about the pace of change in the last six decades. At a more personal level, the more than thirty thousand arduous miles that Doug drove on Bhutan's winding roads made possible some of our most unusual and memorable experiences. So, hang on for the ride. You won't regret it.

When I was born in 1946, even Bhutan's king had no option but to walk if he wanted to travel, unless he rode a mule, horse, yak, or chose to be carried on another's back along a dirt track—the option some officials resorted to in particularly steep areas only a few decades before that. There were no roads at all in Bhutan until the early 1960s. So, in 1958, it took the Prime Minister of India a full week on horseback to get from Bhutan's border with India to Thimphu, which may have encouraged him to subsequently agree to fund a motorable road. In 1983, a friend of mine who works for Save the Children took eight days to go roughly two hundred miles within Bhutan to reach a small settlement where that organization was contemplating a project, and the last day was spent crossing a river many times on the back of an elephant.

A single road lying like a twisted spine across most of the country's east-west width was finally completed in 1986. Although there is still not a single traffic light in the country, the construction of this and over nine thousand miles of subsequent roads have been very consequential. These roads have helped to reinforce the monarchy's centralized power, to unify disparate communities, and to facilitate education, healthcare, trade, and tourism.

In 1959, the National Assembly, which the Third King set up to enact laws, determined that the country's first road should be built south to India to make the import of needed goods easier and cheaper. The fact that China had recently taken over Tibet may have also played a role in this plan. Given that labor was a common form of tax, it was decided that men between eighteen and fifty-four would provide their labor during the seven-month dry season, with the government providing food and the needed tools as well as some salary.

This remarkable effort eventually involved one out of every three people in the country. Thousands of workers were housed and fed in extremely rugged, very lightly populated terrain. A Chinese garage owner and a Manchurian who had operated a mechanical workshop in Tibet were hired to supply needed technical expertise. Jeeps were taken apart, carried on pack mules to sections of the newly constructed road hacked into the mountainsides until they became passable, and then reassembled to transport supplies along them.

At that time, few Bhutanese had ever seen a wheeled vehicle. On seeing jeeps for the first time, "Some villagers ran away, others tried to stroke them and were amazed that the metal beast did not need to be fed with grass. Others were curious to see people sitting in the belly of the beast."[76] Still others, seeing a jeep's bright headlights and hearing its rumbling engine, thought it was a fire-breathing dragon. Interestingly, even sixty years later, there are places in Bhutan where individuals have never actually encountered a car or truck. Indeed, I was told by a colleague that one of her students had never come upon one until he headed from his tiny, isolated village to the college.

Today, distances that used to take twenty days of arduous walking can be covered by car in less than twenty hours. But traveling by road in Bhutan is still an adventure, often presenting unanticipated obstacles. As a newspaper editorial observed, "Located in the young Himalayas, our roads are prone to landslides, mudslides, and falling boulders and in some cases, heavy rain-triggered flooding that washes away bridges or an entire stretch of the road."[77]

One reason the roads were so challenging is that the technology used to build and maintain them has typically been very limited. One of the saddest sights I saw in Bhutan was a thin, bedraggled, female road worker breaking up rocks by pounding them with a hammer while simultaneously teaching her four-year-old daughter how to do the same. In our first year in Bhutan, the only place we saw large earth-moving equipment was as part of an advertising display in Thimphu's main public square, a venue normally used for street fairs, concerts, and the like. However, heavy road-building equipment has recently become quite common on the east-west highway.

Unfortunately, local communities, which have typically been expected to maintain the unpaved farm roads connecting them to the broader national road network, often do not have ready access to such equipment. So, I was not surprised when I heard on the evening news several years ago that about 40 percent of such roads were unusable due to maintenance issues. We experienced the results of poor local road repair practices when a section of the route between the college and our favorite bakery fell into serious disrepair no more than three or four months after it had been resurfaced. To avoid damage to our car, we had to drive slowly around it on a bumpy, muddy track adjacent to the resurfaced but essentially unusable section.

But most road workers do the best they can with the tools they have. A memorable sight was a crew of nine men painting white lines on a road near Bhutan's only international airport. First, a sweeper used an obviously handmade broom to brush gravel out of the way. Then, two other men worked jointly to lay out a straight path for the paint. One, holding a string, moved about forty feet ahead of his teammate and then stretched the string tight along the road's edge. Next, the other took hold of that string where it emerged from the front of a two-wheeled cart supporting a large barrel of white paint. A fourth team member pushed the cart from behind, with an assistant who helped when the grade got steep. Yet another team member collected the string once the paint had been laid down along the path it delineated. Three others accompanied this group, apparently providing support of various kinds or supervising the work. The resulting white line looked pretty good, but I could not help but wonder how many hundreds of man-hours it took to apply a white line to even one mile of pavement this way.

The national east-west highway, often called the lateral road, has been paved from time to time. But in many sections there was little or no remaining evidence of this, and encountering lengthy segments of deep and very slippery mud where the land on one side abruptly dropped off many hundreds of feet was commonplace. Indeed, driving that road gave new meaning to the phrase "have a safe journey," which is often used in the U.S. without serious concern that a departing guest might encounter real danger.

Some sections of that road, which we drove numerous times, had threatening rock outcrops looming above the inner lane, leading me to heave a deep sigh of relief when we had passed under them without damage to ourselves or our car. Where the terrain was particularly steep and unstable, signs warned of "Shooting Boulders" and newspaper reports told of travelers killed by falling rocks. In some places, that road was so narrow that we had to pull in our car's side mirrors to avoid contact with the rock wall on one side or a passing vehicle on the other. It is telling that the word "*lam*" is still used to refer to roads as well as to the paths and mule tracks that it originally designated. Sometimes the distinction did not seem entirely clear, although the east-west highway has recently undergone widening and paving that has improved the situation markedly.

The only road running west to east across the country was commonly blocked by landslides that could take hours to many days to clear.

Slippery mud made roads treacherous, especially during the summer monsoon.

On one trip along this road in 2019, we came around a curve to see that a thin yellow police tape was the only barrier between us and a gaping forty-foot-wide hole where the entire road had simply disappeared down the precipitous mountainside. We had two choices: to head back home or to drive over a narrow, rock-strewn verge between where the road had been and the almost vertical rock wall bordering it, an area barely wide enough for the car's wheelbase. We choose to do the latter. I gingerly crossed that sliver of gravelly rock on foot and, using hand signals, guided Doug as he nursed our car across it with no more than a few inches between the car and the rock wall on one side and the gaping hole on the other.

Driving in Bhutan is hard enough that government officials and others who can afford it routinely have drivers. Just how scary the roads can be was brought home to us when a Royal Thimphu College driver provided for a work-related trip across the country pulled the car over by a shrine at the beginning of a notoriously dangerous section of the lateral road. The drop-offs in this section are particularly long and precipitous and the fog is routinely almost impenetrable in some seasons. Before inching the car through the swirling mist enshrouding it, the driver reverently approached the shrine. Then he carefully lit an incense stick and placed it on the altar before quietly praying for several minutes. He told us that once, when he had driven this part of the road in a particularly dense fog, his passenger had gotten out of the car to walk ahead and provide hand signals to keep him from driving off it into oblivion.

We had another very memorable experience returning from a masked dance festival. Having damaged our car's muffler on the rough dirt road up to the monastery where this tshechu was held the previous year, we decided to take a taxi for the last several miles winding up the steep mountainside. We were warmly welcomed by the monastery's khenpo and escorted to seats under a tent with bright dragons printed on it. The monks, with bare feet, whirled and jumped in their brilliantly colored, centuries-old costumes as a light drizzle turned into a downpour. When it came time to leave, our taxi went only a few hundred feet before slithering off the muddy road into a shallow ditch. This concerned us greatly because the road had many sharp curves, and its other side had a very long, precipitous drop off. It seemed unwise to continue. The taxi driver was less concerned. He observed that the rain was rapidly abating and announced he intended to proceed down home once he got the taxi out of the ditch.

Having decided that discretion was the better part of valor, we trudged back up to the monastery and asked the monks if we could stay there overnight. They agreed but said it would not be very comfortable because they had little in the way of spare bedding or blankets. We decided to remain nonetheless, figuring discomfort was preferable to potential disaster, and we headed back toward the tshechu ground to shelter under the tent for a while. On the way, we encountered a Royal Thimphu College student, who worked part-time as a guide, with a dozen or so Japanese tourists whom he had brought to the event. They had decided to wait for the rain to run off the steep mud-covered road before leaving. He invited us to join them. We gratefully agreed to do so.

Quite a while later, we all piled into their small bus and started down the mountain, but the narrow road was still incredibly slick. The guide jumped out at a particularly perilous turn and began to walk slowly backward down the road. In the thickening darkness, he signaled to the bus driver where to find the rocks in the road that would provide the most traction. When none were available, he scurried off to the road's side and hefted relatively flat rocks into the bus's path to provide traction. The driver then proceeded the next few yards with some degree of safety. Although this technique gave new meaning to the phrase "moving at a snail's pace," we were extremely grateful for it. Finally, after close to an hour of this, the road became less steep and dangerous. The guide, exhausted and slathered in mud, climbed back onto the bus. But he was smiling with satisfaction at a job well done. We smiled as well with relief at having successfully descended the treacherous road and at the welcoming prospect of a bed complete with a mattress and blankets on it for the coming night.

Never-ending curves, including sharp blind ones, are one of the most challenging aspects of Bhutanese roads. In one stretch of the road up to a pass where we enjoyed hiking, Doug counted more than fifty curves per mile, or one about every hundred feet. No doubt this contributed to the fact that in the early days of public bus service, the buses were referred to as "the Vomit Comet," referencing both the stomach-churning consequences of the incessant curves and their speed relative to alternatives like walking.

But curves are not only conducive to stomach upset. They are dangerous, especially when roads are barely wide enough for two vehicles to pass and maneuverability is constrained by dangerous drop-offs. On some sections of road, including parts of even of the national east-west highway, traffic was so light that this rarely posed a problem. For instance, on one trip in central Bhutan, we encountered only eight oncoming vehicles in four hours as we drove east on that highway.

Although traffic is generally very light, you cannot count on being the only vehicle negotiating a curve. Unfortunately, a young driver provided by the college to take us to be judges at a competition at Bhutan's government-funded business college did not keep that sufficiently in mind. As we rounded a blind curve about halfway into our trip, we saw to our horror a large, brightly painted cargo truck decorated with vivid red paintings of racehorses and running athletes bearing down on us.

Both drivers jammed on their brakes, but the vehicles were essentially already upon each other. Another second, and the truck slammed into us with the unnerving screech of collapsing metal. Our car, by far the smaller vehicle, took the brunt of the damage. It was no longer operable, as suggested by the crumpled grill and fender. After the drivers inspected the damage, the truck lumbered slowly backward from its position in the center of the road to its left edge. Given the sheer drop-off of many hundreds of feet on the narrow road's right-hand side, we felt lucky that all of us were alive and apparently uninjured. Only later did we discover that Doug had broken a rib.

Our driver arranged for a tow back to Thimphu. This was more complicated than it sounds because there is no actual towing service in the country. We, however, wanted to continue onward so we could perform our agreed upon duties at the business college. After about twenty minutes, a white van with the logo of a hydropower plant near that college approached. It slowed to a crawl trying to squeeze by our disabled car. We took the opportunity to ask its driver if we could hitch a ride to the college, which was about an hour down the road. He agreed, so we climbed in. We were surprised to find the van half full of large barrels of oil and other supplies. Undeterred, and still rather shaken, we found seats and continued onward, although every blind curve seemed even more ominous than previously.

Given the inevitable challenges of driving on roads carved through terrain so steep that on hikes we often literally pulled ourselves up sections of mountainside by grasping strong, low-lying branches and vegetation, it is vital to find ways to encourage safe driving. One of the things I loved about travelling on the national highway was that, until several years ago, there were slogans posted along it by DANTAK, the Indian organization that builds and maintains Bhutan's major roads. These were sometimes humorous reminders about the dangers of speeding (called over-speeding in Bhutan) as well as driving while drinking, sleepy, or distracted. A few were more general observations about life. Unfortunately, at least from my perspective, most of these have now been replaced by stern directives about proper driving behavior. I couldn't resist listing some of my favorites:

> Be gentle on my curves.
> One who drives like hell is bound to get there.
> Safety first. Speed afterwards.
> Faster will see disaster.
> Speed thrills but kills.
> It is not rally. Enjoy the valley.
> This is roadway, not runway.
> Drive. Don't fly.
> Speed is the knife that cuts the life.
> Better patient on road than patient in hospital.
> Be Mr. Late, Not late Mr.
> Eager to last. Then why fast?
> If you are married, divorce speed.
> Drive fast and try out our recovery service.
> Better late than never.
> Nature does not hurry. Yet everything is accomplished.
>
> Alert
> Avoid
> Accident
> Alert today. Alive tomorrow.
> For safe arriving, no liquor in driving.
> After whiskey, driving risky.
> After rum, driving no more fun.
> Drinking and driving. A fatal cocktail.
> Peep peep. Don't sleep.
> If you go to sleep your family will weep.
> Safety on road is safe tea at home.
> Anytime is safety time.
> Keep your nerves on sharp curves.
> Life is a journey. Complete it.
> Live for today. Drive for tomorrow.

Time is money. But life is precious.
Life is short. Don't make it shorter.
Don't gossip. Let him drive.
Always expect the unexpected.
Drive slow, someone waiting at home.
Let's go green to get our globe clean.
Global warming. We have a solution. Stop the Pollution.
Keep calm. You are in the world's happiest country.
Hard work is the best investment.
Men at work *(Only women were present, breaking up stones with hammers, as is common.)*
We cut mountains but connect hearts.

If you need to get across Bhutan but prefer to avoid the many rigors of the east-west lateral road, the alternative is to drive about five hours south to India from Thimphu in the west. Then, you proceed east through the flat Indian tea gardens before heading north into Bhutan's interior on one of the four roads that wend their way back up the country's precipitous slopes. I did this once on a visit to Bhutan's southeastern corner to give a week-long faculty workshop at Jigme Namgyel Polytechnic, located where the Fourth King had led the Bhutanese army in expelling Indian militants about a decade before. The last time Doug and I had driven on the lateral road, we had averaged less than ten miles per hour on long stretches. This flatter route across the Indian plains can save time as well as avoid some hair-raising driving experiences on the national highway's blind curves. I reasoned it would also allow me to see something of northern India, at least in passing.

This route was not as straightforward as I had anticipated. The parts of West Bengal and Assam in India adjoining Bhutan are far from peaceful. I was told that in some areas the government had very limited control. So, I was advised that if I were robbed, I should bribe the local gang leader rather than contacting the police to retrieve my property. (How I would go about locating such an individual was not made clear.) There were also still occasional reports of armed Indian militants entering Bhutan from those states to steal from Bhutanese living near the border. Later in the same year I made the trip, two Bhutanese road building projects near that area were halted due to border security concerns. Strikes, sometimes involving violence that paralyzed transport and/or commerce, were also common in this part of India. Indeed, in the year of my trip, almost seven and a half million days of work were lost to strikes over job-related and political issues in West Bengal.

Up until the year before that, Bhutanese vehicles on the eight-hour route I took through India routinely travelled in convoys with military escorts to protect them from untoward experiences. But that practice was not generally observed when I made the trip in early 2014, although in an interview just a few months later, Bhutan's PM made references to daylight robberies of Bhutanese occurring on that route.

After an overnight stay on the Bhutanese side of the border, the driver Royal Thimphu College provided for this trip took me to the Indian immigration post to complete visa formalities. As I waited for him, a wizened Indian taxi driver approached me and asked where I was headed. When I told him, he advised, "Madam, if you want to be safe, be sure not to stop anywhere. Just go straight on."

Most of this trip was on a new four-lane divided highway, with cars and trucks whizzing by pedestrians, bicyclists, donkeys, and achingly thin, scantily dressed farmers pulling heavily laden carts in the broiling sun. Tall smokestacks from kilns baking bricks stood in fields near tiny, often dilapidated villages. Every once in a while, we encountered an "Elephant Crossing" sign, although I did not see any of the elephants that terrorize and sometimes kill workers in the nearby tea gardens.

At one point, we passed a row of trucks that extended literally half a mile or more pulled over alongside the road. I was astonished by its length. The driver informed me that this was the line for customs between West Bengal and Assam which trucks, but not cars, have to go through. I remarked that some trucks must be there for a day or more given the glacial pace at which the lengthy line was crawling. He responded, "Well, it all depends on how you treat the customs officer." He went on to say that a bottle of whiskey and some cash might get a driver through in two to four hours. The wait would be much longer without such "gifts." He also observed that one shouldn't judge the officers demanding bribes too harshly, because they needed to pass a share of their illicit takings on to their superiors to keep their jobs.

The highway, although quite straight and wide, was very much a work in progress. For example, the two lanes in which cars normally travelled east or west were often closed off so that the driver had to cross the median strip and go the wrong way in one of the two lanes on the other side of it. Generally, it was clear when vehicles were supposed to return to their usual side of the road. But a couple of times, the signage was unclear or missing, so the drivers had to guess which of the two sets of lanes they were supposed to use. On a few occasions, I saw cars going in what appeared to be the wrong direction, directly toward oncoming traffic so light they had not yet encountered it.

A few hours into this trip, the driver pulled over and quickly relieved himself by the side of the road, while I nervously looked around, remembering the taxi driver's warning. I also suddenly remembered that not far from where we were stopped a Bhutanese acquaintance had been kidnapped by an Indian gang. He was released only after days of negotiation over his ransom. (I found out later that he was one of more than a dozen people who had been kidnapped in that area in recent years.) I was not sure whether or not to be reassured by having already seen heavily armed Indian paramilitary along our route. My tension abated when the driver hopped back and started the car. After another couple of hours, the driver pulled into the parking lot of a café without warning and insisted on stopping for a snack and another bathroom break.

I welcomed the break but was anxious about stopping until I saw two men in ghos finishing off a large pile of samosas. I then noticed that most of the half-dozen cars parked in front of the café had Bhutanese license plates. This was apparently an oasis well known to Bhutanese travelers along this route. Almost a week later, after the workshop, we took a break at this same restaurant on the way back to Royal Thimphu College. I was glad to be able to travel at all on that day. I had heard from workshop participants that a rumored upcoming strike could make travel very dangerous—or even impossible—for a day or two. But no problems materialized.

Since completing the lateral road in the mid-1980s, Bhutan has very substantially increased the areas that can be accessed by vehicle. Extensive work has been undertaken to extend its major road network to reach more of the country as well as to build farm roads, basic dirt roads connecting previously isolated communities to the main road system. But, given the rugged terrain, this process has been slow. For example, when we arrived in Bhutan in 2009, there were enough places that were unreachable by vehicle that a government official's daily stipend when travelling depended upon how many days' walk their destination was. This was sensible given that about 40 percent of the population lived more than a two-hour walk from the nearest road of any sort and that many lived several days' walk from one. Indeed, until 2018, it was not possible to reach a southwestern district, Samtee, by car without first exiting Bhutan and driving west across the Indian plains and then back up north.

One factor impeding road building is the low population density in many parts of Bhutan. For example, when hiking in the vast Phobjikha valley in central Bhutan, we met the principal of a local school. Although there were just under four hundred households spread out across this broad valley in about thirty miniscule villages, he expressed delight in having been assigned to such a heavily populated area. His previous school was a three-day walk from the nearest road, and he sometimes had to sleep in the forest coming and going if he did not time his departure to encounter a farmhouse near nightfall.

When we first arrived in Bhutan, Gasa, one of Bhutan's twenty districts, did not have even a single motorable road due to its high and challenging terrain and small population. The altitude, roughly 9,500 feet, makes it hard to grow crops. So, for many years, Gasa was the country's poorest district. But life in highland areas became easier for many after 2004 when the government lifted its ban on collection of a parasitic fungus, cordyceps sinensis, which are found there. Cordyceps grow inside caterpillars during the winter and spring. In the summer, the fungus then bursts out through the caterpillar's head, killing it. For this reason, it is known locally as Yarchagumba—"summer plant, winter insect."

Known more broadly as "Himalayan Viagra," cordyceps are thought to increase sexual prowess as well as to cure ailments from headaches to cancer, kidney, and lung problems. In 2010, this tiny fungus sold in China for the remarkable sum of over 45,000 USD a pound. In 2019, it was still literally worth more than its weight in gold there. Although prices are somewhat lower now, many highlanders have become richer than their lowland neighbors by trekking to high meadows during the summer and inching painfully along the still chilly ground searching for the short, slender cordyceps shoots hiding in the grass. However, over-harvesting of cordyceps, the most valuable fungus in the world, suggests that this prosperity may be temporary.

After a forty-five-mile dirt road north to Gasa town from Punakha, Bhutan's old capital, was completed in 2011, we decided to drive there for the district's annual tshechu. Having had considerable experience with Bhutanese roads, before departing, we checked the two spare tires we kept in our trunk. A few hours later, we passed Punakha's extraordinary traditional suspension bridge and beautiful dzong, the massive fortress first built by Zhabdrung Ngawang Namgyel in the early 1600s. Then, we continued north to our destination which was almost exactly one mile higher in altitude than the dzong we had just passed.

We drove up and up through increasingly isolated countryside, mostly dense forest of hemlock, oak, birch, walnut, and rhododendron. We stopped at one point to chat with a team from Bhutan Green Power, which was placing poles and stringing wire to bring the first electricity to the area. Later, we passed a sixty-foot waterfall and travelled alongside an aquamarine stream rearing into white plumes when it encountered massive boulders in its path.

As expected, the road to Gasa was unpaved. So, its many extremely rough patches provided a pounding, sometimes ruefully called a Bhutanese massage. Unfortunately, one of our tires was not as well-padded as our posteriors, and it went flat under the road's assault. After a quick tire change, we were on our way. (Doug had changed an average of three tires a year in Bhutan by that time, so he completed the process in less than eight minutes.) But then, when we still had many miles to go, an ominous sound alerted us to a second flat tire. Holding our breaths in fear of yet a third flat in sparsely populated countryside with no remaining spare, we finally arrived in Gasa, a town of under one thousand people. Black yak-hair nomadic tents along the road signaled that we were not the only visitors arriving for the festival.

There were no hotels or guest houses in town, so we were lucky to be generously hosted by a friend of the Royal Thimphu College's dean who was Gasa district's *Dzongda* (governor). We were surprised to learn that it was his job to open the festivities by riding an elaborately decorated white horse down a long, steep, stone stairway from the Gasa dzong's courtyard. He was flanked by several attendants to keep the horse from stumbling and him from ignominiously falling off if it did. Sitting straight in the saddle after reaching the bottom of the steps, he and several other dignitaries on horseback led a parade of a couple of hundred chattering local officials, monks, nomads, and villagers of all ages to the festival. It snaked in a multicolored line up from the dzong to the higher ground in a local temple's courtyard.

Adding additional vibrant color to the procession, about a dozen men carried large orange, white, blue, turquoise, and green flags. Female nomads

The Long and Winding Road 155

Women, wearing the clothing and hats typical of this high and cold area, sing and dance for the crowd.

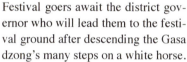

Festival goers await the district governor who will lead them to the festival ground after descending the Gasa dzong's many steps on a white horse.

were decked out in black long-sleeved jackets and full-length skirts. Their outfits were brightened by multiple long strings of coral and turquoise beads and, at waist level, large, finely wrought metal brooch-like disks. Perched on their heads were tiny bamboo hats vaguely resembling upside-down waffle cones with pencil-like shafts sticking out their tops and bands of bright beads suspended at the back. Maroon and saffron robed monks sported red miter-shaped hats. A group of about a dozen men, who would later dance, wore intensely orange robes over their ghos with fat circlets of rolled yellow cloth on their heads. Other villagers proudly displayed their best ghos and kiras, in every imaginable combination of colors and patterns.

Once the parade reached the festival ground, the performances began. Oboe-like instruments and drums accompanied dancers who wore fulllength royal blue and gold robes covered by decorative red aprons. Their heads were adorned with large red caps with gold Chinese-looking designs from which hung dozens of thin, foot-long, rasta-like black braids.

After numerous dances by various beautifully clad groups, everyone helped themselves to a buffet which included tremendous mounds of a Bhutanese specialty, red rice, a nutty pinkish rice we often enjoyed. It was complemented by potatoes, stewed carrots, and whole hard-boiled eggs fried in batter. Attendees then resumed their seats on the grass bordering the tshechu

Local men perform in front of a huge thangka (painting containing Buddhist deities, scenes or mandalas) unfurled at a temple by the Gasa festival ground.

Monks playing the *lingm* (six-holed flute), one of many traditional instruments that are commonly used in religious ritual and festivals.

field. As the dances resumed after lunch, holes in the clouds previously enveloping the valley appeared. They revealed an astonishing view of jagged snow-covered peaks looming impossibly high above the horizon where I had expected to see nothing but the sky.

The next morning, we tried to get our flat tires fixed before setting out on the rough, lonely road back to Punakha. To our dismay, there was no place where a tire could be even minimally repaired. Our host told us that residents of Gasa with flat tires had to arrange a ride three or four hours down to Punakha, which also had the nearest available gasoline and cooking gas cylinders. In desperation, we finally located a hand pump and did our best to inflate both flat tires. Then we bid goodbye to our wonderful host and his family.

On the route back, we briefly visited the Gasa *tshachu*, or hot springs, one of several similar areas in the country where communal bathing pools have been built where hot water bubbles up to the earth's surface. Such springs are believed to have almost miraculous healing powers that help cure an extraordinary variety of aliments including arthritis, ulcers, rheumatism, and indigestion if individuals soak in the waters long enough. This tshachu had a roofed soaking pond for each of four different ailments, each one big enough for about a dozen occupants. Since there were no hotels anywhere nearby, many visitors had pitched tents for overnight stays. Being the only Westerners at the hot springs, we caused quite a stir. Bathers in two of the ponds motioned animatedly to us to join them. But needing to get back to Thimphu, as well as knowing that skin diseases and tuberculosis are also thought to be cured by soaking, we declined the warm invitations with thanks.

On our return trip, Doug did his best to dodge every possible sharp rock, which had us swerving back and forth across the road's narrow span like a ball ricocheting off the sides of a pool table. A check in the trunk, which showed that one of the hand-pumped tires had gone flat just lying there, increased such efforts. To our relief, we managed to get both tires repaired in Punakha before heading back across the 10,200-foot Dochula pass on the route back to Thimphu.

Doug's driving in this way reminded me of a time when a friend driving an underpowered but fully loaded Indian car had zigzagged back and forth across the road leading up to Royal Thimphu College. He did this to help the engine get the car up the hill by slightly decreasing the elevation gain accompanying each foot of forward progress. This approach did not work very well, and ultimately, a couple of the passengers squeezed out of the tiny car's back seat and walked the rest of the way back to the college to lighten the load enough for the car to achieve gradual, laborious progress up the steep incline.

A few months after our excursion to Gasa, we learned that the town was again inaccessible by vehicles because a bridge and a quarter mile of the road had washed out. It was cut off for more than two months. Such washouts are common. They disrupt not only travel but access to essential imported supplies. So, when a stretch of the main road to India which brings in food and gasoline washed away, the Fifth King and the prime minister themselves went to observe the placement of a bailey bridge over the 160-foot gap. Those who absolutely had to travel that route despite the situation walked over a narrow ledge along the precipice created by the washout. Residents in Thimphu, worried by the almost week-long blockage, created traffic jams as lengthy lines formed at gas stations in fear of shortages. They also had to manage without meat and several kinds of vegetables in the market.

In a southern village called Maokhola, every winter for thirty years, villagers have constructed a long bridge that then washes away in each summer monsoon. In a similar area, villagers donate their labor roughly three times a month in the rainy season to construct a temporary bamboo bridge so that children can get to school, patients can get to a local Basic Health Unit, and goods can be conveniently transported. In 2016, heavy rains ruined bridges, swept away more than six-hundred-foot stretches of road in half a dozen places and caused dozens of other landslides and roadblocks.

Such landslides can cause serious problems. As a newspaper described it when there were almost fifty places where a seventy-five-mile road was blocked in a southern region, "A vehicle ... is of no use on this highway. ... Mud, stones, large trees and growling streams fill areas of what used to be a part of the highway."[78] Doug had his own experience with landslides when he, the college's founding director, and another staff member drove south from Thimphu to the border to supervise a large consignment of furniture being shipped in from China via India for the college. About six hours of that two-day round-trip were spent waiting for roadblocks caused by landslides to be cleared.

But creativity can sometimes minimize the impact of such disruptions. An acquaintance encountered a landslide that completely blocked the road when she was headed from her home near Thimphu to the airport by taxi, usually just over an hour west in Paro. Since a substantial portion of air travelers live in Thimphu, the blockage could have resulted in half-empty outgoing flights and many disgruntled arriving passengers stranded on their way home. But a clever solution was found. Those determined to get from Thimphu to Paro left their taxis or the public bus at the landslide and cautiously lugged their baggage over the rubble-strewn area. Alerted to the slide, taxi drivers from Paro had arrived to ferry travelers to the airport or other destinations. They decanted their passengers heading from Paro to Thimphu, who caught rides with the abandoned transport on the Thimphu side of the block, and then picked up the Paro bound ones.

Some problems caused by landslides are less easily solved. A professor coming from India to join the Royal Thimphu College's faculty was caught on the road overnight when the bus he was on heading from the Bhutanese border town of Phuntsholing to Thimphu was trapped between two landslides for more than twelve hours in a very isolated area. When he finally arrived at the college, he exclaimed emphatically, "This country is not for me!" The next morning, he was still so upset by the experience that he caught a bus back down the same road in order to return home to India. Replacing him two days before the semester started was not easy.

In sharp contrast, one of the things that makes Bhutan very much "a country for me" are the often-remarkable experiences facilitated by time spent on its roads. There are too many of these to describe here, including teaching at Nalanda Buddhist Institute, hiking at Chele La pass, and visiting with nomads in a remote area, described in Chapter 9. Often just the views from the roads of scarlet poinsettia, wispy grey-green tendrils of moss clinging to fir trees, glistening white peaks, and fields of intensely pink buckwheat or golden rice are worth the effort. There are also fascinating destinations aplenty including monasteries, festivals, and special events like the Royal Flower Exhibition, featuring not only extraordinary floral displays but large, intricate, wooden models of famous Bhutanese buildings.

One thing I especially treasure about Bhutan's roads is the opportunity they provide to meet, even if briefly, a cross-section of the population including students, monks, and villagers of all ages. Many people in rural areas walk wherever they need to go along whatever route is available. Those walking along roads are almost always glad for a lift whether or not they can speak the same language as those providing it. Doug estimates that over the years we gave rides to at least six hundred people. Because so many Bhutanese speak at least some English, providing rides was a treat for us as well as a help to them.

A number of these individuals were especially memorable. One was an ancient monk who started fingering his prayer beads and quietly murmuring prayers the minute he got into the car. He didn't stop for a moment until we dropped him off at his destination. (Doug insists these prayers were not a response to his driving skills.) Another was a woman with a large bag of potatoes whose clothing smelled so strongly of wood smoke that its pungent lingering aroma reminded us of her whenever we used the car for several days thereafter. We also met about a dozen prisoners high up on a deserted mountain road. They told us they were on their way to a monastery to help repair it to accumulate good karma, but their truck had gotten stuck in deep mud. They were struggling to dig it out, hoping to manage to arrive before nightfall.

Then there were the ten little boys we met in the high glacial valley of Phobjikha who had unwisely taken a dip in a stream in November when the air temperature couldn't have been above 50°F and the water was no doubt colder. Having just emerged from the stream a couple of kilometers from their village, they shivered miserably with chattering teeth in the rapidly darkening afternoon. One of them had tried to warm himself by removing all his sopping wet clothes. But that had not stopped the trembling of his skinny, thoroughly chilled legs. Although we always wear seatbelts and ask passengers to do the same, we loaded this entire group into the car. Several of the smallest boys stood up in the rear of our hatchback, still shaking with cold. The remainder piled quickly into the back seat to get home before hypothermia set in. We turned the heater on full blast and drove them to their village. Once there, they rushed home, trailing behind shouts of thanks and having discovered, I hope, that winter swimming is only a good idea for polar bears.

Occasionally, our unexpected experiences on the road involved people we already knew. Once, we waited for an hour or more in a long line of cars delayed by construction work on the lateral road. As we sat in our car talking quietly, there was a loud knock on our window and a male voice sternly commanded, "Show me your license and registration now!" As I leaned forward to get our documents from the car's glove compartment, much to my amazement, Doug burst out laughing and our interlocutor did the same. Doug had rolled down the window and for the first time saw the face of the supposed police officer—the abbot of Nalanda Buddhist Institute who grinned broadly at his joke. We had a lively chat until we resumed our respective journeys when the road closure ended.

Another time, we pulled over on that same road at a village vegetable market. We were in our car discussing which vegetables to purchase when someone banged on the car door and inquired, "Do you want to buy my chilies?" We were very surprised because Bhutanese vendors virtually always wait for customers to approach them rather than soliciting a potential buyer's patronage. As we turned to respond in the negative, because neither of us is partial to Bhutan's most loved edible, we saw that the supposed vendor was the president of one of Bhutan's two colleges of education, whom I had first met we served together on a university committee. He had stopped to buy a specialty of this particular region, dried mushrooms gathered in nearby forests. Again, we were all on our way after an enjoyable conversation.

There is an amusing scene in the movie *Travelers and Magicians,* written and directed by the Bhutanese lama, Khyentse Norbu, in which a truck stops to pick up a hitchhiker. Half a dozen of the hitchhiker's compatriots, initially masked by trees from the driver's view, hastily pile into the pickup truck's bed, lugging in all sorts of baggage as well. We had a couple of similar experiences. The first was on a work-related trip across the country when we were in a pickup truck. We pulled over to give a middle-aged man a ride. Before we knew it, several people materialized from the thick forest adjacent to the road and hopped in the truck's open bed, smiling and waving to us as they pulled on board the heavy bags containing their belongings.

The second such incident occurred on a hot Sunday afternoon as we drove down the meandering road from Nalanda Buddhist Institute on our way home from teaching young monks English. A young woman sat by the roadside, miles from the lateral road, looking as if she wanted a ride. We stopped and she jumped up quickly, saying "thank you," although she clearly knew little English. We were surprised that she did not get in immediately. Rather, she hesitated, gazing across the road to where another young woman emerged looking hopefully at us. We nodded our acquiescence, and the newcomer trotted across the road and jumped in the back seat.

But our first prospective passenger lingered outside, still looking across the road to where a middle-aged man appeared hauling an old cement sack so heavy he could barely lift it to his waist. This was definitely more than we had bargained for. But the back seat of the car had seatbelts for three, so we indicated he could join us and opened the relatively empty trunk for him to deposit his load. After doing so, he scurried back across the road.

To our growing consternation, he returned several times with additional hefty, bulging sacks. After the first couple of bags had been put in the trunk, we noticed with dismay that blood was leaking slowly out of one of them from what turned out to be a recently butchered cow. But, by then, we were totally committed. One passenger was sitting in the car, some sacks had already been loaded and more were on their way across the road. We frantically grabbed the rubber floor mats from the car's front seat and a couple of stray pieces of cardboard, placing them under the bags to protect the car from their leaks.

After the trunk was full and the last bag had been piled in the back, the first young woman took the remaining space in the back and the man disappeared back into the forest. As Doug drove the heavily loaded car down the winding road, the smell emanating from the bags increased. The first woman smiled apologetically, ostentatiously held her nose and repeated several times, "Smell. Smell." I could only agree. Occasionally, she changed her utterance to, "Thank you, Sister!" After about an hour's drive, our passengers indicated they wanted to disembark in front of a modest home not far from a local market. We pulled over, relieved as they lugged their odoriferous luggage out of our car.

Then, the first woman offered her mobile number and indicated she would like mine. Bhutanese we met casually often did this. Even though it seemed unlikely we could have much of a conversation, I gave my number to her. Since I did not know her name, I entered her number under "Sister Beef." We waved goodbye, and she said a final, "Thank you, Sister." But this was not the last we heard from her. About thirty minutes after we arrived back in Thimphu, my phone rang. It was Sister Beef asking, "Safe home?" Language differences, then, and in the several additional times she called in the following months, precluded much conversation. But the calls themselves were welcome, communicating her warmth and reminding me that I never knew what unexpected sights or adventures I would encounter on Bhutan's roads.

Chapter 9

Land of Yaks and Yetis

Bhutan is often called the Land of the Thunder Dragon, but to me it is also the Land of the Yaks and Yetis. The yaks, enormous shaggy beasts with massive horns, make life possible for small highland communities that for centuries have eked out a living in one of the most challenging environments in which humans survive, the frigid Himalayan terrain just below year-around glaciers and snow. Some of our most memorable experiences featured yaks, whether it was a lost baby yak forlornly trailing after us or huge, handle-bar-horned adult yaks thundering down a steep trail we were hiking. Widely shared stories of yetis, the elusive and fabled beings sometimes known as the Abdominal Snowman or Bigfoot, reflect the fact that much of Bhutan is so remote from the outside world that fact and fiction are sometimes hard to distinguish, especially in a culture where unseen beings play such a major role in peoples' lives. Our trek to the Sakteng Wildlife Preserve, set up in part to protect the habitat of the yeti and the home of many yak herders, was one of our most unusual experiences.

Yaks were first domesticated around ten thousand years ago on the Tibetan plateau. Called "camels of the snow" or sometimes "grumbling ox" because of the strange grunting noise they make when breathing hard, they can survive in temperatures down to -40°F due to their heavy coats and boxy build. They don't go snow-blind even in the fierce Himalayan sun, and they have three times the lung capacity of a cow, which suits them well for high-altitude terrain. They are sure-footed when plowing through snow, and they can carry at least twice as much as a horse. As a result, yaks have been vital to the barter economy, which let Bhutanese herders trade with Tibetans for salt, tea, and other items for centuries. Yaks are also very strong, with it sometimes taking up to four men to restrain them when they are being loaded.

Traditionally, yaks have provided herder communities with almost everything they need. Their coarse outer hair is excellent for braiding into ropes and weaving into tents, and it is also used to shield highlanders' eyes from the intense sun. The softer inner hair is spun into yarn for clothing. Yak bones make tent pegs and jewelry, while their butter is used as lotion to prevent dry skin and as fuel to illuminate herders' tents. When wood is scarce, as it often is in very high areas, dried yak dung can be burned for cooking and warmth. Unfortunately, the black carbon produced by this is a clear contributor to climate change, which is melting the Himalayan glaciers.

Yaks' dried hides can be sewn into boots or sacks. Even their tails find multiple uses, including as fly whisks and brooms. They also decorate pony trappings and the tops of prayer flag poles. Back in the early 1800s, yak tails were even used, along with blankets, ponies, and gold, to pay the British for use of several tracts of land in the south. Rather improbably, at one time they were even exported to make Santa Claus beards, and yak hair is still used in theatrical wigs.

Yak horns are so strong that they can dig though heavily crusted snow to reveal grasses underneath. These horns can be a full yard across and are often used to adorn ritual objects. In 2018, a sorcery case involving yak horns reached Bhutan's High Court. The accused was said to have stuffed papers with the names of two men and incantations to harm them inside a yak horn.

Yak butter, yogurt, and cheese from fat-rich yak milk are important parts of herders' diets. Butter is an essential ingredient in the pinkish salted tea Bhutanese enjoy, as well as being useful for cooking. It is also often employed in making the intricate and beautiful butter and flour sculptures found in virtually all Bhutanese temples. Small, rectangular pieces of smoked hardened yak cheese, strung like beads on thin strings made from yak hair, are for sale all over Bhutan. A piece of that cheese smaller than half of my little finger took more than two hours to dissolve in my mouth, even with some vigorous sucking. It remained too hard for me to dare chew, so finally it just dissolved in my mouth.

But these are far from the only uses of yak products. Yak meat is an ingredient in dog snacks as far away from Bhutan as the U.S. and Japan. It can also be cooked fresh or fermented, processed into sausage, preserved as jerky, or ground into burgers for tourists. No more than sixty or seventy years ago, yak meat was even used to pay taxes, and the mother of a well-known Bhutanese man, who was one of an early group of students conscripted to go to school, bribed an official with a leg of yak meat and some yak butter not to take his brother to school as well.

Yaks used to be ridden frequently and still are on occasion. When Jawaharlal Nehru visited Bhutan in 1958 before the country had any roads, he rode a yak. Aum Kunzang Choden, the previously mentioned writer who grew up in a feudal manor house in a high part of central Bhutan, tells of riding yaks when she was a child. I was excited about riding a yak at a festival organized by local communities an hour or so outside of Thimphu. The festivities were held in a lovely park with forty-six species of rhododendron and a lake in which villagers leave offerings. After arriving, Doug and I headed to the area where I saw a large black yak with a white tail tied to a tree with a yak hair rope. He was adorned with a lei of artificial flowers around his neck, pompoms between his formidable horns, and a colorful yak-hair saddle blanket on his broad back. I approached the villager standing nearby, saying that I had heard there were yak rides on offer. He looked at me, shook his head resignedly and replied, "Yes, but he's in a bad mood today, so I would not suggest trying to take one." It was the word "trying" in his response that sealed my decision to heed his advice, as it conjured up a vision of me ignominiously flying off a bucking, horned beast many times my size.

When Doug and I first arrived at Royal Thimphu College, I did not realize that yaks, which grazed in the thick bamboo jungle immediately above the college, would also occasionally join the cows, horses, and dogs that wandered freely around the campus. Even though adult yaks are rather frightening because of their prodigious size and menacing horns, baby yaks, like so many very young animals, are extremely appealing. The first time I saw one was on a day when work at the college was suspended because the first day of snowfall in Thimphu each year is a public holiday there. Those who have lived in the capital city for many years say there used to be much more snow. Now, the first snowfall is typically in late January and even as late as March, when the wild plum and peach trees are beginning to bud gloriously.

Doug and I decided to make use of the unexpected day off by hiking up a path behind the campus that climbs steadily through the forest to a yak herder's rustic cabin before heading up to a steep, 12,500-foot ridge. As we emerged from our apartment, we saw an Indian faculty member dancing exuberantly as whirling snowflakes covered his hair and disappeared into his open mouth. He was incredibly excited because he had never experienced snow before.

Doug and I walked along the forest path, delighting in the sun gilding the snow-cloaked branches of the thick bushes lining it. After about fifteen minutes, I heard more than the usual rustling in the dense bamboo thicket along the path's right side. I peered intently into the impenetrable foliage, wondering what could be producing the sound. Suddenly, just about five feet in front of us, a downy baby yak emerged, smaller than a large dog. It stood glued to the spot, its dark eyes searching around uncertainly. Doug and I remained still, not wanting to alarm it. But my heart began to thud in my chest, because mother yaks are extremely protective of their calves. After a very long minute or two, Doug and I slowly moved to the far side of the path and walked ahead, past the bewildered knee-high calf.

To our great surprise, the baby yak began trotting along right behind us. Doug, who loves photography, stopped again and again to take photos of the glittering snow-covered landscape. Each time, the baby yak stopped as well, standing patiently within a few inches of my knees until we resumed our hike. He then scurried along close behind me. At one point, our pace slowed because a stream that runs down the path's center for a couple hundred feet had created slick icy patches. Our young companion slowed as well. I was deeply touched, but also a bit concerned. Would a worried five-hundred-plus pound mother yak suddenly charge out from the forest using her horns to retrieve her offspring? Was the little yak old enough to survive by grazing or did it need its mother's nourishing milk? What would we do when it was time to return to our apartment where baby yaks were certainly not allowed as pets, no matter how endearing they might be?

We decided to continue up to the yak herders' cabin, but upon arriving, we discovered it was deserted. The tiny cottage, where we had once had tea with the herders, was locked with no obvious signs of recent habitation. Even more concerning, the large corral where the yaks normally gathered when not grazing was completely empty. So were the adjoining fields. But the little yak appeared to recognize the place, following us right up to the cabin's door and waiting there hopefully. We thought the herder family and the rest of the yaks would probably return in the evening. So, we turned quietly and walked quickly out of the fenced-in area surrounding the cabin, firmly closing the gate behind us. The baby yak turned around to watch our retreating figures, but it did not try to follow as we disappeared on the path back into the forest. The next morning, we made the ninety-minute hike up to the cabin again, in case the little yak was still locked inside the corral by itself. To our delight, all was well. The herd had returned.

We had two other unanticipated and very memorable encounters with yaks—much, much bigger ones. The first was on one of our favorite hikes, a walk up to the Lungchuste *gompa* (temple) which sits above the Dochula pass at almost twelve thousand feet. The trail to it from the pass meanders through an almost magical forest of gigantic hemlocks and junipers, as well as massive rhododendron trees with copper-colored bark. Long, intensely green strands of moss hang from the trees. In good weather, you can see the Gasa dzong from the temple, about thirty miles north, as well as the world's highest unclimbed peak on Bhutan's border with Tibet. But swirling mist that comes and goes often creates a mystical atmosphere that reminds me of the Buddhist emphasis on impermanence.

The hike is usually remarkably peaceful. Few people live in the immediate vicinity and tourists typically spend their time at Dochula pass itself, exploring the 108 picturesque shrines called *chortens* or photographing the long chain of snow-capped Himalayan peaks visible on clear days. Those wanting to visit a temple normally go to one immediately adjacent to the chortens. One of its many attractions is a fascinating painting depicting His Majesty the Fourth King in the jungle leading the fight against Indian insurgents that was discussed in Chapter 5. This painting is near a mural showing monks with laptop computers, a remarkable sight because most temples' walls are covered with very traditional artwork.

But one of our hikes up to the higher Lungchuste temple turned from peaceful to frightening in a moment. As we crested a curve in the trail leading to it, we were suddenly confronted with a dozen or more yaks stampeding downwards towards us, their herder racing along far behind them. They were surging forward in a scraggly line less than one hundred feet from us, some two or three abreast. It did not look as if they intended to detour around us. The closer they came, the more lethal their horns looked. Some had red pom-poms frantically bobbing up and down on their foreheads and others had saddle blankets with bright geometric designs flapping wildly on their backs. But we did not have time to admire their trappings. Doug and I simultaneously raced off the path in different directions, taking shelter behind trees much wider than us. We breathed heavy sighs of relief as the yaks thundered past us and down the trail, leaving billowing dust in their wake. I had never seen yaks move so fast and had no idea what caused their frenzied flight. Although I usually love watching these behemoths as they graze serenely on miniature bamboo or other vegetation, I could not have been happier to see this group disappearing rapidly down the trail.

Another memorable "close encounter of the yak kind" occurred when Doug and I set off with an American colleague to climb Talakha peak, which is almost fourteen thousand feet high. This trek starts from the Talakha monastery, which we often hiked to directly from the college. Alternatively, it can start from the end of a rough logging road. We decided on the latter because it shortened the arduous hike a bit. Our friend, who had access to a 4WD vehicle, drove the three of us up the most difficult road we had travelled in Bhutan. Most places it was a rutted single lane, which was concerning since large logging trucks sometimes use it. It was rocky or muddy virtually everywhere. A few places it was even icy, since it was late November. The forest was deep, dark, and almost mystical, even on a spectacularly clear fall day.

We had scouted the route on a previous visit to Talakha monastery, so we knew where the trail and the logging road intersected. That turned out to have been wise. Some acquaintances who later tried to climb this peak never succeeded because they were unable to find the trail, which is quite faint in places. We walked with our friend for a couple of hours on a clear but rocky path, heading up almost continually, but not too steeply. As we got higher, increasingly spectacular views appeared one after the other. Looking down, we could see the massive, gilded, ten-story-tall Buddha statue that gazes serenely over the capital city from a promontory on the mountain that forms one of the Thimphu valley's flanks. From so far above, it looked like a tiny sentinel guarding the city from a diminutive watchtower. Looking north, we could see the saw-toothed chain of frosted peaks bordering the Tibetan plateau. At first, the tallest ones barely peeped over the heavily forested and nearer lower mountains. But as we passed thirteen thousand feet and our perspective changed, the string of glacier-clad mountain looked like a long lacy necklace floating above the misty horizon.

Soon we saw a small, rustic cabin with stones weighing down its shingled roof. A large, fierce-looking black mastiff sitting next to three black and white yaks calmly sunning themselves signaled that it was a yak herder's home, which explained why we had begun encountering so many yaks along the trail. Occasionally, a group of these huge beasts claimed the path, and we simply detoured around them through the fir trees along its side. Some of the female yaks, called *dries,* were trailed by smaller young ones, at least twice the size of the little yak that had adopted us on our snow holiday hike.

Soon thereafter, near a curve in the trail, we came to a five-foot-high barrier across its path. It was clearly intended to keep the yaks grazing in that area from wandering onto the land beyond it. Constructed of roughly hewn logs, it was heavily fleshed out with tree branches and prickly dried bushes. The spiny fingers of the protruding vegetation were guaranteed to catch the clothing of the unwary. Doug and our friend, both of whom have much longer legs than I, climbed over first. As I considered the best footing through the pile of thorny brush, I heard a noise behind me. Coming around the bend in the path, and rapidly closing the thirty or forty feet between us, were three enormous male yaks. Although yaks are not generally aggressive, I was petrified to see several thousand pounds of horned yak rushing straight toward me. I leapt up into the tangled bushes, thrusting one foot and then another on branches to gain height and leverage. Seeing my plight, Doug reached out and speedily hauled me over the top of the spiky barrier. I was so busy disentangling myself from the briars that I never even saw where the yaks causing the commotion went. The only real damage done was to my sunglasses, which never recovered from the beating they took when they fell off my nose during my frantic scramble to safety.

We stopped for a quick picnic at an area called "the beach," which takes its name from large sandy patches showing through the wheat-colored scrub at a point above the tree line. Doug decided to stay there and take some photos, because the views of the mountains from this spot were extraordinary and it had been a long climb even to that point. Our friend, at least twenty years younger than us and very fit, virtually dashed to the very top of the nearly fourteen-thousand-foot peak, since it was clear that we would have to turn around shortly to get down the treacherous logging road before nightfall. I opted to forge ahead at a more moderate pace. The views became increasingly remarkable. As I continued, I could see more and more of Bhutan's second-tallest peak, the sacred Mt. Jhomolari, thrusting up into the crystalline sky at more than twenty-four thousand feet. Beyond it to the west, I could see Sikkim as well as Nepal's majestic Kangchenjunga, the world's third highest mountain, at over twenty-eight thousand feet. Time constraints led me to reluctantly turn around no more than ten minutes or so from the summit. But I considered the day an absolute success when we safely reached the bottom of the daunting logging road just as darkness fell. We headed back home, both exhilarated and exhausted.

Some yak herders can be found in many of the high areas not far from Thimphu town, like the ones living just above the college or those whose home we saw on the trail to Talakha peak. However, entire communities of yak herders are farther afield, generally at high altitudes in the west in the Haa district, in the north in Gasa, and in the east where Bhutan borders India's Arunachal Pradesh. Most of these areas were closed to tourists when we first arrived in Bhutan. However, in late 2010, a high area in the far east, including the seminomadic village of Sakteng in the Sakteng Wildlife Sanctuary, was opened for tourism. It was widely acknowledged to be one of the most remote parts of this remote country. The people living there have their own unique Brokpa language and culture. They have been characterized as being among "the most archaic and exotic ethnic components of Bhutan."[79] So we decided to seize the opportunity to visit.

Arranging a trip there was not easy, since tourism had barely commenced. We had great difficulty locating even one Bhutanese who had visited this remote area personally. Nonetheless, with the help of some friends, we finally arranged for a guide. Since there were no hotels or guest houses on the three-day trek to our destination from where the national highway ended in the east, we also arranged for packhorses to carry tents and other camping equipment.

The logistics got increasingly complicated. For example, we had to hire more horses than initially planned because fires are not permitted in that area, so we needed an extra horse to carry a thirty-five-pound propane cylinder to have hot food or drink on the week-long trek. Then, the horseman insisted on bringing his wife along to assist him as well as to cook. But finally, by May 2011, just over six months after the Sakteng area was opened to tourists, we had arranged a trek there with our oldest daughter, who was visiting us at that time.

The three of us made the arduous but breathtakingly beautiful trip east across the country by car in three days. The night before the trek began, we stayed in the village of Rangjung at a simple hostel near a large temple. The next morning, we continued by car to the small village of Phongmey at the absolute end of the east-west road. There we met our guide as well as the horseman and his wife who were loading their six equine charges. Our guide urged us to start along the trail, saying he would help load the horses and then catch up with us. We initially demurred, saying that we did not know the trail. He countered, casually revealing that he had only walked the trail once many years before. But he assured us that it was quite clear. So, a bit reluctantly, especially since we had heard that both bears and wild boars frequented the area, we set off by ourselves.

The three-day hike up to Sakteng village was an extraordinary experience. The trail, which is used by the nomads for trading with lower settled communities, was barely wide enough for two horse or yak trains to pass each other, even at its widest point. Most places, as promised, its path was quite clear. However, before we were reunited with our guide late on the first day, we came to several forks where decisions had to be made. At first, I was concerned about wandering off on a side path and getting separated from our tents and supplies in such a remote area, as once happened to an acquaintance trekking elsewhere in Bhutan with a European tour group. However, we discovered through trial and error that these forks led to steeper shortcuts

We encountered this impressive yak on our path while hiking.

A Brokpa woman returns home to Sakteng with her horse that is laden with goods she bartered for yak butter.

that eventually reunited with the main trail. After that, wandering along with just our daughter gave us a great sense of freedom and adventure.

On the first day, every time we reached the top of an incline, we had to start down again toward another river crossing hundreds of feet below. The bridges on our route varied tremendously. On one 150-foot steel suspension bridge, we encountered a pony train. It started across when we were in the middle and it barely managed to squeeze by without pushing us deep into the wire mesh fencing anchored rather precariously to the bridge's sides to keep travelers from inadvertently falling off into the icy water rushing below. But most of the bridges were shorter and wooden, including one made of three planks with numerous large rocks covering gaping holes in each. A rough-hewn log marked each edge of that bridge, but nothing except careful footing and a good sense of balance kept us from tumbling into the frothing water below. Many of these bridges were decked with blue, white, green, red, and yellow prayer flags, which are commonly hung near rivers and streams on the theory that the water will carry the prayers to the broader world beyond, which I found a lovely idea.

The first night, we camped on one side of the trail. The next day's hike also had many ups and downs, although we clearly gained significant altitude overall. Our guide went ahead with the horses in the morning, saying that he needed time to prepare lunch. Some places were so steep that the trail consisted of switchbacks or seemingly endless flights of extremely uneven stone steps. We encountered several groups of oncoming villagers taking yak products to barter for goods like salt and rice in local towns. I was amazed that their heavily laden ponies were able to climb and descend the irregular, rocky steps of such stairways without stumbling. In the afternoon, we came upon a diminutive schoolhouse to one side of the trail in a tiny village called Thrakthrik. A few children playing outside ran to greet us. Then, a teacher in his thirties emerged from the small structure. After chatting with us for several minutes and learning we were from Royal Thimphu College, he led us inside to meet his students.

We were delighted to do so. More than a dozen pairs of blue galoshes of varying sizes rested on the school's porch. Inside, we saw about twenty barefoot students of widely different ages, quickly standing up behind their desks as we entered. The oldest looked about thirteen. One baby-faced girl who barely reached the waist of the older girl standing next to her appeared

Land of Yaks and Yetis

The boys in Thrakthrik's multigrade classroom are in traditional Brokpa dress. The girls' have short haircuts that have distinguished female Bhutanese from Tibetan women for centuries.

Brokpa women wear a traditional hat with yak hair braids which protect their heads in bad weather by draining off raindrops.

only about four or five years old, although the official age for school enrollment was six at that time.

About a third of the children were dressed in the clothing made from wool and yak hair that is worn by the Brokpa nomads—a maroon belted tunic over warm black leggings for males and a pinkish stripped tunic for females topped by a jacket, often woven with bright geometric designs. The other students wore ghos and kiras of various colors and designs. Such clothing was very unusual for school children because most students are required to wear uniforms of ghos and kiras in a specific color combination identifying their school.

The teacher explained that this was one of the many multigrade classrooms for elementary school children in the country's most sparsely populated areas. The room was clean, and light streamed in from several traditional arched windows. The walls were decorated with posters featuring English and Dzongkha vocabulary. A poster, labelled "Parts of the Body" showed a young boy wearing shorts with labels on his arms, legs, face, etc. A poem, "The Clothes Line" by *Charlotte Druitt Cole*, was handwritten on another poster. It is used in the sixth-grade curriculum in some schools in the U.S. I was rather surprised by this choice since it contains relatively advanced English words like "restive" and "caper." However, it also contains some lovely imagery likely to appeal to children everywhere.

The teacher told students that we were from Royal Thimphu College, writing its name on the board because it was unlikely that they would have heard of it. He then gave them our names and asked us to provide a short English lesson, which we did. After the students were dismissed, the teacher showed us his office. It contained a desk and a couple of chairs, many reports, and several dozen large black binders used for record keeping that were organized neatly in a bookshelf. Through the windows, we could see tumultuous smoke-colored clouds gathering ominously, suggesting that rain was likely soon. With typical Bhutanese graciousness, the teacher invited us to stay in the classroom overnight and we gratefully accepted. We pushed some of the small desks and chairs to the walls and spent the night on the schoolroom floor. Around 2 a.m. I awoke very aware that the school had no heat source, although the climate there was cool enough that many of the Brokpa we encountered wore woolen jackets most of the day even though it was May.

We got underway early the next morning, in order not to disrupt the students' schedules. A few hours later, as we neared Sakteng village, we encountered the first yaks on the trail. They were heavily loaded with goods for barter or sale and accompanied by a single elderly nomad. They wore bells hanging from red neck bands decorated with cowry shells. Each set of shells resembled a white flower with four petals. Historically, cowry shells are abundant in the Indian Ocean and they have been used as money in many parts of the world. Exactly how they ended up decorating yaks in such a remote village in Bhutan remained a mystery to me.

Cresting a final slope on the trail at over nine thousand feet, we emerged at the top of a large open area, where the vegetation had been cropped short by grazing yaks and sheep. Below we saw the village of Sakteng, with a modest number of outlying homes scattered around on the surrounding slopes. Some of these houses were constructed of stone. Most had whitewashed walls and the elaborately carved and painted window frames that are an integral part of Bhutanese architecture. Gigantic piles of split wood filled the space under protruding second-floor balconies.

Somewhat incongruously, these very traditional-looking homes had roofs made from corrugated galvanized iron (CGI) sheets that glinted brightly in the sunlight instead of the more typical wooden shingles dotted with stones. We learned from a forest ranger that the World Wildlife Fund had subsidized this roofing to reduce the amount of wood cut in the area's forests for shingles, which needed to be replaced frequently. However, a couple of years after our trek to Sakteng, concerns arose that the flashes of light reflecting from the metal roofs disturbed animals and that the sun warmed the metal roofing too much for birds to rest comfortably on it. Furthermore, metal roofing was inconsistent with the goal of promoting economic development through tourism because it was quite unattractive. Thus, the CGI sheets were covered with shingles to restore the homes' traditional appearance.

Excitedly, we hurried toward the village and began to explore. There was a temple and a school large enough for two hundred to three hundred children. Beyond the village, before the mountains rose again on the other side of the valley, was a wide, rocky riverbed. It was relatively dry since the monsoon season would not start for more than a month. Yaks wandered on the rock-strewn lanes between houses and loitered in front of the town's few small shops. The exterior of the first store we entered was gaily painted red, blue, and yellow, with prayer flags hanging across the front wall of the second story where the proprietor lived. Its stock was extremely limited. Numerous plastic containers containing penny candies wrapped in bright paper lined a low counter, savvy marketing to young students heading to the nearby school. On higher shelves along the wall behind the proprietor was a modest collection of canned and bottled goods, including tuna fish, juice, and sodas, as well as crackers and bars of soap. The offerings at the other shops were remarkably similar. Most noteworthy was the remarkable amount of alcohol for sale in each. Although it takes five days to bring beer to Sakteng on the back of ponies, we saw thousands of empty beer bottles piled up in backyards, apparently accumulated during the decade since bottled beer was first brought into the village. A shopkeeper there averred that the village stores would die out in no time without their bars, which he said were crowded in the summer when the herders are back in town. In a sign of changing times, payment could be made with cash as well as through barter for butter or other yak products.

Although we could hear the voices of children wafting over from the school, the rest of the village had an eerie, deserted feel to it. A couple of elderly people went slowly about daily chores and some young children stared intently at us and giggled as we strolled by. But there was almost no other activity. So, we were pleased when an elderly woman leaned out from a second-floor balcony and motioned us inside. She nodded and smiled as we entered her home and then gestured vigorously for us to sit down on the floor with her. She spoke no English and we, unfortunately, did not speak, Brokpa, the local language. Our hostess immediately took out an old juice bottle full of ara. She then gave us cups filled to the brim with the strong drink and filled her own as well. Since neither of us normally drinks much alcohol aside from occasional wine, we took modest sips to be polite. Doug pulled out the package of photos that usually facilitated interaction in situations in which we could not converse easily. But our hostess was intent upon our enjoying her ara. Every time we took a couple of sips, she whipped out the juice bottle to refill the cups almost to overflowing. Clearly, we were not drinking quickly enough, because she began gesticulating while loudly urging us to drink more.

The woman raised such a commotion that a neighbor about her age arrived to see what was going on. She also took a cup of ara, from which she drank thirstily. Then, she added her voice to the clamor, shouting at us and motioning for us to drink more. Realizing that our cups would never be empty before we consumed more than we could possibly handle, we thanked our hostess profusely and staggered out. When we mentioned the experience to a friend from a nearby area of eastern Bhutan, he replied with a grin, "Oh, you were lucky. In a village near there they will pinch you if you don't drink enough." Perhaps we were lucky, because I later learned that another practice at gatherings in that region is for one person to hold another's hands captive while still others pour ara down the reluctant drinker's throat.

We discovered why the village was so quiet later that afternoon when visiting the school. Most adults in this seminomadic community accompany the yaks and sheep to their grazing grounds for about eight or nine months a year. Basically, only school children, their teachers, and the elderly are left in the village during that time. As one parent explained, "We have to go away with our herd, which is the only source of our livelihood. If we remain back in the village with our children, we will have nothing to eat."[80] School is free, but each student is required to supply six bundles of firewood. The local gup, the equivalent of a mayor, estimated that about 60 percent of the children were totally on their own, 10 percent were in the care of neighbors and 30 percent were with family members, normally grandparents.

The year we visited Sakteng, its primary school was transformed into a lower secondary school so it could accommodate students through the eighth grade. Children must leave the valley for a government boarding school if they continue their education beyond that. But often, their parents prefer that they remain with the family so they can help with the livestock and other responsibilities. For example, less than a year before we visited, an article in a newspaper quoted a Sakteng father of nine as saying, "I had to keep my sons out of school to help me. … We can earn if we rear the cattle [a term referring to yaks], whereas sending them to school incurs expenses and I can't afford that."[81] A mother of seven, who sent just two of her children to school, raised another concern asking, "If we send all our children to school, who'll take our place and carry forth the traditions and culture we've long cherished and lived by?"[82]

A reporter's interview with a thirteen-year-old boy in Sakteng who had never attended school demonstrates just how much children of that age can contribute to their families' livelihoods and how all-consuming that task can be:

> Interviewer: What do you want to do when you grow up?
> Pema: I want to be a rich yak herder with many yaks. …
> Interviewer: What do you do after your work?
> Pema: Work never ends. Every evening I have to churn the milk, make cheese and butter, then cook and finally sleep to get rest for next day's work. Life is a never-ending chain of work for me. …
> Interviewer: When did you start herding yaks?
> Pema: I was born in the forest with yaks and I will die in the forest with yaks. …
> Interviewer: Can you tell me something about your family?
> Pema: I am the eldest son and I have a younger brother. I live with my parents, but most of the time I am in the forest with yaks.
> Interviewer: When was the happiest moment in your life?
> Pema: I don't know when it was, but I feel happy when a female calf is born because I can become a herder with many yaks.
> Interviewer: When do you feel sad?

Pema: I feel sad on seeing my yaks dying of diseases and accidents. It is really unbearable to see them dead.[83]

The mother quoted in a previous paragraph was clearly concerned about preserving local traditions, many of which are quite different from those in the rest of Bhutan. The Brokpa believe that their ancestors fled from Tibet to their current valley after they killed a harsh ruler who ordered them to remove the top of a hill that shaded his dwelling from the morning sun. A female villager is said to have inspired that revolt with a song suggesting that it was easier to cut off someone's head than to dismantle a hill. Brokpa women, who play a major role in family decisions, worship the goddess who is said to have led their ancestors safely to Bhutan by undertaking an annual pilgrimage to a high peak thought to be her home. A special five-day dance drama honors the goddess by telling stories of people known for their piety or special achievements.

Male Brokpa have special traditions as well, included a *terchham*, or naked dance. Every third year they gather in a temple, and following two days of rituals dedicated to the tertön, Pema Lingpa, they emerge in the evening. Some are completely naked. Others have bamboo leaves, a piece of chili, or a condom dangling over their private parts. Barefooted, they perform a sacred dance. A lama wearing a fierce mask and a dancer carrying a torch accompany them to each house in the village to chase evil spirits away. Householders offer them wine and white scarves in gratitude. Around midnight, the dancers roll on the ground by the crematorium. The markings they make are believed to create a border beyond which the evil spirits cannot pass. By 3 a.m., they head back to the temple, having protected the village from illness and misfortune for the next three years.

Another of the Brokpa's most iconic traditions is a dance that pays homage to yaks. A dummy yak, ridden by another dummy representing a protective deity, is carried by men dancing to the sound of cymbals and drums. Other men sing a story about the origin of the yak and praise it for the great benefit it has brought the community.

The Bhutanese government accepts and even encourages Brokpa and other highland traditions. The Brokpa are allowed to wear their distinctive clothing even on occasions when most others are required to wear ghos or kiras, as was evident in the multigrade classroom we visited. Unfortunately, the wool used to make essential parts of these outfits is in increasingly short supply due to wild dogs preying on sheep, which has led many Brokpa to discontinue raising them.

In fact, when the king and queen visited Sakteng in 2015, the Fifth King charged the Brokpa with the responsibility for protecting their unique cultural heritage. Unfortunately, in recent years, the dance drama and the yak dance have not been performed as often as they used to be. Previously, dancers were exempted from taxes and/or given other incentives to compensate for the substantial time it took to learn the complex moves. When that ceased, and as greater contact with the outside undermined tradition, such events became less frequent.

In spite of some lessening of tradition, many Brokpa do still cherish their cultural heritage. For example, when singers at Bhutan's Royal Academy of Performing Arts began to perform a song believed to have been composed by their guardian deity, the Brokpa objected, upset that their sacred tradition was being turned into entertainment for others.

During his visit, the Fifth King also told the Brokpa that, as a people living near the border, they have the responsibility to help protect the nation's security and sovereignty. His words took on new meaning in 2020 when, for the first time, China claimed that the Sakteng Wildlife Sanctuary was a disputed border area. Bhutan's government responded promptly, saying boldly, "Bhutan totally rejects the claim … Sakteng Wildlife Sanctuary is an integral and sovereign territory of Bhutan."[84] What led to China's new assertion of rights over more than 10 percent of Bhutan's territory is not clear. But this development was worrying for Bhutan, and most especially for the Brokpa.

After exploring the shops, school and other parts of village, we spent a cold rainy night in a tent pitched near the Sakteng Wildlife Sanctuary park ranger's office. This almost three-hundred-square-mile preserve contains more than two hundred species of trees and shrubs as well as globally threatened and endangered species like the red panda, the capped langur, Himalayan black bear, and musk deer. As we signed the visitor's register, the park ranger told us we were the first foreigners to visit in the four months he had been posted there. So, I was not surprised to learn that a survey conducted at about that same time found that more than one-third of the people of Sakteng had never seen a Westerner in person, let alone interacted with one. A few years later the newspaper reported that a total of twenty-nine tourists had visited Sakteng and/or a neighboring village during the year.

The next day we further explored the village and its surroundings. At the local Basic Health Unit, we learned that respiratory infections are the most common problem, followed by skin, eye, and then digestive problems. That suggested there has been considerable recent progress regarding food safety, since a middle-aged adult in Thimphu told me that when he was growing up, he thought diarrhea was the normal state of affairs for the human digestive tract.

We also greatly enjoyed time spent with a group of older Brokpa women with heavily weathered skin sitting in the spring sunshine. They held drop spindles in their right hands to make yak hair into yarn, which they gathered into balls in their left hands. They waved for me to join them for a photo. One of them removed her distinctive black yak-hair felt hat and motioned for me to put it on. These unique head pieces, known as a *tsipee cham,* were perched on their heads like shallow, upside-down soup bowls. Each had several thin five- or six-inch braided tufts sticking out from its round core like the skinny legs of a spider. These apparently protect the head from rain by draining it off the hat's core.

Later that day as we hiked in the village's periphery, we came upon a large log cut in half with the words, "Welcome to Sakteng Village Sanctuary: Entering to Big Foot (Migoi) Valley" painted on it. We kept a close lookout for a yeti as we hiked, although we were still a couple of thousand feet below the extremely high altitudes where local hunters and herders have reported sighting them. Those living in the Himalayas have believed in the *migoi,* or yeti, for centuries. In fact, a pre-Buddhist ritual in Tibet calls for the blood of a migoi. Also, the lyrics of a song about a famous fifteenth century saint and engineer who crisscrossed Bhutan building bridges depict him using a migoi as a porter.

Aum Kunzang Choden, who wrote an entire book relating tales and legends about yetis, observed in it, "The Brokpa do not question the existence of the yeti."[85] Indeed, the yeti is enough of a reality in the Bhutanese highlands that it has numerous additional names including "strong man," "great man," "glacier man," "snow goblin," and "mountain goblin." The fact that yetis are rarely sighted is explained by the extremely high, lonely regions they are believed to inhabit. In addition, they are said to walk backwards when pursued to fool those tracking them by their footprints. Yetis are real enough that a villager who found what he believed were yeti droppings gave them to the king. About a year after our visit to Sakteng, a park ranger filed an official report about finding yeti scat there.

Westerners ranging from a British traveler in Tibet in 1903 to a Greek zoologist in 1925, a Polish soldier escaping from a prisoner of war camp in 1942, and a world-renowned Italian climber in 1986 have claimed to have encountered a yeti. Western interest in yetis was strengthened when one of the world's leading experts on DNA analysis examined hair found on a 2001 yeti hunting expedition in Bhutan. He concluded, "It's not a human, not a bear, nor anything else we have so far been able to identify. ..."[86]

However, numerous Western expeditions mounted by individuals ranging from the mountaineer Sir Edmund Hillary to an American oilman have searched in vain for the elusive beast. Like most of those who have hunted for the yeti at more propitious altitudes, we returned to our camp without seeing one. The weather that evening turned cold and rainy, so the park ranger generously invited us to sleep in his storeroom rather than in our tent. We happily snuggled down in our sleeping bags surrounded by sacks of rice and bottles of cooking oil as rain pelted loudly on the metal roof of the unheated space.

We followed the same trail on our return trip from Sakteng as we had taken on the way there, past foaming waterfalls and through forest studded by hundreds of brilliant scarlet rhododendron blossoms. Contributing to the sense of adventure as we chose our route and encountered new sights, our guide, the horseman, and his wife usually trailed or preceded us at some distance, staying behind to pack up the camping equipment or going on ahead to begin meal preparations. As we descended to a lower, warmer altitude, we saw flowering fruit trees and farmers using wooden plows on tiny, relatively flat pieces of land. Linked by wooden yokes, study animals called *dzos*, the progeny of female yaks and male bulls, pulled the plows preparing the fields for planting. Coming changes in this isolated region were foreshadowed by the heavy rolls of coiled electric wire strapped on the backs of both male and female nomads heading to Sakteng in preparation for the upcoming electrification of the area. Such changes were also signaled by the large red and yellow plastic toy car strapped to the pack horse of a man wearing the Brokpa's unique maroon clothing, with a jerkin of yak hide adding extra warmth.

The trip back to Thimphu along the east-west road was just as long and bumpy as the trip out. But it seemed shorter because we had so many wonderful memories of our experiences in Sakteng to discuss. As the car labored to surmount each of the seven mountain passes on our route, I kept a sharp eye out for the hulking black and white yaks that had come to be such an iconic symbol of Bhutan for me. I spied them occasionally, grazing on miniature bamboo or sitting in the sun. Sometimes they deigned to return my gaze, but more often they ignored me. Keeping a sharp eye out for other denizens of those high places, I also saw a variety of birds and a small, brown, furry animal that was probably a marmot, but I did not see a yeti. Perhaps that is just as well. Mystery and legend enrich life by reminding us that there is always more of what is known to be learned and of the unknown to be discovered. One of the joys of living in Bhutan was to realize just how much I had not previously known or experienced and to begin to develop new knowledge and understanding from encountering ways of life so different from my own.

Chapter 10

Is Happiness a Place?

When Doug and I were preparing to leave the U.S. for Bhutan in 2009, we constantly encountered people who asked, "Where is that?" or remarked, "I've never heard of it." A couple of my students asked if Bhutan was in Africa. When we were arranging to send about two thousand books that I had collected in a book drive at my U.S. university to Bhutan to start the Royal Thimphu College library, some of the transport companies had never even heard of the country. One of them mistakenly provided an estimate for sending the books to Bataan in the Philippines.

Recently, when we mention Bhutan to Westerners, the reply is more typically something like, "Oh, yes. Isn't that the happiest country in the world?" Fostering happiness has long been a stated goal of the Bhutanese government. Way back in 1629, the country's first legal code asserted that "if the Government cannot create happiness (*dekid*) for its people, there is no purpose for the Government to exist."[87] However, for foreigners, the association between Bhutan and happiness typically reflects the international attention that the idea of Gross National Happiness (GNH) has brought to the country. This concept originated in the 1970s when Bhutan's Fourth King asserted that Gross National Happiness was more important than Gross National Product. (Some say that was at least partly because Bhutan did not have dependable data on GNP at that time.) However, it took more than three decades for this idea to become widely known and influential outside of the country.

In 2011, the UN General Assembly passed a Bhutanese resolution encouraging countries to emphasize happiness and wellbeing when measuring social and economic development. The next year, it adopted another Bhutanese resolution declaring an annual International Day of Happiness and initiated a highly publicized annual World Happiness Report. The link between happiness and Bhutan was both reflected and reinforced when the country's tourism council adopted the slogan, "Happiness is a Place."

Bhutan's most recent ranking in the international World Happiness Report places it somewhat below average in happiness, ninety-fifth out of 156 countries that were ranked by how positively individuals rated their lives. The strongest predictor of such ratings is a country's per capita GDP, which is well below the world average in Bhutan. Another important predictor on which Bhutan is also below the world average is healthy life expectancy. Such facts may help to explain the country's modest ranking despite its long emphasis on happiness.

Happiness as understood in GNH goes well beyond individuals' ratings of how their lives compare to an ideal one or the simple conception of happiness reflected in a ten-year-old Bhutanese boy's comment to me that "In mango season people are happy." Specifically, it consists of four elements, called its four pillars: sustainable and equitable social and economic development, preservation and promotion of culture, conservation of the environment, and good governance. Several domains are nested under each of these four pillars, with numerous variables measuring each.

In 2008, Bhutan's Planning Commission was renamed the GNH Commission, and it began to screen policies for consistency with GNH. One of the reasons Bhutan did not join the World Trade Organization (WTO) was the GNH Commission's concern about the compatibility of WTO membership with attainment of GNH.

Bhutan conducted national surveys measuring GNH in 2010, 2015, and 2022. These focused heavily on conditions thought to be conducive to happiness, rather than on individuals' reported happiness or satisfaction with their lives per se. Some questions had a very Bhutanese twist. For example, one measuring psychological wellbeing asked, "Do you consider karma in the course of your daily life?"[88] Questions under the cultural preservation pillar measuring the community vitality domain asked about labor contribution to religious buildings as well as to construction and repair of others' homes. Under the socioeconomic pillar, the education domain was measured by items about knowledge of local legends.

GNH provides a useful framework for discussing some of the most striking changes that have occurred in Bhutan as well as numerous fundamental aspects of current day Bhutan. Changes in the first pillar of GNH, socioeconomic development, have been dramatic. In the last four decades, Bhutan's per capita GDP has gone up almost ten times, with much of that increase in the last two. Correspondingly, Bhutan's poverty rate dropped dramatically from 73 percent to 8 percent between 2003 and 2022.

Consistent with the first pillar of GNH's emphasis on fostering equality, Bhutan's income inequality is somewhat lower than average for countries around the world. However, the inequality that still exists is striking. A well-off student of mine who volunteered at a scouting program in a poor area of eastern Bhutan wrote about her experience, saying, "Their bare feet made me guilty for wanting Nike shoes. Their faded clothes made me guilty about my full closet. Their sore hands made me wonder why I had my nails painted. … Their aim was to serve the country and their parents, while mine was to be a successful person who worships Korean actors and artists. The camp was planned for those children to learn values from the volunteers, but we ended up learning from them."

One very visible indication of the growth in wealth in Bhutan has been the explosion in the number of cars plying its improving, but still challenging, roads. In the 1970s, there were so few cars that two-digit license plate numbers sufficed. A Canadian volunteer told me that even in the mid-1980s, there were only about twenty-five cars in Thimphu and no more than fifty to sixty in the entire country. By 2011, there were about fifty-eight thousand cars in Bhutan. By 2024, there were over 127 thousand vehicles in the country, including roughly one car for every three people in the capital city.

Rather ironically, given that GNH highlights the importance of environmental and cultural preservation, a newspaper article on measuring GNH shared the front page with an article titled, "The Big Car Mania." The latter observed that very large and expensive vehicles like Prados and Land Cruisers "define the very identity of Bhutanese bureaucrats."[89] A few years later, an editorial asserted, "Car culture, which is heavily associated with social status and standing in the society, is becoming stronger by the year. People continue to sell their land and family heirlooms so that they can drive a car.

... The Bhutanese penchant for cars is as strong as our weakness for chilies."[90] Indeed, one Bhutanese remarked that when he used to drive a Hyundai, the brand of car that Doug and I drove, he bowed his head to those in expensive vehicles. After he started driving a much bigger more expensive vehicle, people acknowledged him as he passed.

But wealth, which lets individuals purchase cars, is only one domain under GNH's first pillar. Education and health, which are almost exclusively the purview of Bhutan's government, are also nested there. Although formal education is not required, the constitution promises all citizens a free tenth grade education. In 2020, eleventh and twelfth grade were made free as well. Currently, just under 25 percent of college-age youth are enrolled in higher education.

In sharp contrast, literacy and numeracy levels in earlier generations were extremely low. Fifty years ago, only about 15 percent of Bhutanese youth could read and write. The writer Aum Kunzang Choden recalls a yak herder she knew as a child who counted in units of fifteen because he did not know numbers beyond that, although some of his contemporaries could count in units of twenty. To improve such skills for those who did not get a formal education, the Ministry of Education has, for more than thirty years, provided a very successful basic literacy and numeracy program that has served over 190 thousand individuals fifteen to fifty years of age.

GNH goes beyond valuing education that imparts skills like literacy and numeracy. For example, in 2009, the Ministry of Education launched a holistic program, Educating for GNH, which included, among other things, increased attention to moral, environmental, spiritual, and aesthetic issues. Some Bhutanese were fervently in favor of this. Others saw it as a branding effort or pointed out inconsistencies in the concept, such as the simultaneous emphasis on democracy and the symbols of hierarchy. But the initiative did have some impact. For example, many classes now start with a few moments of meditation, which reinforces the link with Bhutan's spiritual heritage. Even management meetings at Royal Thimphu College often started this way.

Healthcare, also part of the first pillar of GNH, has seen dramatic changes in just a generation or two. Before the widespread introduction of allopathic (Western) medicine in the last few decades, Bhutanese typically relied on traditional medicine, Sowa Rigpa, which is based heavily on Buddhist philosophy. It uses cupping, steaming, minor surgery, acupuncture, herbal medications, commonly made from a rich variety of local plants, and other approaches. Although allopathic medicine is increasingly popular for many purposes, Sowa Rigpa is recognized as Bhutan's official medical tradition. Practitioners are trained in three- and five-year programs at the Institute of Traditional Medicine and Sowa Rigpa services are offered in all of Bhutan's twenty districts. It still holds enough sway that it was front page news when the Ministry of Health produced a report based on it recommending indulgence in sexual activities only once every two weeks during some months, but once every three days in others.

Shamans, whose approach is generally to determine which spirits or deities are causing illness, are still also commonly consulted as well. A middle-aged friend explained that when he was growing up, the shaman "who treated all the diseases and kept so many supernatural beings in good humor" was regarded "as next to God." Finally, there are over two thousand local healers who still "hold a significant place in the hearts of the people" according to a recent news report.[91] They handle a wide range of problems including headaches, stomach aches, sore throats, jaundice, and fractures with treatments including sucking body parts and blood, administering herbal concoctions and setting bones.

The first Bhutanese who was a fully graduated allopathic doctor did not begin his practice until 1954. Now, over 650 outreach clinics, more than two hundred Basic Health Units, and several hospitals are available in Bhutan. Between 1950 and 2024, life expectancy more than doubled from about thirty-two to seventy-three years. Polio and smallpox were eradicated during that period, leprosy was virtually eliminated, and malaria was drastically reduced. Goiters, which plagued almost two-thirds of the population as recently as the 1980s due to iodine deficiency, have all but disappeared.

Nonetheless, substantial health problems remain. One-fifth of Bhutan's children under five are physically stunted, and two-fifths are anemic. Also, religious beliefs sometimes undercut effective medical treatment. People may, for example, seek cures from lay monks for problems better handled through allopathic medicine, such as venomous snake bites. Hundreds of people need corneal transplants, but not a single donor has given corneas to the cornea bank that opened in 2014, at least partly because so many believe that their souls will not rest in peace if a body part is missing.

Several very creative approaches have been used to promote public health. In 1955, for instance, the country had no roads or airports when a trade dispute with Tibet cut off its supply of salt. An airdrop of bags filled with salt from India was arranged. As another more recent example, a lecturer at the Royal Institute of Health Sciences, concerned about the possible spread of HIV/AIDS, distributed free condoms supported by a small grant from the Ministry of Health. His van, with a license plate reading "Condom Man," displayed his phone number and health-related messages. We would see him in Thimphu wearing eye-catching clothing urging, "Use Condoms." He became so well-known that the newspaper articles and social media posts proclaimed, "Everybody in Thimphu … knows Tshewang Nidup, a.k.a. 'Condom Man.'"[92] At that time, free condoms were also placed in hotels and other public places. A friend told me this practice was discontinued because weavers were using the condoms' lubricant to soften thread or to pick up lint and some were using it as face cream as well.

Another innovative approach to broadening access to health services was the 2017 initiation of a helicopter service to ferry those in isolated villages to emergency medical services as well as to provide sightseeing excursions for high-end tourists. We enjoyed hearing the helicopter pilots' stories at pizza parties held at a hotel near the airport, especially since Doug is a private pilot and I have done some flying as well. The pilots were bemused to hear that one of my students told me that her father had literally cried in terror when he first saw a helicopter overhead, believing it was a dragon coming to destroy their village.

A truly remarkable amount has been accomplished in the last several decades to improve healthcare in Bhutan. But trained individuals and financial resources remain very limited relative to existing need. In a televised interview, a weary doctor reported having treated almost two hundred patients that day at his hospital. Luckily, Doug and I did not need to make much use of health facilities in Bhutan. The experiences we did have, however, suggested that despite extraordinary progress and much hard work, a great deal remains to be done. The only time I visited a physician in Bhutan, his examining table still had traces of the prior patient's blood on it. Almost equally disconcerting to someone used to U.S. standards of hygiene, there was no soap or water in the Thimphu hospital's bathroom. Doug waited for more than a month for an MRI because the machine needed was broken and a repair technician was not available, which was not an unusual experience. The X-ray machine in another hospital was out of service for more than ten months with no solution to the problem in immediate sight.

The dentist Doug saw for a root canal had neither X-ray film nor Novocain. Doug personally went to three other dental clinics searching in vain for the film before finally getting some from a health-worker acquaintance at a hospital. He came home from one of the four painful sessions it took to complete the root canal joking that he had made a major contribution to GNH that day. A large plate glass window right near the hospital entrance gave passersby a clear view of him in the dentist's chair. A sizeable crowd had gathered, enjoying the rare sight of a large foreigner undergoing prolonged dental treatment. Unfortunately, the root canal had to be redone when we returned to the U.S.

For many years, Bhutan's government has paid considerable attention to the second pillar of GNH, the promotion and preservation of traditional culture. When the country finally opened for tourism in 1974, it set a limit of two hundred tourists a year, fearing the impact of large numbers of tourists on its culture and environment. As tourism's potential for economic development became clear, the strict limit on the number of tourists under the country's initial "High Value Low Volume" policy was lifted. But requirements designed to maximize revenue while limiting the impact of tourism, such as a high daily minimum tariff and the requirement that tourists be accompanied by both a guide and driver, were maintained. So, in 1992 when we first visited Bhutan, annual tourist arrivals were still only about three thousand, fewer than the average number of guests arriving at Disneyland in California every hour and a half, night and day.

But over time, despite such policies, tourism has become Bhutan's largest source of foreign exchange and its second largest source of revenue after hydropower. Indeed, in 2019, the country hosted over 300 thousand tourists, including almost 250 thousand regional tourists from India, Bangladesh, and the Maldives and about seventy thousand from elsewhere, mainly the U.S., the EU, and China. A massive rise in regional tourists in the years right before the COVID-19 pandemic created urgent calls for action, especially because they were not subject to the substantial daily fee that other foreigners paid. Post-COVID tourism policy is still in flux, as policymakers deal with complex tradeoffs related to tourism income, cultural and environmental preservation, and international relations.

A continuing and very challenging part of the government's effort to preserve its culture is its fostering of Dzongkha, the official national language for around fifty years. Historically, Bhutan's rugged terrain severely limited interactions between communities and led to the development of nineteen different languages in this tiny country. Only about 30 percent of Bhutan's population of 800 thousand, mainly those in the west, are native Dzongkha speakers. A great many of them cannot fluently read and write Dzongkha, which has its own script. Nepali, common in Bhutan's south, and Tshangla, common in the east, are each the native tongue of roughly another quarter of the population. Many other less common mother tongues are also still spoken.

With this tremendous linguistic diversity, English became the de facto language of the civil service, white-collar workers, and educated people outside of monasteries. As Bhutan's prime minister put it in 2019, "English has become the official language in every official meeting and daily order of business in every agency."[93] Its having been the language of instruction in Bhutan's education system for decades no doubt contributed importantly to this. English also opens the possibility for study or work outside of the country, for employment in the tourism industry, and for communicating readily with those with other mother tongues within the country. Dzongkha is also taught in the schools. However, the majority of students are unable to correctly spell in Dzongkha things as simple as their own names and the names of their parents, schools, and villages.

In addition to teaching Dzongkha in schools, much has been done to promote it. The Dzongkha Development Commission has constantly worked on simplifying the language and promoting uniformity in grammar and spelling. It also develops new words for modern concepts. So, for example, "power tiller" is now rendered in Dzongkha with words meaning "mechanical ox," "carbon dioxide" is referred to as "dirty air," and soccer is "foot play kick and roll." Despite the proliferation of such new words, I was often struck to hear English words such as "computer" and "democracy" in the middle of sentences in situations where there either was no Dzongkha word for a concept, or the speaker did not know it.

Another strategy to promote Dzongkha has been to require its use in electoral campaigns and National Assembly debates. This, however, has created problems for those who do not speak it fluently. Some who want to run for parliament, or who have been elected, must take Dzongkha lessons to campaign and/or to speak effectively in the National Assembly. Some citizens skip meetings with candidates because they cannot understand their

Dzongkha presentations. After a couple of elections, a compromise was reached that now allows candidates to interact with attendees at their campaign events briefly in another language after their formal presentations in Dzongkha. A 2020 editorial reviewed the situation and concluded that despite much effort, "From our experience with promoting Dzongkha, nothing seems to be working."[94] Nevertheless, the government and many individuals continue to feel it is important to keep trying to foster a national language as a symbol of national identity despite the practical challenges this poses.

Numerous attempts, both small and large, to support the second pillar of GNH through preserving culture in many areas beyond language are also evident. For example, monasteries have begun to lock their religious texts in metal cabinets to protect them from the depredations of rats. For centuries, male royalty and high-level officials wore extraordinarily beautiful leather and brocade boots with upturned toes, called *tshoglhams*, embroidered with images of dragons, flowers, and phoenixes. When it was realized that only one man capable of making these still lived, a half dozen students were sent to him for training to preserve the tradition. Then, the government mandated that civil servants at modestly lower levels must also wear tshoglhams on important occasions to create a market for the apprentices' skills.

Larger scale efforts to preserve culture include replacing the lovely but tiny Bhutan Textile Museum, which opened more than twenty-five years ago, with a much larger National Textile Museum. In addition, in 2005 the Royal Textile Academy of Bhutan was opened under the patronage of a

Traditional elaborately embroidered men's boots have been rescued from possible oblivion by a government program that trained apprentices in the art of producing them.

On their graduation day, Royal Thimphu College students dress in elaborate traditional kiras and ghos, which can take months to weave.

member of the royal family to preserve and promote the country's stunning textile arts. Numerous architectural conservation and restoration projects have also been undertaken. For example, when we arrived in Bhutan in 2009, the Drukgyel dzong at one end of the Paro valley was a derelict ruin atop a hill. Built in 1649 to honor Bhutan's beating back forces from Tibet and Mongolia, it was destroyed by fire in 1951. Now, the tall, whitewashed central tower of the reconstructed dzong with a gold spire on its sloped roof proudly surveys its surroundings.

A very different attempt at preserving tradition was not so successful. Women's clothing has evolved substantially. For example, in urban and southern areas many women now wear a half kira, a long straight skirt, with a blouse and tailored cloth jacket rather than the traditional full-length kira described earlier. Also, with increasing prosperity, the strip of cloth worn over a woman's left shoulder when in government offices or monasteries, called a rachu, became more elaborately woven or embroidered. In addition, it also began to appear in more colors than the red customarily used by all commoners in earlier times. In 2016, the Ministry of Home and Cultural Affairs announced that only the earlier, plainer rachu was acceptable, except for female members of the royal family. Perhaps reflecting the changes brought about by democracy, the outcry that followed, especially on social media, led to a cabinet-level decision reversing this fiat.

Numerous efforts to preserve culture through creating new traditions that reinforce attachment to the nation's history and culture have also been undertaken. For example, in 2011, I attended the very first Druk Wangyal festival, developed to commemorate Bhutan's success in the 2003 campaign described in Chapter 5 to dispel Indian militants from its territory. In developing the festival's music and choreography, Dasho (a male honorific) Dr. Karma Ura incorporated time-honored Bhutanese dances and costuming as well as some elements from other traditions. Performers, clad in an astonishing variety of costumes, included everyday citizens, monks, and army personnel. One dancer, bare in the icy weather except for a mask and a white cloth like loose swim trunks around his hips, portrayed a famous eleventh century Buddhist mystic and saint to the sound of horns and cymbals. Others, with green leafy circlets on their heads and round rhinoceros-skin shields, portrayed Bhutanese soldiers stalking through the jungle in search of Indian militants.

I arrived at this festival as an eager crowd streamed into an open field at the 10,200-foot Dochula pass. Mist and snowflakes swirled around us, alternately hiding and revealing the dancers and lending an otherworldly atmosphere to the proceedings. The Fourth and Fifth Kings, other members of the royal family, the head of the Central Monastic Body, and several cabinet ministers sat under a large tent emblazoned with images of dragons.

I found a place on the freezing ground with ordinary members of the audience, putting a piece of cardboard under me to protect my clothing and cut the chill. My neighbor during this four-hour event was a woman who I guessed, based on her white hair, bent back, and leathery wizened face, must have been over eighty years of age. We did not share a language, but part way through the performance she pulled out a bag of walnuts and silently offered me one. As I looked on, she put the intact shell of another walnut in her mouth and quickly crunched it open despite numerous missing teeth. Having once had to work hard to open similar walnuts with a hammer, I pantomimed thanks to her and offered her some crackers I had with me. Then I put the walnut away for a time when I could open it without risking a trip to the dentist.

Preserving a unique culture is not easy in a country open to the outside world. Rapid urbanization has increased this challenge. For example, young people who move from rural areas to a city sometimes drop customs honoring local deities and fail to make the often difficult and time-consuming trip back to their villages for annual festivals. Challenges to ancestral ways are obvious on the streets of Thimphu and at the college as well. Many male students sport Korean hair styles very different from the close-cropped look common among their male elders. Many female students are entranced by Korean beauty products. Some who can afford it buy Korean skin care products costing more than a laborer earns in two days. As a newspaper article put it, "K-pop was the first invasion. … Then came … K-Beauty. Bhutanese girls and women took to it like fish to the water."[95] I wondered how the Fifth King reacted when he read a wedding felicitation from a fourth-grade student saying, "King, you are very lucky. … Your queen is looking like Korean girl."[96]

Western influence in clothing and female hair styling choices is also apparent. Many female Royal Thimphu College students lightened their lustrous black hair to a medium brown or treated it to produce auburn highlights. DVDs, TV, and the internet all brought Korean, American, and Indian films and music to the campus. Students created rap songs and breakdance routines for presentations at college cultural shows. However, many more still performed traditional Bhutanese, Nepali, and Tibetan dances, providing solace for the conservative members of the faculty and staff, who winced at witnessing foreign-influenced performances.

Village membership, as well as family membership, has historically been important in Bhutan. Thus, one important domain under GNH's second pillar, cultural promotion and preservation, is community vitality, which includes things such as volunteerism, family relationships, and a sense of safety. Not too surprisingly, Bhutan's GNH survey found that community vitality is stronger in rural than in urban areas. For example, urbanites were much more likely than those in rural areas to feel unsafe from harm by other humans when walking alone in their neighborhood after dark.

I had my own experience with lack of safety in an urban setting, although I still feel much safer in Thimphu than in most U.S. cities. As Doug and I headed to our car around 9 p.m. after seeing a movie shown by a friend who is a lama in Thimphu, two tall young men snuck up quickly behind me and tugged insistently on my purse. I was so astonished that I froze and did not utter a sound. I fell hard onto the deserted asphalt road as they pulled on the purse which I reflexively clung to until they gave up and ran away. Doug, who had walked around our car to the driver's-side door before the would-be thieves struck, could not immediately figure out where I had disappeared to. After I got my breath back and rose from the pavement, we headed home to ice the rapidly developing lump on my head. Because crimes must be reported in Bhutan, a college official informed the police of the incident the next day, although I had no way of identifying the miscreants. We were told that I was the first Westerner to ever report such an experience.

Of course, humans are not the only potential source of danger in Bhutan or elsewhere. The percentage of GNH survey respondents feeling "completely unsafe" or "unsafe" when alone at night due to humans (30 percent) is not strikingly different from those feeling "completely unsafe" or "unsafe" from wild animals (27 percent) or ghosts/spirits (25 percent).

Two time-honored aspects of Bhutanese civic life strongly related to community vitality are providing neighbors with assistance for activities (like building houses or planting rice) and mandatory labor contributions for community projects (from building roads to digging irrigation ditches). Much such activity continued during our years in Bhutan. However, I heard laments that households have started sending the most easily spared member of their family for mandatory work, even for tasks requiring heavy labor, a practice less common in earlier times. Also, many longstanding customs or festivals are waning, because local communities have trouble finding enough young men to perform the dances or other activities essential to such events.

Nonetheless, the striking success of the Dessung, or Guardians of Peace, suggests that volunteerism is alive and well in Bhutan, even in urban areas. In 2011, the Fifth King initiated this program which trains volunteers to assist in natural disasters, religious events, and other situations where additional trained persons are needed for civic purposes. Consistent with the idea of GNH, this training emphasizes not only specific skills which can be useful in the job market, but also the importance of harmony, civic responsibility, and community service.

In roughly fifteen years since then, over fifty thousand Bhutanese have been trained as Dessups, including many living in urban areas. Trainees included members of the royal family and a former prime minister as well as many ordinary citizens. Wearing distinctive bright orange jumpsuits, they

The Druk Wangyel festival, first performed at Dochula pass in 2011, is unique because it mixes traditional culture with elements of Chinese opera and African tribal dances, reflecting Bhutan's growing contact with the outside world.

A monk who lives at Druk Wangditsi lhakhang which Dessups helped restore to its former glory.

have assisted in situations ranging from the disastrous 2015 earthquake in Nepal to forest fires, the COVID-19 pandemic, and a religious gathering where they helped to cook, collect trash, and deal with emergencies for two hundred thousand attendees.

The Dessups not only provide needed skills and services, but they also inspire others to contribute as well. For example, on a hike to the Wangditse temple near Thimphu, Doug and I encountered a dozen or more Dessups serving as a human chain to move large rocks needed in the reconstruction of this building. A faculty colleague, who was not a Dessup herself, had organized some friends to help her provide lunch and other refreshments for the hard-working group, donating both the food and the work it took to prepare and transport it by foot to that temple, which does not have road access.

The third pillar of GNH, conservation of the environment, is one of the hallmarks of Bhutan's identity as a nation. Indeed, Bhutan's name came first on a list of "The World's Most Unlikely Climate Heroes" after a 2015 UN-sponsored meeting on climate change. Its constitution requires maintaining 60 percent of its land area under forest cover as well as preserving and even improving the country's environment. Currently, Bhutan is one of only three carbon negative countries in the world, with its forests absorbing about six million tons of carbon dioxide a year. The government even provides rural citizens with a modest amount of free electricity to replace firewood, and it exports large amounts of clean energy produced via hydropower to India.

Despite Bhutan's contributions to the struggle against climate change, climate trends have impacted the country significantly. Perhaps the biggest threat is the impact of warmer weather on Bhutan's glaciers, which are receding at about one hundred to two hundred feet per decade. This melting has heightened the possibility of destructive glacial lake outburst floods and could also undermine the supply of water for hydropower as well as for agriculture, which currently employs much of the country's population.

Government policies are vitally important in mitigating climate change. But citizens' beliefs also impact environmental sustainability. Importantly, 80 percent of Bhutan's GNH survey respondents reported feeling "highly responsible" for protecting the environment. Unfortunately, individuals' behavior is not always consistent with their attitudes. Repeated government efforts to ban plastic bags due to environmental concerns met with very modest success, and I routinely collected a dozen or more carelessly discarded plastic water and juice bottles on the forty-minute walk I took near the college most mornings.

However, some Bhutanese do go to unusual lengths to preserve the environment. For example, a man named Gopilal Acharya, who lived near the auto repair shops outside of Thimphu, reacted to the fact that there was no garbage pickup in his area of the capital city by taking his trash to the city's central market to put in their bins. He was told by officials that he could not deposit it there because too many people were doing that and causing the bins to overflow, which brought packs of dogs and subsequent complaints from VIPs. He was advised to take his trash to his office downtown and then to carry it out to the garbage truck when it made its rounds in that area.

A core precept in the Tibetan Buddhism practiced in Bhutan is compassion for all sentient beings, with that term typically being understood to include insects and plants as well as animals and even some inanimate objects. Such compassion has strong implications for environmental sustainability because it encourages minimal disruption of individuals' surroundings. Recall, for example, the earlier discussion of Yarney, the forty-five-day annual summer retreat during which monks stay inside monasteries to avoid inadvertently killing insects. This same concern leads many to feel that farming, especially the use of pesticides, leads to bad karma which should be avoided, or at least expiated. Also reflecting compassion for insects, an acquaintance told me about a friend who would not eat honey because it was stolen from the bees. Another woman told me she no longer admired President Barack Obama after he seemed pleased to have killed, with a quick slap, a fly that landed on his forearm during a televised interview.

Consistent with this emphasis on compassion for other beings, many government policies attempt to reduce meat consumption. For example, with strong support from the Central Monastic Body, selling meat during two holy months in the Buddhist calendar as well as on additional holy days each month is not allowed in Bhutan. Many deal with this by stocking up on meat which they dry or store in freezers for later use, because most Bhutanese are not vegetarian.

Indeed, despite religious scruples, Bhutanese eat more meat per capita than those in any other South Asian country and only about 15 percent of Royal Thimphu College students requested the vegetarian meals available to them. As one newspaper article put it, "As a Buddhist country, we discourage killing, even if we like eating meat."[97] When the government made the hardheaded decision to set up a meat processing plant near Thimphu to reduce foreign exchange expenditures on imported meat, the public outcry was so loud that the plan was quickly dropped. Similarly, a government plan to have Bhutan produce 90 percent of the meat consumed in the country was impossible to realize, due mainly to the stigma related to killing animals.

Religious scruples related to killing other species as well as legal and reputational considerations clearly shape many individuals' behavior. Raising animals for meat is not generally approved of, although villagers can butcher an animal that has died naturally without opprobrium. Perhaps this accounts for the fact that I have heard talk of cows committing suicide by falling off a cliff. Explaining the low level of meat production compared to consumption, a meat vendor observed, "Many people enjoy eating meat, but ... if farmers turn into butchers then the people ostracize them."[98] An acquaintance who started raising chickens to sell eggs left the business because she could not afford to feed the older hens that had stopped producing, but she felt it morally wrong to sell them for meat.

People in some remote areas, still influenced by pre-Buddhist Bon practices, engage in rituals involving animal sacrifice, with the animal then being eaten. Back in the late 1980s, the head of the Central Monastic Body decried such practices, and they have gradually become less common. For example, an annual festival in the western region of Haa used to feature the sacrifice of one or more yaks in honor of a deity, Ap Chundu. About a decade ago, this practice was given up after prayers to the local deity by a monk and a shaman were followed by a roll of the dice by the local mayor, which produced results suggesting this deity accepted the change.

The complex interplay between the religious injunction to have compassion for all sentient beings, longstanding practices, and economic motivation is illustrated by the issues arising in the work of Semchen Tsethar Tshogpa, an organization which purchases and relocates yaks, cattle, and sheep that would otherwise be killed. Indeed, it has even bought out entire livestock farms to rescue their animals.

However, some profit-oriented individuals buy young yaks for a low price and then demand exorbitant amounts from such groups not to kill them, essentially holding them for ransom. Unfortunately, sometimes herders paid to take care of ransomed animals do not fulfill that responsibility. Then the animals may be caught and resold for meat. Also, such animals sometimes wander away, eating villagers' hard-won crops and posing a danger to unwary drivers. In one area, sheep released by an animal rescue organization were attacked and eaten by dogs. Then the dogs, having discovered that sheep were easy prey, began to kill sheep owned by villagers. Balancing religious sentiments, individual freedom, economic interests, and GNH's third pillar, environmental conservation, is not easy. Nonetheless, both Bhutan's government and the majority of its people clearly recognize the importance of efforts to protect and sustain the country's extraordinary environment, including its fauna.

From my perspective, there are times when the urge toward compassion combined with the custom of deference to authority can create problems for a country like Bhutan, in which the government plays a tremendous role in so many areas of life. For example, after five civil servants were charged with corruption, the Minister of Economic Affairs opined that they should not be put behind bars if found guilty because that would be difficult for their families. The Minister of Health suggested simply changing their jobs or demoting them if they were guilty rather than firing them. Yet, in that very same legal system, ordinary people were jailed for three years for not having a tax receipt for tobacco and those vandalizing religious structures could even receive life sentences.

The fourth and final pillar of GNH is good governance, measured in surveys by questions about the government's promotion of the other three pillars of GNH as well as about political participation, anti-corruption efforts, lack of discrimination, and service delivery. Ratings of various areas under this pillar varied substantially. However, the majority of individuals were reasonably positive about government services and there was a substantial improvement in this area between 2010 and 2022, which was not surprising. With rapidly increasing prosperity during the past two decades, governments at various levels in Bhutan have undertaken a wide variety of efforts to improve the infrastructure and services that importantly impact daily life.

One of these has been the expansion and improvement of the road system. A second was the expansion of access to electricity from under one-third of the population to almost everyone. In fact, in recent years, we found that one reliable way to locate monasteries hidden high up in the mountains when hiking was to look for the massive towers bringing them electricity. Ready access to electricity in most areas has also made light at night possible as well as the use of TVs, computers, rice cookers, and electric fencing for crop protection.

Electricity has also greatly facilitated the spread of cell phones. When we first arrived in 2009, villagers would sometimes walk for hours just to recharge their phones. A creative individual discovered that a nearly depleted basic cell phone battery could be recharged for a couple of hours by slipping a blade of grass between the phone and the battery electrode and then simultaneously switching the phone on and pulling out the grass. Another discovered that a bank note did the trick as well. The story made the newspaper since cell phones were so useful in areas without electricity for everything from healthcare to contacting urban relatives.

Communication from rural villages was extremely difficult before the arrival of cell phones. One friend told of using smoke signals when he was young. Those in other villages used conch shells, which produce a deep resonant sound that carries for long distances. An acquaintance described a relay system in which someone with a strong voice would go to a hillock and shout toward the next village, where someone else would then pass the message on in the same way. Another friend recalled that deaths were announced in a special somber tone, which he always found chilling as a child, especially because villages were so small that he was very likely to know the deceased.

The postal system has been available for written communication since the 1960s. It started with mules, postal runners, and a few vehicles. Then, in 1997, it added a bus service for passengers as well as mail. However, when we arrived at Royal Thimphu College, there was still a postal runner ferrying mail to a high, distant part of the Thimphu district using a tortuous trail covered with snow in the winter and requiring the crossing of raging streams during the summer monsoon. His trials and tribulations were captured in a fascinating documentary called Price of Letter, which won a prize at the Brooklyn Film Festival in New York.

Even in the capital city of Thimphu, postal delivery did not start until 2015, and it then covered only 124 buildings on three streets. Contributing importantly to this situation, most streets in Thimphu had no names at that time. Even when they had names, most were generally unknown even by long-time residents. Efforts toward street naming began as early as 2001 when much of the population was still illiterate, and a later exercise in 2013 was also not generally welcomed. Another was announced in 2020 and presented to the nation's cabinet for approval in 2021. It remains to be seen whether this more recent effort will be more effective than earlier ones. As an editorial described the situation at that time, "The capital's residents are not used to streets and lanes even if we have named streets. Apart from Nor-zin and Changlam, not many know the other streets by their name."[99]

So how do Thimphu's residents find each other? They give directions using various landmarks, such as government offices, banks, and schools. Not surprisingly, police and fire fighters often have trouble figuring out where exactly to go when they receive a call for help. Similarly, when Thimphu underwent a sudden strict lock down during the COVID-19 pandemic, the plan was to deliver food to those needing it. But it sometimes took more than an hour to locate a specific household, which obviously was not scalable in a city of around one hundred thousand inhabitants. Once, when we were invited to visit an acquaintance's home, we were told to proceed to a water tower and then to telephone her so she could come get us. Another time we were given instructions to a friend's home that ended with turning left immediately after a yellow bulldozer. After driving around unsuccessfully for a considerable time, we finally called our hostess in desperation, only to have her notice that the bulldozer had moved since she had shared the directions.

Shortly after we arrived in Bhutan, we approached the post office with a problem that was almost miraculously solved. An acquaintance in the U.S. had a young pen pal in Bhutan to whom he asked us to bring a gift. The only address we had for her was her name and "Thimphu." When we approached the postal counter and explained the problem, the clerk replied with a smile, "Oh, that's my daughter and she's here." We chatted with the daughter and gave her the package. When we returned to the U.S. for a vacation, we took a gift from her back to her pen pal.

Later, we saw how the post office got mail to extremely remote locations when we sent a photo to a monk who lived in a monastery high above the secluded Tang Valley in central Bhutan. Almost nine months later, we received a thank you note from him. In it, he said that the photo had taken several months to get to him because Doug's letter had stayed at the district post office until employees encountered someone planning a trek up to the distant monastery and asked him to deliver it.

The Thimphu post office provided us with the solution to another problem—what I could readily send to my ninety-six-year-old mother in the U.S.

for her birthday. One unique service it offers is creating usable stamps with the customer's image on them. The person wishing to be pictured goes there and has their photo taken, or, these days, brings a digital image. In a few minutes, stamps are produced with their likeness. Since my mother was not in Bhutan herself, I pasted a blow-up of a digital picture of her on a cardboard placard. The postal clerk took a picture of it and created some stamps. My mother very much enjoyed this unique gift, remarking that totally new experiences were a rare treat for someone of her age.

Despite our good experiences with the post office, I was very surprised to learn that, in the early 1970s, it contributed more revenue to the government's coffers than any other source. In the late 1950s, the Third King wanted to undertake a number of development projects. But the World Bank turned down Bhutan's request to fund them. A man named Burt Todd, generally believed to be the first American to visit Bhutan, had met a member of the royal family while studying at Oxford. Although Bhutan was not producing stamps at the time, Mr. Todd suggested that the country could raise money by producing unusual stamps as collectors' items. This idea was approved, partly because the stamps might also bolster Bhutan identity as a sovereign country.

By 1967, this project had created the world's first 3-D lens-shaped stamps. Rather ironically, for a country that barely had roads, this series also featured images of astronauts. Other innovative stamps soon followed, including the world's first scented stamp, the first bas-relief stamp, the first extruded plastic stamp, as well as the first stamps ever printed on metal and silk. In 1972, a set of stamps that were tiny, one-sided vinyl records that could be played on a normal turntable were produced. They contained Bhutan's national anthem, folk songs, and historical information in Dzongkha and English, the latter narrated by Burt Todd himself. By 1973, stamp production was called Bhutan's principal industry, although, to be honest, there was not much competition in that category. When Doug and I were first considering joining the college, Doug had the pleasure of meeting Mr. Todd at his home in the U.S. and seeing his extraordinary collection of Bhutanese stamps. Shortly thereafter, Mr. Todd passed away at the age of eighty-one, still enthusiastic about his many experiences in the tiny, faraway country.

Rather remarkably, in just over ten years, Bhutan progressed from being a reclusive country unknown to most of the outside world to one in which its king and other members of the royal family received prestigious international awards, its prime minister gave a well-received TED Talk, its diplomats successfully sponsored UN resolutions, and its people won recognition in the Guinness Book of World Records for environmental accomplishments.

Much more importantly, for most Bhutanese the quality of life has improved quite dramatically during the span of less than one lifetime. Longevity has markedly increased, and poverty decreased. Education and healthcare have improved dramatically, with regard to both the proportion of the population that benefits from them and quality. Improvements in roads, sanitation, electrification, communication, and other areas have also eased suffering for many and expanded individuals' horizons.

At the same time, although most are very proud of their country, many Bhutanese recognize that clichés like "The Last Shangri-La" and sobriquets such as "The Happiest Country in the World" are not accurate. Progress has been impressive in many realms, but much remains to be accomplished. Indeed, the week I started this chapter, the Fifth King made a speech on Bhutan's national day calling for major reforms in the country's education system as well as in its civil service; and there is considerable room for improvement in areas such as healthcare and youth employment as well.

However, our decade in Bhutan suggests that the country's leadership was wise in recognizing that attention to the array of factors included in GNH is more likely to steer it on the path to promoting the wellbeing of its people than one which focuses solely on GNP. So, although happiness is more a state of mind than a place, Bhutan has been admirably successful in moving relatively quickly from being an isolated, absolute monarchy with high levels of poverty and disease to a democratic constitutional monarchy that has vastly improved the life chances of most of its people. Thus, the path it has chosen is indeed one worth paying attention to and I, for one, am happy that Bhutan has brought the idea of GNH onto the world stage, not only earning attention for itself, but also making an important contribution to the wider world that it has so recently joined.

Afterword

Much of this book was written during the COVID-19 pandemic, when Doug and I were unexpectedly unable to return to Bhutan after having gone home to the U.S. for Royal Thimphu College's lengthy winter break. To protect itself from the pandemic, Bhutan instituted a ban on foreigners entering the country in March 2020, just a day or two before our return flight for the college's spring semester. Living up to its tradition of emphasizing community, the Bhutanese government nonetheless organized repatriation flights for over nine thousand citizens working or studying abroad who wished to return to their homeland. It also covered the cost of twenty-one-day quarantines for all of them to protect the broader community.

Displaying the warmth and welcome Doug and I experienced when living in Bhutan, the Bhutanese spared no effort in treating the first COVID-19 patient in their country, a seventy-six-year-old American tourist, Bert Hewitt. He received medical care in Bhutan which probably saved his life, according to a doctor who treated him once he had been airlifted back to the U.S. He also received a pair of blue silk pajamas and a coverlet from the Fifth King as well as kind letters and flowers from the Bhutanese public.

I have missed my colleagues, students, and friends in Bhutan. But being away from Bhutan for much longer than any other period since 2009 has also given me both time and distance from my years there, which have been helpful in reflecting on my experiences in the country. One of the things I appreciate most about Bhutan is how sensitive many people are to the interdependence between various components of the environment. That was reflected in everything from the belief in spirits living in trees and lakes to the practices of praying for all sentient beings and protecting wildlife—even at a substantial cost to humans. I still recall being introduced to the idea of interdependence in fifth grade, with a picture of a rabbit sitting under a raspberry bush in a book about ecology. But I have never seen it evidenced so clearly in so many aspects of individual and societal functioning as I have in Bhutan.

The Buddhist emphasis on interdependence combined with its focus on compassion has a marked and very positive impact on many aspects of social life in Bhutan. I recognize that, as a foreigner in my sixties or seventies, I was often given special treatment. But the warmth and generosity Doug and I experienced, even from total strangers, was touching. We were invited into complete strangers' homes dozens of times. When our car had a flat tire one evening near dusk, three young men in another car pulled over so they could change it for us. In the U.S., I would have felt frightened or at least uncertain as the group piled out of their car and approached us on a lonely road. In Bhutan, it did not even occur to me to be concerned about their intentions. At the college, colleagues contributed financially to help each other with expensive rituals when others faced the death of family members. All this contrasted very sharply with my previous experiences living in a suburban neighborhood in the U.S. and working at a U.S. university, despite the valued friendships formed in those environments. Life in Bhutan highlighted for me the richness that a broad, supportive community can add to one's life, even as it very reasonably expects something in return.

I also came to a newfound appreciation of stillness in Bhutan. I have always lived an active and busy life, spending much of the time preparing for the next phase. I worked hard in high school to get into a good college, and in college to get into a good graduate school, and in graduate school to lay a good foundation for obtaining a challenging job. I actively pursued a demanding professional career while raising three daughters with Doug, which also kept me moving constantly from one thing to the next. And I enjoyed all that greatly. But, in Bhutan, I learned to sit quietly and listen to the wind in the trees and the splash of a stream. I learned to just absorb the richness of the sights and sounds of spectacular festivals without wondering how to get a great photo to show to friends or having my mind wander to what I would be doing that evening.

Finally, over the years in Bhutan, the Buddhist emphasis on impermanence also influenced me greatly. Lama Shenphen, a monk who works with young drug addicts in Thimphu and who became a friend of ours, often emphasized the importance of understanding this concept. Recognition of impermanence leads to accepting the inevitability of loss but also to recognizing the continuing possibility of positive change, thus greatly increasing the equanimity with which one can face the inevitable vicissitudes of life.

During the pandemic, Doug and I contributed to the college as we could from a distance. We looked forward to returning and resuming our work there when it seemed wise, given our age, the mandatory three-week quarantine for those returning to Bhutan, and our concern about the potential availability of needed medical treatment should we contract COVID there. But then, just as we were beginning to consider returning before too long, our home in Colorado and all its contents burned to the ground in a huge wildfire, which decimated over one thousand homes in our community and a neighboring one.

Much of the time since then has been taken up by extremely onerous efforts to deal with the consequences of the fire that crowded out a great deal of our long-distance, college-related work. So, we decided in the fall of 2023 to return to Bhutan for six weeks to vacate our apartment there, transfer work-related materials to the individuals who had taken on many of our responsibilities, visit some favorite places, and say goodbye to the many friends we had made there.

This was a wonderful but excruciatingly bittersweet journey. Being back in Bhutan reminded me vividly of the things I so love about it. At the same time, the purpose of the trip was to bring that chapter of our lives to a close. One of the treasures our time in Bhutan gave me, the increased awareness and acceptance of impermanence, helped me deal with the conflicting emotions evoked by this experience.

In this book, I have emphasized those aspects of Bhutan that are different from my experience in the Western world. These are the things that were most striking to me as a Westerner and I believe they are most likely to be of interest to readers. I should emphasize, however, that living in Bhutan also gave me a profound sense of how much human beings share, even when their experiences are incredibly different. The importance of family and friends, the desire to be acknowledged and valued for who we are, and the hope to live a happy and comfortable life are all fundamental aspects of human experience that most people share despite cultural differences.

In closing, I encourage you to spend some time exploring this intriguing and inviting country if at all possible. Although not perfect, it is a truly special place. If you wish, you can learn more online about Royal Thimphu College (www.rtc.bt) or visit it, because the college is glad to host guests if that is arranged in advance. But even if you never have the good fortune to experience this fascinating land or Royal Thimphu College in person, I hope the vicarious visit to Bhutan this book has provided leaves you with new perspectives and lasting memories.

Glossary

Ara: home-brewed whiskey
Ashi: an honorific used preceding the first name of female nobles or royalty
Atsara: a jester
Aum: an honorific used preceding the first name of highly respected women
Bomena: a tradition in which a male sneaks into the home of a female at night to court her
Dasho: an honorific used preceeding the first name of a highly respected man
Doma: a mild stimulant made from areca nut and slaked lime wrapped in betel leaves
Desi: sweet white rice with butter, sugar, raisins and saffron served on special occasions
Driglam namzha: rules of etiquette regarding speech, dress, and other behaviors many of which pertain to appropriate behavior toward individuals of higher status
Dzo: offspring of a cow and a yak
Dzong: a huge fortress serving as a center for secular and religious authorities
Dzongda: a district governor
Dzongkhag: a district or province
Gho: male clothing consisting of a knee-length robe tied tightly at the waist
Gup: a mayor
Gompa: a monastery

Glossary

Kabney: a large scarf worn by men which indicates their status from commoner to king

Khenpo: a abbot

Khadar: a long narrow cloth, usually silk, presented to another to indicate respect, welcome, goodbye, congratulations, condolences, etc.

Kidu: benefit, such as citizenship, money, or land, granted by the Bhutanese king to a subject

Kira: female floor-length clothing made from a large piece of cloth fastened at each shoulder with broaches and a tight belt at the waist

Lam: a path or road

Lhakhang: a Buddhist temple

Je Khenpo: Head of the Central Monastic Body

Rachu: a long narrow strip of cloth worn over the shoulder by women when in a monastery or government office or at a tshechu

Rinpoche: an honorific for a highly respected Buddhist religious figure, literally meaning precious one

Semso: a gift a money to a bereaved individual

Tashi lebey: a dance in which all join hands and circle repeatedly which signals the end of an event

Tercham: a naked dance or treasure dance

Tertön: a treasure finder with special spiritual powers to find and/or leave messages in places ranging from rocks and cliffs to dreams and visions

Thangka: a painting on cloth with Buddhist iconography such as mandalas and deities.

Torma: a sculpture, often very large, intricate, and colorful, made by monks from butter and barley flour

Tshachu: a hot springs

Tshechu: a religious festival usually including masked dances by monks

Tshoglham: a traditional elaborately embroidered men's boot

Tsipee cham: a Brokpa woman's hat like an upside-down soup bowl with yak hair braids

Tulku: a reincarnated spiritual master often identified when a child

Yarney: a 45-day period when monks stay in their monastery to protect insects from harm

Woola: required community service

Zhabdrung: a Tibetan Buddhist rinpoche who unified Bhutan in the 1600s and laid down its first laws

Book Club Questions for *Discovering Bhutan*

1. Of all the information and anecdotes in the book, what has stayed with you the most and why?
2. What do you think the author might wish us to learn or think about?
3. What was the most surprising thing you learned from this book?
4. What, if anything, do you think those in your country could learn from Bhutanese culture that would improve their lives or the culture more generally? What, if anything, do you think the Bhutanese could learn from your country's culture?
5. Bhutan evolved in just a few years from being an absolute monarchy, in which the king could set aside court decisions and grant individual petitions, to a constitutional monarchy with power vested in a democratically elected parliament. At the time of that transition (2006-08), just over 50 percent of the population was illiterate. Do you think there are any conditions under which an absolute monarchy is preferable to a democracy? If so, what conditions? If not, why not?

6. Did reading this book about how the author spent the decade from her mid-sixties to her mid-seventies impact your thoughts about aging or what you might do in retirement?
7. What questions would you ask the author about the book or her experiences in Bhutan if you met her? Why?
8. In contrast with the traditional measure of development, GNP, which focuses solely on economic productivity, Bhutan developed and promoted the philosophy of Gross National Happiness (GNH) that includes environmental and cultural preservation, good government, community vitality, and improved health outcomes as development goals. In a country where poverty is still common, is aiming for GNH desirable and realistic? Is it fair and/or desirable for wealthy countries, like the U.S., to encourage poorer countries to focus on noneconomic goals?
9. Given what you read, would you like to live in Bhutan for several months or more if you could deal with the practical issues of being away from your home? Why or why not?

If you wish to see if I am available to talk with your book group or to speak about Bhutan, please contact me at DiscoveringBhutanBook@gmail.com

Photo Credits

All photos were taken by Douglas Schofield, with the exception of the photo of the Royal Thimphu College faculty with His Majesty Jigme Khesar Namgyel Wangchuck in Chapter 5, which was taken by Gelay Jamtsho.

Acknowledgements

I gratefully acknowledge the many individuals who have contributed importantly to making this book possible. First, I thank Ashi Kesang Wangmo Wangchuck and Tenzing Yonten for their vision in founding Royal Thimphu College and their dedication to making the college an inspiring reality. The one-year commitment my husband and I made to help establish the college turned into a wonderful decade working in Bhutan to help further develop it. This book would never have been written without the exposure to this stunningly beautiful country and its fascinating culture that our time at the college provided. I also most sincerely thank other Bhutanese colleagues and friends, too numerous to name individually, who contributed so much to my understanding of the country as well as to the richness of my experience and my enjoyment of our time there.

Numerous others have also contributed substantially to this book. A college classmate, Claudia Van der Heuvel, volunteered her outstanding skills as an experienced copyeditor. Susan Chipman, Ellen Cooney, Julia Hough, Marge Riddle, Ann Schofield, and Laura Shapiro provided useful feedback on the manuscript. Numerous others, including Ellen Hume, Linda Leaming, Susan Levenstein, Bob McGahey, Linda Greenhouse, Francine Prose, and Mary Eccles, provided helpful information regarding various aspects of the publishing process. In addition, I thank the capable staff of Sentient Publications, especially Deborah Weisser and Marissa Cassayre, who did so much to make this book possible.

I would also like to thank my husband, Doug, for sharing the adventures and experiences which shaped so much of this book as well as for his patience with all the time I devoted to writing it. He was the prime mover in initiating our move to Bhutan from Pittsburgh, where we had lived for most of our adult lives. To me, the move felt like jumping off a cliff. But it resulted in a very happy landing, both personally and professionally.

Finally, I also want to thank our daughters, Alanya, Heather, and Emily, the latter of whom was still a college student when we left the U.S., for their patience with their wandering parents. Initially, technical issues in Bhutan made communication less easy, dependable, and frequent than desirable. Their flexibility regarding that issue and their support for our unusual choice of a place to live and work meant a lot to me, as did their thoughtfulness in coming halfway around the world for visits.

Endnotes

Bhutanese Buddhists typically have one to three names, none of which is a surname. So, their names are presented in full here, unlike those of the other authors cited whose first initial is presented before their surnames.

1	M. Chester, "The Remote Country of Bhutan," Christian Science Monitor, March 2, 1981, https://www.csmonitor.com/1981/0302/030253.html.

2	J. Polsky, "English Speaking, Chili Eating," Kuzuzangpo, Inflight Magazine, April-May 2018, 42-50.

3	M. R. Dhital, "Editorial," The Journalist, August 26, 2012, 2.

4	D. Rizal, The Royal Semi-Democracy of Bhutan (Lanham, MD: Lexington Books, 2015), 42.

5	Phurpa Tenzin, "The Education Saga," Bhutan Observer, April 2-9, 2010, 3.

6	M. Windischgraetz and Rinzin Wangdi, "The Black-Slate Edict of Punakha Dzong," 2019, https://www.academia.edu/39877892/The_Black_Slate_Edict_of_Punakha_Dzong.

7	J. Strachey, M. Solms, and S. Freud, The Revised Standard Edition of the Complete Psychological Works of Sigmund Freud (Washington, D.C.: Rowman and Littlefield Publishers, 1924), 274.

8	Karma Phuntsho, *The History of Bhutan* (Haryana, India: Penguin Books, 2013), 562.

9	J. Gettleman and J. C. Hernandez, "China and India Agree to Ease Tensions in Border Dispute," The New York Times, August 28, 2017, https://www.nytimes.com/2017/08/28/world/asia/china-india-standoff-withdrawal.html?searchResultPosition=19.

10	S. Parasjar and S. Datta, "Ties Strained as India Cuts Fuel Subsidy to Bhutan," Times of India, July 6, 2013. https://timesofindia.indiatimes.com/india/Ties-strained-as-India-cuts-fuel-subsidy-to-Bhutan/articleshow/20936874.cms.

11	Thinley Namgay, "Tshechus to Be an Indoor Affair," Kuensel, September 10, 2020, 1. https://kuenselonline.com/tshechus-to-be-an-indoor-affair/.

12	New Agriculturalist, "Country Profile: Bhutan," January 2014. http://www.new-ag.info/en/country/profile.php?a=3177.

13	Françoise Pommaret, "The Journey of Bhutan Through a Life Lens," lecture at Royal Thimphu College, Thimphu, Bhutan, October 10, 2012.

14	"The Never-Ending Chilli Issue," Kuensel, January 22, 2021, 4.

15	Editorial, Constitution of the Kingdom of Bhutan (2008), 11. https://www.nab.gov.bt/en/business/constitution_of_bhutan.

16	Ibid, 9.

17	Ibid, 9.

18   "Bhutan to Have Its First Hindu Temple," Times of India, October 11, 2011. https://timesofindia.indiatimes.com/world/south-asia/Bhutan-to-have-first-Hindu-temple/articleshow/10318138.cms.

19   V. Arora, "Bhutan Makes Condoms Available to Buddhist Monks to Stop Spread of STDs," Huffington Post, March 29, 2013. https://www.huffpost.com/entry/bhutan-makes-condoms-available-to-monks-to-stop-spread-of-stds_n_2976401.

20   T. Limbu, "Bhutan Takes a Second Look at Phallus Worship," The Washington Post, March 3, 2014. https://www.washingtonpost.com/national/religion/bhutan-takes-a-second-look-at-phallus-worship/2014/03/03/1e9ff838-a310-11e3-b865-38b254d92063_story.html.

21   Sonam Kinga, "Why Phalluses Are Everywhere," in Speaking Statues, Flying Rocks, ed. Sonam Kinga (Thimphu: DSB Publication, 2005), 157-171.

22   Kunzang Choden, Bhutanese Tales of the Yeti (Bangkok: White Lotus Press, 2007), xiii.

23   Tashi Dema, "Accepting Tradition," Kuensel-K2: Weekend Magazine 2, no. 29 (July 28, 2012): 22.

24   Ibid, 9.

25   Rinzin Wangchuk, "For Divine Intervention," Kuensel, June 14, 2014, 1.

26   Tashi Dema, "Spirit Possession Accepted as Circumstantial and Corroborative Evidence in Trongsa Double Murder Case," Kuensel, July 3, 2018. https://kuenselonline.com/spirit-possession-accepted-as-circumstantial-and-corroborative-evidence-in-trongsa-double-murder-case/.

27   Tashi Dema, "High Court Sentences Two to Life for Murder," Kuensel, February 14, 2015. https://kuenselonline.com/high-court-sentences-two-to-life-for-murder/.

28   Chencho Dema, "Poison Givers: Forbidden Tales of Suffering," Business Bhutan, July 11, 2017. https://www.businessbhutan.bt/2017/07/11/poison-givers-forbidden-tales-of-suffering/.

29   Younten Tshedup, "Headhunter Rumor Goes Viral in Eastern Bhutan," Kuensel, May 5, 2018. https://kuenselonline.com/headhunter-rumor-goes-viral-in-eastern-bhutan/.

30   Phuntsho, *The History of Bhutan*, 223.

31   Khandu Wangchuk, "Distinguished Guest Lecturers Series," lecture at Royal Thimphu College, September 18, 2021.

32   Jigme Wangchuk, "It's No More Around," Bhutan Observer, September 16-23, 2011, 4.

33   "A Tribute to a Visionary Monarch: The People's King," Bhutan Today, October 31, 2010, 4.

34   Jigme Khesar Namgyel Wangchuck, "Coronation Speech," November 7, 2008. https://www.europarl.europa.eu/meetdocs/2004_2009/documents/dv/dsas20081202_bhutan_/DSAS20081202_Bhutan_EN.pdf.

35   Needrup Zangpo, "Children Speak Their Hearts," Bhutan Observer, October 21-28, 2011, 2. https://www.bmf.bt/children-speak-their-hearts/.

36   Phuntsho, *The History of Bhutan*, 9.

37   Sonam Jatso, "What Makes Us Bhutanese," The Bhutanese, November 7, 2015. https://thebhutanese.bt/what-makes-us-bhutanese/.

38   Siok Sian Pek-Dorji, "Nurturing Civil Society – Building Legitimacy, Ensuring Relevance," The Druk Journal 2, no. 3 (Winter 2017). http://

drukjournal.bt/nurturing-civil-society-building-legitimacy-ensuring-relevance/.

39   Hofstede Insights, "Country Comparison—Bhutan," n.d. https://www.hofstede-insights.com/country-comparison/bhutan/.

40   J.C. White, Sikkim and Bhutan: Twenty-One Years on the North-West Frontier 1887-1908 (Varanasi: Pilgrims Publishing, 2009), 157-158.

41   Kinley D. Tshering, "The Flogging Drum Diary," The Journalist, August 2012, 8-9.

42   "The DPT, PDP Syndrome," The Bhutanese, June 22, 2012. https://thebhutanese.bt/the-dpt-pdp-syndrome/.

43   Sonam Pelden, "PM This Week," Bhutan Observer, September 18-25, 2009, 17.

44   Tashi Penden, "My Say - Appeal for Inclusive Royal Kidu," Kuensel, June 30, 2020, 4.

45   B.K. Todd, "Bhutan, Land of the Thunder Dragon," National Geographic Magazine 52, no. 6 (December 1952): 713-754.

46   "Good Communication," The Bhutanese, May 26, 2012, 4.

47   Sithar Tenzin, "Work Culture Needs to Be Overhauled," Bhutan Observer, August 13-20, 2010, 3.

48   Pema Khandu, "Keep the Discourse Alive," Bhutan Observer, May 14-21, 2010, 2.

49   Tempa Wangdi, "Growing Democracy Among Youth: Facing the Social Media Wall," Bhutan Centre for Media and Democracy Blog, January 8, 2019. https://bcmd.bt/growing-democracy-among-youth/.

50	Tshering Cigay Dorji, "Basis of Bhutanese Values: Reflections of a Bhutanese Man," May 30, 2010. http://cigay.blogspot.com/2010/05/basis-of-bhutanese-values.html.

51	Ministry of Education, Royal Government of Bhutan, Bhutan Education Blueprint 2014-2024 (2014), 78. https://www.globalpartnership.org/content/bhutan-education-blueprint-2014-2024.

52	Tara Limbu, "Mechanical Learning Is Not True Education," Bhutan Times, September 6, 2009, 16.

53	Chewang Rinzin, "A Vision in Realization," Kuensel, April 25, 2020. https://kuenselonline.com/desuung-a-vision-in-realisation/.

54	L. Leaming, *A Field Guide to Happiness* (New York: Hay House, 2014), 85-87.

55	Namgay Zam, "Media and Democracy," lecture at Royal Thimphu College, Thimphu, Bhutan, May 21, 2013.

56	Kuenzang Norbu and J. J. P. Wouters, "Tertiary Education, Students' Experiences, and Future Imaginations in Bhutan," Rig Toshoel, Research Journal of Royal Thimphu College 3, no. 1 (2020): 13.

57	Phuntsho, *The History of Bhutan*, 568.

58	Kinley Dorji, "What Is the 'Bhutanese-ness' of the Bhutanese People?" Druk Journal 1, no. 1 (2015). http://drukjournal.bt/what-is-the-bhutanese-ness-of-the-bhutanese-people/.

59	Ibid.

60	Lucky Wangmo, "Put Religious and Racial Differences Behind, Worry More About Economic Disparity Says HM to the Graduates," Business Bhutan, July 16, 2011, 22.

61   Khagengra, "Our GNH Country—Bhutan," Bhutan Youth, September 3, 2011, 11.

62   Lilly Yangchen, "Being a Bhutanese Means Being a GNH Citizen," Druk Journal 1, no. 1 (2015). http://drukjournal.bt/being-a-bhutanese-means-being-a-gnh-citizen/.

63   Jamyang Khyentse, "Shangri-La May Be the Problem," Bhutan Observer, June 3-10, 2011, 4.

64   Jamyang Khyentse, "What Makes You Not a Bhutanese?" Druk Journal 1, no. 1 (2015). http://drukjournal.bt/what-makes-you-not-a-bhutanese/.

65   Sonam Chuki, "Marriage in Bhutan: At the Confluence of Tradition and Modernity" (2013), 64. https://www.google.com/search?client=firefox-b-1-d&q=Sonam+Chuki+%282013%29+Marriage+in+Bhutan%3A+At+the+confluence+of+tradition+and+modernity.

66   Tashi Phuntsho, "Business Bhutan, Free Pullout," Business Bhutan, December 3, 2011, 1.

67   Tshering Zam, "Alcohol Becomes the Top Killer in Bhutan," Bhutan Broadcasting System, January 20, 2017. http://www.bbs.bt/news/?p=66360.

68   Sonam Pelden, "Gangs Pledge to Disband," Bhutan Observer, August 27, 2010, 1.

69   Kinley Wangmo, "A Change in the Trend of Youths Rushing for Civil Service Jobs," The Bhutanese, January 11, 2020. https://thebhutanese.bt/a-change-in-the-trend-of-youths-rushing-for-civil-service-jobs/.

70   Kuenzang Norbu and J. J. P. Wouters, "Tertiary Education, Students' Experiences, and Future Imaginations in Bhutan," Rig Toshoel, Research Journal of Royal Thimphu College 3, no. 1 (2020): 14.

71   "A Solution for the Joblessness," Kuensel, July 2, 2020. https://kuenselonline.com/a-solution-for-the-joblessness/.

72   Ugyen Wangmo, "Foreign Workers Sorely Needed," The Journalist, December 11, 2011, 8.

73   Lucky Wangmo, "RCSC Tries to Restructure PCS (Position Classification System) to Value Seniority," Business Bhutan, November 20, 2010, 18.

74   Staff Reporter, "Old Is Gold," Bhutan Today, November 17, 2011, 5.

75   R. Suhonen, "I Didn't Know What I Was Capable Of: The Voice of a Bhutanese Youth," Druk Journal 2, no. 2 (2016). http://drukjournal.bt/i-didnt-know-what-i-was-capable-of-the-voice-of-a-bhutanese-youth/.

76   Gross National Happiness Commission, Twelfth 5-Year Plan 2018-2023: Just, Harmonious and Sustainable Society through Decentralization (Thimphu: Royal Government of Bhutan, 2019), 27.

77   "Keeping Our Roads Open," Kuensel, June 23, 2020. https://kuenselonline.com/keeping-our-roads-open/.

78   Tshering Tashi, "Major Roadblocks Between Zhemgang and Gelephu Lead to 33 km Long Walks," The Bhutanese, July 30, 2016, 9.

79   Phuntsho, *The History of Bhutan*, 39.

80   Staff Reporter, "To Study as Children of the Nomads," Bhutan Observer, July 10-17, 2009, 16.

81   Tshering Palden, "Where Tradition Discounts Education," Kuensel, May 22, 2010, 12.

82   Ibid.

83   Sonam Rinchen, "The Adolescent Dreams," Bhutan Observer, May 11, 2007, 4.

84   Geeta Mohan, "Bhutan Demarches China on Its Claim to Sakteng Sanctuary, Beijing Reiterates Position," India Today, July 6, 2020. https://www.indiatoday.in/world/story/china-bhutan-territory-dispute-demarche-chinese-embassy-new-delhi-sakteng-sanctuary-1697392-2020-07-06.

85   Kunzang Choden, Bhutanese Tales of the Yeti (Bangkok: White Lotus Press, 2007), 129.

86   Tandin Zangmo, "The Abominable Snowman 'Drops' by Thrumshingla," The Bhutanese, September 12, 2012. https://thebhutanese.bt/the-abominable-snowman-drops-by-thrumshingla/.

87   GNH Centre Bhutan, "The History of Gross National Happiness," 2019. http://www.gnhcentrebhutan.org/what-is-gnh/history-of-gnh/.

88   Centre for Bhutan Studies and GNH Research, A Compass Towards a Just and Harmonious Society: 2015 GNH Survey Report (Thimphu, Bhutan: 2016), 303. https://www.bhutanstudies.org.bt/a-compass-towards-a-just-and-harmonious-society-2015-gnh-survey-report/.

89   Dekey Choden Gyeltshen, "The Big Car Mania," Bhutan Times, May 24, 2009, 1.

90   Editorial, "Untitled," Bhutan Observer, August 2, 2013, p. 2.

91   Kinley Dem, "Local Healer in Deling, Phuentshogling Treats Illnesses Free of Charge," Bhutan Broadcasting System, July 2, 2023. https://www.bbs.bt/news/?p=188371.

92   The Global Fund, "Meet Condom Man!" Facebook, May 15, 2024. https://www.facebook.com/theglobalfund/photos/meet-condom-maneverybody-in-thimphu-the-capital-city-of-bhutan-knows-tshewang-ni/10152436935299511/?paipv=0&eav=Afa0pqZr9FaLg0FMGxafkSa1UDLWeRi7x6QBTbB_aZRKIzVwJevHZAswyWm_MRNtPLo&_rdr.

93   Editorial, "Promoting Dzongkha Everyone's Responsibility: PM," Kuensel, January 10, 2019, 4. https://kuenselonline.com/promoting-dzongkha-everyones-responsibility-pm/.

94   Editorial, "A Solution to Promote Dzongkha?" Kuensel, June 24, 2020, 4. https://kuenselonline.com/a-solution-to-promote-dzongkha/.

95   Yangyel Lhaden, "K-Beauty Craze Among Bhutanese," Kuensel, July 20, 2020, 1. https://kuenselonline.com/k-beauty-craze-among-bhutanese/.

96   Needrup Zangpo, "Children Speak Their Hearts," Bhutan Observer, October 21-28, 2011, 2. https://www.bmf.bt/children-speak-their-hearts/.

97   Editorial, "Saving Animals," Kuensel, March 29, 2019. https://kuenselonline.com/saving-animals/.

98   Ibid.

99   Editorial, "Worth the Wait?" Kuensel, July 31, 2021. https://kuenselonline.com/worth-the-wait/.